The Bhakti-yoga Handbook

A Guide for Beginning the Essentials of Devotional Yoga

By
Stephen Knapp

Dedicated to my own spiritual master,
His Divine Grace Srila A. C. Bhaktivedanta Swami Prabhupada
who gave me the inspiration to follow this path
and the guidance to continue it,
the results of which have made all the difference

Copyright © 2013, by Stephen Knapp

All rights reserved. No part of this book may be reproduced without written permission from the copyright owner and publisher, except for brief quotations for review or educational purposes.

Published with the Support of
The World Relief Network,
Detroit, Michigan

ISBN-10: 149030228X
ISBN-13: 978-1490302287

Cover Photo: The highly decorated deities of Sri Sri Radha-Kunjabihari (Radha-Krishna) in the Detroit Iskcon Krishna Temple, Devesadan Mandir. This is typical of most altars in the way the lineage of gurus, or the *parampara*, are on the lower shelf, with the smaller or *utsava* deities in front of the main larger deities. (Photo taken by Stephen Knapp)
    The gurus in front, from left to right are, Srila A. C. Bhaktivedanta Swami Prabhupada, Srila Bhaktisiddhanta Thakur, Srila Jagannatha das Babaji, and Srila Bhaktivinoda Thakur.

You can find out more about
Stephen Knapp
and his books, free ebooks, research,
and numerous articles and photos,
along with many other spiritual resources at:
www.stephen-knapp.com
http://stephenknapp.info
http://stephenknapp.wordpress.com

Other books by the author:
1. The Secret Teachings of the Vedas: The Eastern Answers to the Mysteries of Life
2. The Universal Path to Enlightenment
3. The Vedic Prophecies: A New Look into the Future
4. How the Universe was Created and Our Purpose In It
5. Toward World Peace: Seeing the Unity Between Us All
6. Facing Death: Welcoming the Afterlife
7. The Key to Real Happiness
8. Proof of Vedic Culture's Global Existence
9. The Heart of Hinduism: The Eastern Path to Freedom, Enlightenment and Illumination
10. The Power of the Dharma: An Introduction to Hinduism and Vedic Culture
11. Vedic Culture: The Difference it can Make in Your Life
12. Reincarnation & Karma: How They Really Affect Us
13. The Eleventh Commandment: The Next Step for Social Spiritual Development
14. Seeing Spiritual India: A Guide to Temples, Holy Sites, Festivals and Traditions
15. Crimes Against India: And the Need to Protect its Ancient Vedic Tradition
16. Destined for Infinity, a spiritual adventure in the Himalayas
17. Yoga and Meditation: Their Real Purpose and How to Get Started
18. Avatars, Gods and Goddesses of Vedic Culture: Understanding the Characteristics, Powers and Positions of the Hindu Divinities
19. The Soul: Understanding Our Real Identity
20. Prayers, Mantras and Gayatris: A Collection for Insights, Protection, Spiritual Growth, and Many Other Blessings
21. Krishna Deities and Their Miracles: How the Images of Lord Krishna Interact with Their Devotees.
22. Defending Vedic Dharma: Tackling the Issues to Make a Difference.
23. Advancements of the Ancient Vedic Culture.
24. Spreading Vedic Traditions Through Temples.

Contents

INTRODUCTION   1
    The Purpose of this Book

PART ONE: GETTING STARTED ON THE PATH OF BHAKTI-YOGA

CHAPTER ONE: 4
THE SECRET OF BHAKTI-YOGA

CHAPTER TWO: 11
UNDERSTANDING THE ESSENTIALS
    At the Temple or at Home * The Basic Process * The Regulative Principles

CHAPTER THREE: 18
STARTING OUR DAY
    The Sacred Brahma-muhurta Hour * Offering Obeisances * Bathing * Putting on Tilaka * Going to the Temple Program or Starting our Program at Home * Hatha-yoga and Pranayama

CHAPTER FOUR: 25
STANDARD SONGS USED IN THE KRISHNA TEMPLES
    Sri Sri Gurvashtaka * Additional Songs Sung During Mangala Arati * The Pancha-Tattva Maha Mantra * The Hare Krishna Maha-Mantra * Prema-Dhvani or Pranam Prayers * Shri Nrisimha Pranam * Tulasi-Arati Kirtana * The Ten Offenses in Chanting the Holy Names * Shri Vaishnava Pranam * Sri Sri Shikshashtaka * Jaya Radha-Madhava * Mantras Chanted Before Class * Mantras Chanted Before Class Commentary * Additional Pranam Mantras * From the Brahma-Samhita * Sri Guru-Vandana * Sri Nama-Kirtana * Other Nice Songs * Prasada-Sevaya * Additional Kirtanas * Shri Shri Shad-Goswamy-

Ashtaka * Nama-Sankirtana * Gaura-Arati * Shri Damodarashtaka * Saparshada-Bhagavad-Viraha-Janita-Vilapa * Shri Jagannathashtaka * Gurudeva * Savarna-Sri-Gaura-Pada-Padme Prarthana

PART TWO: A DEEPER LOOK INTO THE BASICS

CHAPTER FIVE: 70
ON CHANTING HARE KRISHNA
    How to Chant Hare Krishna

CHAPTER SIX: 79
THE PANCHA-TATTVA MANTRA
    Who is Sri Chaitanya Mahaprabhu

CHAPTER SEVEN: 88
GREETING THE DEITIES IN THE TEMPLE
    The Significance of Deities and Deity Worship

CHAPTER EIGHT: 92
IMPORTANCE OF READING DEVOTIONAL TEXTS
    As You Read and Study with Your Spiritual Practice

CHAPTER NINE: 95
TULASI DEVI–THE SACRED TREE
    How to Offer Tulasi Devi Worship (Puja) * The Importance of the Tulasi Plant

CHAPTER TEN: 103
PRASADAM–THE POWER OF SACRED FOOD

CHAPTER ELEVEN: 106
RULES FOR TEMPLE ETIQUETTE
    Dancing in the Temple * Learning the Instruments

CHAPTER TWELVE: 110
EKADASI–THE APPEARANCE AND PURPOSE OF THIS
SPECIAL DAY
      Additional Information * Other Special Days and Festivals we Observe * Chaturmasya

CHAPTER THIRTEEN: 120
THE NINE PROCESSES OF BHAKTI-YOGA

CHAPTER FOURTEEN: 125
A FEW ADDITIONAL POINTS TO UNDERSTAND
      The Purpose of Having a Guru * What is "Namaste" * Why Red Dots are Worn on the Forehead * What is Tilaka or Forehead Marks * Why ring Bells in the Temple * The Significance of the Arati Ceremony * The Reason Lamps are Used * Why a Conch Shell is Blown * Why Coconuts are Offered * The Purpose of Circumambulating Temples or Deities * Why the Lotus is Sacred * The Purpose of Fasting * Who May Practice Sanatana-dharma * What is a Sari * What is a Dhoti * Why Many Devotees Wear White * Why Many Swamis Wear Saffron Colored Cloth * The Significance of the Shikha (Tuft of Hair) * The Meaning of the Sutra or Sacred Thread * The Purpose of Touching our Head to the Floor * What are the Vedic Texts

PART THREE: UNDERSTANDING A FEW BASICS OF THE PHILOSOPHY

CHAPTER FIFTEEN: 146
WHO AM I? THE VEDIC DESCRIPTION OF THE SOUL

CHAPTER SIXTEEN: 150
WHAT IS REINCARNATION

CHAPTER SEVENTEEN: 154
WHAT IS KARMA

Contents

CHAPTER EIGHTEEN: 158
WHO IS KRISHNA

CHAPTER NINETEEN: 163
WHY BE VEGETARIAN
    Beyond Vegetarianism

CHAPTER TWENTY: 170
VEDIC CULTURE–AS RELEVANT TODAY AS EVER

PART FOUR: PRACTICING BHAKTI-YOGA AT HOME

CHAPTER TWENTY-ONE: 176
ESTABLISHING AN ALTAR AT HOME

CHAPTER TWENTY-TWO: 182
THE BASIC ARATI CEREMONY
    Consecrating Water for Purification (Samanya-Arghya) * Establishing General Arghya Water (Samanya-Arghya-Sthapana) * Doing the Achamana Procedure * Doing the Arati Ceremony * Mantras for Obtaining Forgiveness for One's Offenses

CHAPTER TWENTY-THREE: 194
MAKING OUR COOKING PART OF OUR YOGA
    Shopping * Cleanliness * Cooking * Offering

CHAPTER TWENTY-FOUR: 201
CARING FOR TULASI DEVI IN YOUR HOME
    Techniques for Caring for Tulasi Devi * Important Points * Potting * Light * Temperature * Controlling the Enemies of Tulasi Devi * Planting * Additional Points * Prayers

CHAPTER TWENTY-FIVE: 212
ADDITIONAL STEPS FOR HOME DEITY WORSHIP
    Bringing the Deities to Your Home * Qualifications for Doing Deity Worship * Your Deity Program * Waking the Deities * Bathing

and Dressing the Deities * Putting the Deities to Rest * If You Must Leave the Deities at Home

CONCLUSION: WHAT TO EXPECT FROM YOUR PRACTICE	225
GLOSSARY	227
REFERENCES	235
INDEX	238
ABOUT THE AUTHOR	242

Introduction

THE PURPOSE OF THIS BOOK

Parts of this book have been written earlier, while other parts were written specifically for this book alone. But now I have put them all together in one volume to fulfill the purpose of this book, which is to provide easy access to the most important information so anyone can begin the practice of bhakti-yoga, whether they be in the temple ashrama or practicing at home.

Over the years I have seen many versions of a "Bhakta Handbook," most of which were compiled at various Krishna temples for the use of new members in the ashrama. In many ways, they were a good start, but were also rather simple since those who would be using it would be guided first-hand by others who were more experienced and also living in the ashrama. Today, such versions would be in want of further explanations, especially for those who might be practicing bhakti-yoga at home and not in close proximity to those who are more advanced, which in this day and age is the main way most people live. After all, most people are not joining the ashramas as in years ago, but are raising a family or pursuing a career and living at home. Many may be attending the temple services regularly, while others may live a long way from any temple and will only visit it on special occasions. So this book is to help get people or new bhaktas started wherever they may be.

This book is meant to first cover the main external practices of bhakti-yoga and the attitude or mind-set with which they are done. This is called *sadhana*, or regular spiritual practice. The purpose of *sadhana* is to purify our activities, which then purifies our consciousness. So if you want to purify or spiritualize our thoughts, desires, words, and consciousness, we first have to begin by spiritualizing our activities. By spiritualizing our externals, or our actions, this begins to purify our internals, meaning our mind, desires, thoughts, words, etc. In bhakti-yoga, *sadhana* is centered around hearing and discussing about the Supreme Being, Lord Sri Krishna and His pastimes, qualities, character, and His *avataras*, and chanting His holy names. The more we hear and chant His holy names, then the more our consciousness is spiritualized by this form of meditation. Then the more in tune we become to the spiritual strata.

By continuing to work in this way, our consciousness becomes increasingly spiritualized, until we actually begin to perceive and then gradually even enter into the spiritual dimension. This means as our consciousness is raised to the spiritual level, we begin to perceive and interact with the spiritual platform and see what goes on there. The spiritual dimension is all around us, like radio or television waves or frequencies that remain unnoticed until we get a proper receiver. Similarly, when our consciousness becomes spiritualized, we can have the proper reception to witness the spiritual strata within and around us. This is the purpose of our *sadhana* in bhakti-yoga, called *sadhana-bhakti*.

Another purpose of this book is that it will coincide with another book that I plan to make available that will deal with more of the internal and spiritual understanding of practicing bhakti-yoga. This book will be *The Easy Path of Devotional Yoga*. It will summarize and explain the whys and what-fors of our spiritual practice in bhakti-yoga. Even though much information has already been provided in my books, such as *The Secret Teachings of the Vedas*, or *The Heart of Hinduism*, and others, *The Easy Path of Devotional Yoga* will work hand-in-hand with this present volume, *The Bhakt-yoga Handbook* and go further into the process of *sadhana* in bhakti-yoga and its philosophy.

Furthermore, we will base most of the elements of our daily program on the example found within the Iskcon (International Society for Krishna Consciousness) Krishna temples, since they offer what many have accepted to be a genuine and thorough understanding of what is and how to perform bhakti-yoga. Iskcon is part of the Brahma-Madhva-Gaudiya *sampradaya* or lineage that can be traced back from Srila Prabhupada through numerous spiritual masters to Sri Chaitanya Mahaprabhu, and on back to Lord Krishna Himself. However, even within these temples there are particular variations in schedules. So we may outline a general itinerary for our daily spiritual activities but find that it changes from one place to another, and especially for those who practice at home, we can certainly adopt the schedule that fits us best.

PART ONE

GETTING STARTED ON THE PATH OF BHAKTI-YOGA

CHAPTER ONE

The Secret of Bhakti-yoga

There are various kinds of yoga; such as Karma-yoga, based on purifying our activities for the higher good; Jnana-yoga, based on acquiring spiritual knowledge and insight to differentiate between what is matter and spirit; Raja-yoga or astanga-yoga, the mystical, eight-fold process of yoga meant for raising our life-airs to the top of the head and then reach *moksha* by leaving the body in this way; and Bhakti-yoga, attaining union with God through love and devotion. From these yoga systems, additional systems have also developed. But these four basic forms of yoga are all discussed in the primary and essential Vedic text of the *Bhagavad-gita*. But out of all of them, Lord Krishna specifically directs us toward engaging in Bhakti-yoga, love and devotion toward Him. So why is this so special?

Bhakti-yoga is the devotional service performed for Lord Krishna, or one of His avataras, such as Lord Vishnu, Lord Ramachandra, Vamanadeva, etc. Lord Krishna explains that, "Work done as a sacrifice for Vishnu has to be performed, otherwise work binds one to this material world. Therefore, O son of Kunti [Arjuna], perform your prescribed duties for His satisfaction, and in that way you will always remain unattached and free from bondage." [1] This means free from karma, which is an important point in our spiritual progress.

Sri Krishna goes on to relate that "Those who know Me as the Supreme Lord, as the governing principle of the material manifestation, who know Me as the one underlying all the demigods and as the one sustaining all sacrifices, can, with steadfast mind, understand and know Me even at the time of death. [2] And whoever, at the time of death, quits his body remembering Me alone, at once attains My nature. Of this there is no doubt. Whatever state of being one remembers when he quits his body, that state he will attain without fail. Therefore, Arjuna, you should always think of Me in the form of Krishna and at the same time carry out your prescribed duty. With your activities dedicated to Me and your mind and intelligence fixed on Me, you will attain Me without doubt."[3]

In this way, we can begin to understand that devotional service ultimately brings us to the level of being able to see Lord Krishna directly. It is by this method that numerous other saintly sages and yogis have come to be able to directly see the Lord. The point to remember is that the more spiritual we become, the more we can perceive that which is spiritual. The more purified our consciousness is, or the higher the vibrational level upon which our consciousness functions, the more we can see and enter into that higher level of existence or reality. It awakens our transcendental senses that exist within us. So the process of continued service to Krishna and His devotees will bring about the purification which will allow us to enter into Krishna's domain, even within this very lifetime, if we are fortunate enough.

As Lord Krishna further relates, "The form which you are seeing with your transcendental eyes cannot be understood simply by studying the *Vedas*, nor by undergoing serious penances, nor by charity, nor by worship. It is not by these means that one can see Me as I am. My dear Arjuna, only by undivided devotional service can I be understood as I am, standing before you, and can thus be seen directly. Only in this way can you enter into the mysteries of My understanding. One who is engaged in My pure devotional service, free from the contaminations of previous activities and from mental speculation, who is friendly to every living entity, certainly comes to Me." [4]

"One can understand the Supreme Personality of Godhead as He is only by devotional service. And when one is in full consciousness of the Supreme Lord by such devotion, he can enter into the kingdom of God." [5]

Lord Krishna also explains in the *Bhagavata Purana* that the residents of both heaven and hell want to take a human birth on earth since such a human life provides the best facility to achieve transcendental knowledge and love of God. Neither heavenly nor hellish bodies provide the efficient means for such opportunity. [6] This is the fortunate nature of life on this earth planet and in these human bodies, which we often take so much for granted.

Furthermore, Lord Krishna describes in the *Bhagavata Purana* the highest level of happiness that can be attained when we have a taste for serving Him. He says that if you fix your consciousness on Him, giving up your material desires, you will share a happiness with Him that cannot be experienced in any way by those who remain engaged in merely trying to gratify the senses. If you do not desire anything of this world, and have achieved peace through controlling the senses, and if your consciousness is equipoised in all situations, and when your mind is satisfied in Him, you will find happiness wherever you go.[7] If or when you are without any desire for personal gratification, and when the mind is attached to Him, peaceful and without false ego, merciful to all living beings, and when your consciousness is not affected by the prospects for gratifying the senses, then you can find a happiness that cannot be known or achieved by those who lack such qualities. [8] In other words, this is beyond anything that a common man may experience.

With the explanations that follow we can understand that a separate endeavor for engaging in the mystic yoga tradition is not needed. Whatever spiritual goals you may wish to attain can be acquired simply by engaging in devotional service to the Supreme. Sri Krishna explains this: "One who can control his senses by practicing the regulated principles of freedom can obtain the complete mercy of the Lord and thus become free from all attachment and aversion. [9] And of all yogis, he who always abides in Me with great faith, worshiping Me in transcendental loving service, is most intimately united with Me in yoga and is the highest of all.[10] He who meditates on the Supreme Personality of Godhead, his mind constantly engaged in remembering Me, undeviated from the path, he, O Partha [Arjuna], is sure to reach Me... One who at the time of death, fixes his life air between his eyebrows and in full devotion engages himself in remembering the Supreme Lord, will certainly attain to the Supreme Personality... [11] After attaining Me, the great souls, who are yogis in devotion, never return to this temporary world, which is full of miseries, because they have attained the highest perfection." [12]

This is the powerful effect of the process of thinking and dedicating your activities to Lord Krishna. However, the same result can also be acquired by proper association with those who are spiritually advanced. In this regard, the Supreme Lord personally told Uddhava that it is by associating with His pure devotees that you can destroy your desires for the objects that can gratify the senses. It is this purifying association that can bring the Lord under the control of such a devotee. You may perform the astanga-yoga system, engage in philosophical analysis of the elements of material nature, or practice nonviolence and other ordinary principles of piety, like dig wells, give in charity, plant trees, or other public welfare activities. You may even chant the Vedas, perform penances, take up the renounced order of life, worship the demigods, chant confidential mantras, or visit the holy places. But all such activities cannot bring Him under your control. [13] Even though you may engage with great endeavor in the mystic yoga system, or philosophical speculation, or charity, vows, penances, rituals, or even studying the *Vedas* and teaching the Vedic mantras to others, still you cannot achieve Him by these means alone. [14]

However, by example we can see that as the residents of Vrindavana, headed by the gopis [cowherd girls devoted to Krishna], were always completely attached to Him with the deepest love, they could not find any other comfort or happiness in their separation from Him when Krishna's uncle Akrura took Him and Balarama to Mathura. All of the nights in which the gopis spent with Krishna in Vrindavana went by like a moment. And now, bereft of His association, the gopis felt those same nights drag on forever, as if each night were a day of Brahma. Just as the great sages in yoga trance merge into self-realization, just like the river merging into the ocean, and are thus oblivious to any material names and forms, in the same way the gopis of Vrindavana were so completely attached and absorbed in thought of Him that they did not think of their own bodies, or of anything of this world, not even of their future. Their complete consciousness was simply absorbed in Krishna. Though they were not completely aware of His actual position, by their thoughts and association with Him, they all attained Him, the Supreme Absolute Truth.

Therefore, as Lord Krishna goes on to explain in the *Bhagavata Purana*: "Abandon the Vedic mantras as well as the procedures in the supplementary Vedic literature and all their injunctions. Simply take shelter of Me alone, for I am the Supreme Personality of Godhead situated within the heart of all conditioned souls. Take shelter of Me wholeheartedly, and by My grace be free from fear in all circumstances."[15]

An example of such fearlessness for devotees on the path of spiritual progress is related as follows: Those who are yogis learn how to control their lives so that they pass away from this world at the right moment, and in the right consciousness, so that they will not take birth in this world again. However, Lord Krishna explains this and concludes that for His devotees there is no reason to be overly concerned about such things. "According to the *Vedas*, there are two ways of passing from this world--one in light and one in darkness. When one passes in light, he does not come back; but when one passes in darkness, he returns...[16] Those who know the Supreme Brahman pass away from the world during the influence of the fiery god, in the light, at an auspicious moment, during the fortnight of the moon and the six months when the sun travels in the north. The mystic who passes away from this world during the smoke, the night, the moonless fortnight, or in the six months when the sun passes to the south, or who reaches the moon planet, again comes back.[17] However, the devotees who know these two paths, O Arjuna, are never bewildered. Therefore be always fixed in devotion."[18] Thus, for a devotee who is always thinking of Krishna, there is no reason for any other endeavor or concern in the performance of one's spiritual progress.

Krishna further clarifies in the *Bhagavata Purana* that whatever mystic perfections can be achieved by good birth, herbs, austerities and mantras can all be achieved by devotional service to Him; indeed one cannot achieve the actual perfection of yoga by any other means.[19] Everything that can be attained through fruitive or karmic activities, penance, knowledge, detachment, mystic yoga, charity, religious duties, or any other means of perfecting life can be easily achieved by His devotee simply through loving service to Him. If for some reason His devotee desires to be promoted to heaven or attain liberation, or a residence in His abode, such benedictions are easily achieved.[20]

A similar point is reiterated by the Lord in His form as Kapiladeva when He explains that because His devotee is completely absorbed in thought of Him, he does not desire such benedictions as going to the higher planetary systems, like Satyaloka, nor any of the eight mystic powers obtained from yoga, nor does he desire to be liberated into the kingdom of God. However, the devotee nonetheless enjoys all offered benedictions even in this life, even without asking for them. [21]

In conclusion, everything that can be accomplished by separate endeavors in other processes are not left out of the path of devotion to the Lord. "A person who accepts the path of devotional service is not bereft of the results derived from studying the *Vedas*, performing austere sacrifices, giving charity, or pursuing philosophical and fruitive activities. At the end he reaches the supreme abode." [22]

This is the secret of the potency of Bhakti-yoga.

Furthermore, Bhakti-yoga is not a dry system of philosophy and solitude, but it is the ecstatic way of chanting the Lord's holy names, dancing in bliss, and associating with other devotees and taking Krishna *prasada*, spiritual food that has been offered to Sri Krishna. It is a process of learning to serve the Supreme Being in a multitude of ways, whether through music, the arts, or even technology, through the use of our natural talents and proclivities, and using them all in His service, and to attract others to this process by sharing what we know and do. It is a life of ever-increasing pleasure as we uplift our consciousness to perceive and even interact with the spiritual dimension, which ultimately brings us to the point of entering the spiritual world and even reciprocating directly with the Supreme Being. This is the goal. It is like entering into the mood of the spiritual world, which then brings us into the spiritual strata. This system is not new but has brought many others to the perfectional platform as well.

CHAPTER NOTES
1. *Bhagavad-gita* 3.9
2. Ibid., 7.30
3. Ibid., 8.5-7
4. Ibid., 11.53-55
5. Ibid., 18.55
6. *Srimad-Bhagavatam* 11.20.12
7. Ibid., 11.14.12-13

8. Ibid., 11.14.17
9. *Bhagavad-gita* 2.64
10. Ibid., 6.47
11. Ibid., 8.8, 10
12. Ibid., 8.15
13. *Srimad-Bhagavatam* 11.12.1-2
14. Ibid., 11.12.9
15. Ibid., 11.12.9-15
16. *Bhagavad-gita* 8.26
17. Ibid., 8.24-25
18. Ibid., 8.27
19. *Srimad-Bhagavatam* 11.15.34
20. Ibid., 11.20.32-33
21. Ibid., 3.25.37
22. *Bhagavad-gita* 8.28

CHAPTER TWO

Understanding the Essentials

AT THE TEMPLE OR AT HOME

It may be easier to follow a disciplined lifestyle for regulated yoga practice of any kind while living or staying in an ashrama, but bhakti-yogi can easily be adopted wherever you may be. So I will be pointing out some of the differences of what to do between practicing in an ashrama or at home as we go through this book.

For example, if you are living at home, you may not be able to have time to do everything that is outlined in the morning program, as described later. You will follow what is called "the family schedule." It will be up to you to decide what is best for you to do and how much you can include. I remember staying with one advanced devotee at his home ashrama and he would go through the main parts of the morning program in about a half-hour, including a short *mangala-arati* while worshiping his deity, then do Tulasi *puja*, and then Guru *puja*. Then he would spend more time on his *japa* meditation, and then have a class or a reading from scripture sometime later. So he would pack a lot into his morning very quickly and then have plenty of time later in the day for many other things.

So those of you at home will also have to arrange a morning practice that best fits your schedule and needs, based on what is described later in this book. Then, during those days when you have more time, like on the weekends, you can increase the practices, or even go to the temple to follow the program there.

One thing also is to decrease your time that is spent on television or games, and what could be called useless actions. Do not waste time, especially on temporary materialistic pursuits, which we are trying to free ourselves from, and then use more time for activities in bhakti-yoga and spiritual development. It is a common occurrence that as you begin to get a higher taste from your spiritual practices, you will naturally lose your taste for lower, temporary sensual happiness.

THE BASIC PROCESS

The most basic thing is to rise early enough in the morning to incorporate the essential parts of the morning program and the chanting of your *japa* mediation, consisting of chanting the Hare Krishna maha-mantra on your beads. If you cannot always finish your chanting in the morning, you can wait until later or end your day with the remaining amount of *japa*. The main thing is to be regulated, follow your schedule every day. This chanting is also important in the form of *sankirtana*, getting together with other *bhaktas* or devotees and chanting Hare Krishna and other devotional songs and mantras in a group, which can certainly enliven us. So we should do both, our *japa* meditation, and then from time to time getting together with others to sing and chant together in a group, which is called *sankirtana*. In the temple ashrama you can do this daily.

The next most important part is to take some time everyday to read some of the *shastra*, scripture like *Bhagavad-gita* or *Srimad-Bhagavatam*, to increase your spiritual knowledge and understanding, and to remain conversant in the topic so you can train yourself and talk to others about the philosophy. This is also jnana-yoga, the acquisition of spiritual knowledge. This in itself also incorporates getting the proper association. Rather than taking time for television and radio or other forms of entertainment, or talking gossip with others, which often gives unwanted thoughts and association with the improper and unnecessary images and violence and sexual innuendoes that are displayed or discussed on television, and are but distractions from what we are trying to accomplish, we should instead take the time to read *shastra* which will give us additional clarity on the importance and value of using our time for spiritual pursuits.

The next most important thing is to allow ourselves to have the best association, which is the company of other *bhaktas* and spiritual practitioners who are perhaps far more experienced and knowledgeable in bhakti-yoga than we are. We can discuss the philosophy with them, or talk about our difficulties, and ask advice for what is best for us. Plus, it is always good to be around those who are enlivened and enthusiastic in the process, which often helps us to be more enthusiastic as well, and gives us the opportunity and ideas for doing service or engaging in activities that help ourselves and others.

New *bhaktas* or devotees can and should go to the temple regularly to get association with other and more advanced devotees, or go to home programs where others gather. It is good to put your questions to them for practical answers, and go to the classes as well. Sri Chaitanya Mahaprabhu emphasized association as part of the means of sustaining one's progress:

krishna-bhakti-janma-mula haya 'sadhu-sanga'
krishna-prema janme, tenho punah mukhya

"The root cause of devotional service to Lord Krishna is association with devotees. Even when one's dormant love for Krishna awakens, association with devotees is still most essential." (*Caitanya-caritamrita*, Madhya-lila 22.83)

So, chanting Hare Krishna in *japa* meditation and in *sankirtana*, reading *shastra*, and getting the right association are key to continuing our practice of bhakti-yoga. The next most important thing to understand is the regulative principles.

THE REGULATIVE PRINCIPLES

When we become more serious about making progress on the path, we also incorporate into our lives the regulative principles. There are four, which include: 1. no meat-eating, 2. no gambling, 3. no unnecessary sex, and 4. no intoxication. These are the four "nos", but they can also be accepted as the four "yeses." Why? Because they allow us to develop much more rapidly than if we did not follow them, and help us avoid the bad habits, both physically and mentally, that keep us distracted by that internal conversation that goes on in our mind that always tempts us to indulge in the common everyday addictions that keep us bound to materialistic life. And that is from which we want to free ourselves. You cannot be free when your mind is entangled by these habitual thought patterns. You cannot make spiritual development while still bound by the common materialistic habits that are outlined by these four regulative principles. If you think you can, then you are just a pretender.

Now you may not be able to follow all of these at first, but it is best to know what the proper standard is, and then work your way toward that as best as you can. And if you continue to chant the maha-mantra and read *shastra*, as we have discussed, and as your consciousness becomes increasingly spiritualized and you add proper association with other *bhaktas*, the material life and the bad habits that go with it will soon lose their attraction. Believe me, that is what happened to me. When I first started going to the temple, I decided to chant merely four rounds of *japa* on my beads every day. I was still smoking cigarettes to a small degree at the time, primarily due to bad association in the form of friends who did the same, and then I would go to the temple on Sundays. It was before I ever joined the ashrama. But once I started chanting regularly, I felt an inner strength or power come over me, and I decided to direct that toward quitting smoking. Using the power I got from chanting, I was able to overcome the desire to smoke and I never looked back. The low desire for smoking was replaced by a higher happiness and strength from chanting Hare Krishna. So if you take this seriously, it will also work for you. But you have to be serious. And then your life will progress in a completely new way, and you can reach a higher potential that you may never have known you had. Then so many bad habits can be overcome, not because you have to work at it, but because they simply lose their attraction. They simply become useless. Or you could say you simply outgrow them and you reach a new level of life and existence.

To explain these regulative principles a little more, no meat-eating means to increase our mercy and kindness toward others. It means to give ourselves the facility to recognize that all species of life have souls, and to free us from the cruel practice of animal slaughter and the karma that is rapidly accumulated from engaging in it, whether it is killing animals for the pleasure of the tongue, or buying the meat, or cooking or eating it. You cannot say you have compassion for others if you still have a taste for eating them. Thus, the next step is to take up a vegetarian lifestyle. This frees you from the degrading karma of supporting the cruel animal killing business, or eating them, and lifts you to a healthier state of being by eating more fruits and vegetables. This also lifts you to a loftier consciousness by being free from all of the low energy that comes from eating animals that are slaughtered in a state of fear, and the intoxicating drugs that are often found within meat, along with all of the harmful bacteria that usually accompanies the slaughtering process which is ingested by those who eat such meat. Not only that, but you will find that as you give up meat and its by-products, your taste will change, and you often find yourself appreciating various fruits and vegetables that you never knew or thought you would like. This has happened to many people I have talked to about this. There are many other advantages of a balanced vegetarian lifestyle.

No gambling means to become free from gambling itself, and such games of chance and the losses they often cause and the anxiety and frustration that follows. It also means to be free from unnecessary speculation about trying to make fast money in questionable businesses or investments. This also means to be content through an honest, even if meager, occupation. This frees the mind from so much unnecessary and unwanted trouble from trying to figure out how to get more money, or more anything, by hook or by crook. This generally creates more trouble in the long run than if you simply lived an honest life, being content with what you have through a trustworthy and upstanding way of life. Peace of mind is what we want, especially when traversing the spiritual path, and being free from gambling certainly helps us in this way.

However, this does not mean that we have to be poor. If we are single students living in the ashrama, such matters should not affect us. But if we are householders raising a family, then we should also not be in anxiety over debts and the cost of living. We will still need to have an occupation, but it should be an honest and respectable occupation. Plus, one thing I have always said, you also cannot use your desire for spiritual pursuits as an excuse to give up the family responsibilities you have already accepted. But if you are still single, without many responsibilities or obligations, and you have a strong desire to engage in spiritual practice, then nothing should hold you back from engaging in serious spiritual practice. But make that decision before accepting a wife and children and all that goes with it.

No unnecessary sex means to reach a higher standard of cleanliness both physically and mentally. It means to keep ourselves free from always looking at others for the potential of sex life and how to arrange for it, or how to exploit others for our own pleasure. Becoming free from that is such a liberation from the most common preoccupation of the mind. It is more of an habitual thought pattern than an actual physical need. However, it is not wrong to get married and have a family with children, but the constant preoccupation with sex will keep you busy accomplishing little else than trying to meet the demands of the mind and genitals. They can pull you in any direction if you are not careful. It is like working so hard for so little, and then in the end having practically nothing to show for it. It is better to be happy with one wife, and raise a decent family than to continue to try to play the field, so to speak, and continually end up spending lots of money, or engaged in so much intrigue to satisfy you mind and senses, which is compared to pouring gasoline on a fire, which actually only gets bigger and more out of control. Trying to satisfy your mind and senses in this way is like that, they are never satisfied. They only want more, though they may slowly get worn out from the repetition of one habit or another, but will only devise other means desires for seeking satisfaction in other ways.

This never ends except by acquiring a higher taste, which is the happiness of the soul, which is your real identity beyond the mind and senses. Thus, giving the soul the attention it is seeking is the means for attaining true happiness. Then you can actually attain a state of contentment, not otherwise. Once you are happy on the spiritual platform, it overwhelms whatever happiness you could get on the material or sensual platform. Then all the sensual happiness you could acquire begins to look insignificant, and even distasteful or downright disgusting. But you have to clean your mind and consciousness to reach that stage, you have to take it seriously and work at it. It can be done. And when it happens, you can know a bliss which knows no bounds. It is waiting for you. That is why we follow these four regulative principles.

No intoxication is easy to understand. It means no drugs like heroin or cocaine or other substances like psychedelics, or alcoholic beverages like wine, whiskey, beer, etc. It also means no tobacco or cigarettes, and nothing that causes any form of mental imbalance. The point is that when person becomes even a little intoxicated, you lose your discrimination between right and wrong, good and bad, and you begin to feel that if it sounds good or feels good, why not do it? Then you begin to succumb to all the ideas that we have mentioned above in regard to the other principles we have described. Then you lose your mental balance and spiritual perspective, and you drop back into the bad habits we are trying to overcome.

An intoxicant means it is toxic, it is a poison in more ways than one. Becoming free from intoxicants helps us become free from being a slave of our mind and senses, which take complete control over us when we are intoxicated. Intoxicants make you do things that you otherwise would not do, leaving you often feeling sorry later for what you have done. So we can help ourselves be free from that by remaining free from intoxicants, and keeping our mind steady and fixed on the spiritual goal we are pursuing within the process of bhakti-yoga.

In previous times long ago, there were different forms of austerities that were done to attain spiritual advancement, but these four principles are the main austerities in this age of Kali-yuga, the age of quarrel, confusion, lethargy, and corruption. But following these principles correctly, along with our spiritual practice, will propel one into the happiness of the freedom from material consciousness and the slavery to our mind and senses that such consciousness causes. It also greatly assists us in our spiritual development and the happiness that follows.

So conform to these principles, or at least try as best you can and keep working on it, and with the following spiritual practices that we will outline, you will soon be moving forward on the spiritual path in leaps and bounds.

CHAPTER THREE

Starting Our Day

In practicing bhakti-yoga, we can incorporate some aspect of it in all parts of our day. It is just a matter of learning how to do that. But the most important thing is how we start the day. As anyone knows, how our day begins can make a difference in how the rest of the day proceeds. So the point is to make the day filled, as much as possible, with various ways of devoting our thoughts and activities in our devotion to God. This keeps us connected and united with God, which is the whole goal of yoga, as much as possible. The easy part of bhakti-yoga is that we do not have to remain in a motionless form of meditation, but can actually be engaged in all kinds of activity while still focused on our connection with the Supreme. This may take some practice, nothing is accomplished overnight, but this is how we can begin. And it all starts in the early morning.

THE SACRED BRAHMA-MUHURTA HOUR

Some may question why, especially in the ashramas, it is recommended that everyone rise early and start their spiritual activities and attend the *mangala-arati* (auspicious *arati* ceremony) about an hour-and-a-half before sunrise. This is explained in the *Srimad-Bhagavatam* (3.20.46):

"The time early in the morning, one and a half hours before sunrise, is called *brahma-muhurta*. During this *brahma-muhurta*, spiritual activities are recommended. Spiritual activities performed early in the morning have a greater effect than in any other part of the day."

In the *Archana Padati* it is also described, "Every twenty-four minutes is equal to one *danda*. Two *dandas*, or forty-eight minutes, is equal to one *muhurta*. In the day and the night together, there are a total of thirty *muhurtas*. In the last portion of the night, the time beginning two *murtas* before the rise of the sun up to the rise of the sun, or one hour and thirty-six minutes before the rise of the sun, is called *arunodaya*. Of these two *muhurtas*, the first *muhurta* is called the *brahma-muhurta*. This *brahma-muhurta* is the most auspicious time for devotees seeking success in spiritual realization."

OFFERING OBEISANCES

So when we awake, we first offer our obeisances to our guru and Lord Krishna or our *Ishta-devata*, our personal deity, to show our gratitude for being able to start another day of service to them, and for their blessings of having another day. Then we get up and straighten up our bed and make our way to take our morning bath.

BATHING

It is recommended that anytime you sleep for more than an hour, a quick shower should be taken for cleanliness. So when we get up in the morning, a quick cold or cool shower is recommended. I say cool because in some places to take a cold shower the water is so cold it can jeopardize one's health if you are going to be lathering yourself with soap for a complete scrub down, which you need from time to time.

So this means that first you evacuate if possible, pass water, then brush your teeth, and then you finish with a shower. Do not take a shower and then brush your teeth, because then you are considered unclean again. The mouth is also filled with germs and should be cleaned before your shower. After drying off, we get dressed and then go to mark our bodies with *tilaka* (pronounced teelok), described next:

PUTTING ON TILAKA

The *tilaka* markings on the body indicate that it is a temple of the Lord. So when we see each other with *tilaka* on, it helps us recognize that we are not simply persons, but our body is the original temple of God in which we exist along with the Paramatma, Supersoul. In the Uttara-khanda of the *Padma Purana*, Lord Shiva says to Parvati that in the middle of the "V" of the Vaishnava *tilaka* mark there is a space and in that space reside Lakshmi and Narayana. Therefore, the body that is decorated with *tilaka* should be considered a temple of Lord Vishnu.

The *Padma Purana* also states:

> *vama-parshve sthito brahma*
> *dakshine cha sadashivaha*
> *madhye vishnum vijaniyat*
> *tasman madhyam na lepayet*

"On the left side of the *tilaka* Lord Brahma is situated, and on the right side is Sadashiva, but one should know that in the middle dwells Lord Vishnu. Therefore one should not smear the middle section."

In applying *tilaka* on ourselves, we first pour a little water into our left palm, then take some special clay called gopichandana (mud from Dwaraka) if we can get it and mix it with the water to make a paste in our left palm. Then take your ring finger from your right hand and dip it into the paste and apply it to the forehead. Start just at the bridge of the nose, then bring your finger with the paste upward to the hairline, making two vertical lines. You may have to do this more than once to get it right. Then apply the *tilaka* to the nose in a downward movement, from the bridge of the nose down about two-thirds of the length of your nose, ending in a point.

When marking *Tilaka*, we can refer to the following mantra from the Uttara Khanda of the *Padma Purana*:

> *lalate keshavam dhyayen*
> *narayanam athodare*
> *vaksha-sthale madhavam tu*

Chapter Three

govindam kantha-kupake

vishnum cha dakshine kukshau
bahau cha madhusudanam
trivikramam kandare tu
vamanam vama-parshvake

shridharam vama-bahau tu
hrishikesham cha kandhare
pristhe tu padma-nabham cha
katyam damodaram nyaset

tat prakshalana-toyam tu
vasudeveti murdhani

In accordance with the above mentioned mantra, one should apply the gopichandana with the ball of the ring finger tip to make the *tilaka* marks on the twelve parts of the body. According to the *Brahmanda Purana*, one should not use the fingernail to make the space in the middle of the *tilaka*. One should use the finger tip or place a thin damp cloth over the finger and make the space with that. Thus, when the *tilaka* is applied, the following mantras should be chanted:

The forehead--om keshavaya namaha
The belly--om narayanaya namaha
The chest--om madhavaya namaha
The throat--om govindaya namaha
The right side of the waist--om vishnave namaha
The right upper arm--om madhusudanaya namaha
The right shoulder--om trivikramaya namaha
The left side of the waist--om vamanaya namaha
The left upper arm--om shridharaya namaha
The left shoulder--om hrishikeshaya namaha
The upper back--om padmanabhaya namaha
The lower back--om damodaraya namaha

Finally, after washing one's hand, whatever water is left should be wiped on the top of the head in the region of the *shikha* (tuft of hair) with the mantra: om vasudevaya namaha.

In the *Padma Purana* it is stated:

> *nasadi-kesha-paryantam*
> *urdhva-pundram sushobhanam*
> *madhye chidra-samayuktam*
> *tad vidyad dhari-mandiram*

"That marking (of *tilaka*), which begins from the root of the nose and extends up to the hairline, which has a space in it and is very beautiful, is known as *urdhva-pundra* (*tilaka*). One should know it to be a temple of Lord Hari [Vishnu]." The *Padma Purana* also mentions that the *tilaka* marking should only extend three quarters of the way down the nose from the root of the nose, which is located between the eyebrows. The space in the middle of the *tilaka* should begin from between the eyebrows and extend up to the hairline. The marking on the nose and forehead should be connected. That is a perfect *tilaka* marking.

GOING TO THE TEMPLE PROGRAM OR STARTING OUR PROGRAM AT HOME

Now when we are dressed with *tilaka*, we go to the temple to observe *mangala-arati*, or to get *darshan* of the deities.

When we do not live in an ashrama but live at home, we may have to walk or drive to the temple. In some cases, we may live a distance from any temple, so we may go to our own temple room where we serve the deities in what is most suitable for us. Maybe we have our own *arati* with our family, or go to have a little *kirtana*, or simply greet our own deities if we have some and chant our *japa* meditation in front of Them.

In the temple we will observe or even help serve the deities that have been ritually installed, which means They get full worship with many items, food offerings, and are newly dressed everyday, and so on.

But if we are practicing bhakti-yoga at home, then we may alter or arrange a program or serve our deities according to what we can handle. Instead of serving in the temple for the day, which we would do if we are living full time in the temple ashrama, we may have to go to work at our job in order to support our family. So then we adjust our morning program so we can accomplish the most needful things to do, which may be first chanting our *japa* meditation, which is also like polishing our consciousness so we are protected throughout the day from whatever challenges may take place as we interact with varieties of people and situations.

Doing our *sadhana* or spiritual practice is like arming ourselves with a spiritual armor so we can remain peaceful throughout the day, no matter what life may throw at us. If we can rise early, and then chant the Hare Krishna mantra in our *japa* meditation for a certain number of rounds, and then perhaps read some from the *Srimad-Bhagavatam*, it will fix our consciousness in a way which will help us stay peaceful and in a spiritual awareness. It will keep us focused on what really matters in life. We can also arrange to have a sacred space and environment in our home, such as a prayer room or temple room, and then take some of that atmosphere with us wherever we go when we leave home.

If we do live at home and get up early, or if we live in the temple ashrama, these are the basic parts of the morning program that we can attend or perform.

So, first is *mangala-arati*, which is the most auspicious *arati* of the day, when the deities are worshiped with a variety of items, such as incense, ghee lamp, water conch, a cloth or napkin, a flower, a chamara (yak tail) fan, and a peacock feather fan. If we live at home, maybe we can arrange to do this for our home deities if we have Them.

Then there is Tulasi *puja*, then time for chanting *japa*, then greeting the deities after they are newly dressed, then Guru *puja*, then class in *Srimad-Bhagavatam*, and then breakfast of sacred *prasada* food. The importance and meaning of these will be explained in the following chapters. All of the songs and mantras for these functions are described and provided in the next chapter as well.

However, not all Vedic or Hindu temples will follow the same program as we have outlined here. Some have rituals or a schedule that are quite different. So we are explaining what is most likely to be found at the Krishna temples, and there are many, where the process of bhakti-yoga is followed.

HATHA YOGA AND PRANAYAMA

There are many kinds of yoga or steps of the yoga system, and they can be combined for heightening the effects of one with the other. With bhakti-yoga, we also use mantra yoga with it by our chanting of mantras, and jnana-yoga with our cultivation of spiritual knowledge by our study of sacred texts, and even karma-yoga by dedicating our activities toward God. All of these forms of yoga are included in this process of bhakti-yoga. But there is also no harm in taking a little time during our day, and when we have the space, to do some hatha-yoga or *pranayama* breathing exercises.

Doing hatha-yoga exercises will certainly help keep our body loose, limber and in shape, which also can help us in our activities of devotional service. There is never any harm in taking care of our health, and we need that no matter what we do. It is better to keep one's health intact and live simply and easily than to ignore it and face the consequences of premature disease later on.

By observing a vegetarian diet, keeping a regulated lifestyle, and getting exercise by dancing during the *kirtanas* and getting other forms of exercise by our devotional activities, usually keeps us quite healthy. And our chanting, when done properly, automatically provides the proper breathing exercises. So we may not need much else, but adding a few minutes of hatha-yoga and *pranayama* exercises, or even something as simple as the Surya Namaskar to our daily program, can certainly help.

Furthermore, many people like to learn yoga, which to most means hatha-yoga. So being able to teach this can also attract people to attend such classes, which can then lead into discussions on, for example, *Bhagavad-gita*, or the process of mantra-yoga, or adding bhakti-yoga to what they are already doing. So there is no harm in adding this to your day if time allows.

CHAPTER FOUR

Standard Songs Used in the Hare Krishna Temples

As we participate or engage in the typical morning program followed in many Krishna temples, especially those of Iskcon, these are the standard mantras and songs used therein.

OBEISANCES TO SRILA BHAKTIVEDANTA SWAMI PRABHUPADA
(Said upon entering the temple room by his disciples, and sung during many *arati* ceremonies.)

nama om vishnu-padaya krishna-preshthaya bhu-tale
shrimate bhaktivedanta-svamin iti namine

namas te sarasvate deve gaura-vani-pracharine
nirvishesha-shunyavadi-pashcatya-desha-tarine

Translation

I offer my respectful obeisances unto His Divine Grace A. C. Bhaktivedanta Swami Prabhupada, who is very dear to Lord Krishna, having taken shelter at His lotus feet.

Our respectful obeisances are unto you, O spiritual master, servant of Sarasvati Gosvami. You are kindly preaching the message of Lord Chaitanyadeva and delivering the Western countries, which are filled with impersonalism and voidism.

SRI SRI GURVASHTAKA
(Glories of the Spiritual Master, sung for early morning *mangala arati*, by Srila Vishvanatha Chakravarti Thakura)

(1)
samsara-davanala-lidha-loka
tranaya karunya-ghanaghanatvam
praptasya kalyana-gunarnavasya
vande guroh shri-charanaravindam

(2)
mahaprabhoh kirtana-nritya-gita-
vaditra-madyan-manaso rasena
romancha-kampashru-taranga-bhajo
vande guroh shri-charanaravindam

(3)
shri-vigraharadhana-nitya-nana-
shringara-tan-mandira-marjanadau
yuktasya bhaktamsh cha niyunjato 'pi
vande guroh shri-charanaravindam

(4)
chatur-vidha-shri-bhagavat-prasada-
svadv-anna-triptan hari-bhakta-sanghan
kritvaiva triptim bhajatah sadaiva
vande guroh shri-charanaravindam

(5)
shri-radhika-madhavayor apara-
madhurya-lila-guna-rupa-namnam
prati-kshanasvadana-lolupasya
vande guroh shri-charanaravindam

(6)
nikunja-yuno rati-keli-siddhyai

ya yalibhir yuktir apekshaniya
tatrati-dakshyad ati-vallabhasya
vande guroh shri-charanaravindam

(7)
sakshad-dharitvena samasta-shastrair
uktas tatha bhavyata eva sadbhih
kintu prabhor yah priya eva tasya
vande guroh shri-charanaravindam

(8)
yasya prasadad bhagavat-prasado
yasyaprasadan na gatih kuto 'pi
dhyayan stuvams tasya yashas tri-sandhyam
vande guroh shri-charanaravindam

(9)
srimad-guror ashtakam etad uccair
brahme muhurte pathati prayatnat
yas tena vrindavana-natha-sakshat-
sevaiva labhya janusha 'nta eva

Translation

(1) The spiritual master is receiving benediction from the ocean of mercy. Just as a cloud pours water on a forest fire to extinguish it, so the spiritual master delivers the materially afflicted world by extinguishing the blazing fire of material existence. I offer my respectful obeisances unto the lotus feet of such a spiritual master, who is an ocean of auspicious qualities.

(2) Chanting the holy name, dancing in ecstasy, singing, and playing musical instruments, the spiritual master is always gladdened by the *sankirtana* movement of Lord Chaitanya Mahaprabhu. Because he is relishing the mellows of pure devotion within his mind, sometimes his hair stands on end, he feels quivering in his body, and tears flow from his eyes like waves. I offer my respectful obeisances unto the lotus feet of such a spiritual master.

(3) The spiritual master is always engaged in the temple worship of Shri Shri Radha and Krishna. He also engages his disciples in such worship. They dress the deities in beautiful clothes and ornaments, clean Their temple, and perform other similar worship of the Lord. I offer my respectful obeisances unto the lotus feet of such a spiritual master.

(4) The spiritual master is always offering Krishna four kinds of delicious food [analyzed as that which is licked, chewed, drunk, and sucked]. When the spiritual master sees that the devotees are satisfied by eating *bhagavat-prasada*, he is satisfied. I offer my respectful obeisances unto the lotus feet of such a spiritual master.

(5) The spiritual master is always eager to hear and chant about the unlimited conjugal pastimes of Radhika and Madhava, and Their qualities, names, and forms. The spiritual master aspires to relish these at every moment. I offer my respectful obeisances unto the lotus feet of such a spiritual master.

(6) The spiritual master is very dear, because he is expert in assisting the gopis, who at different times make different tasteful arrangements for the perfection of Radha and Krishna's conjugal loving affairs within the groves of Vrindavana. I offer my respectful obeisances unto the lotus feet of such a spiritual master.

(7) The spiritual master is to be honored as much as the Supreme Lord, because he is the most confidential servitor of the Lord. This is acknowledged in all revealed scriptures and followed by all authorities. Therefore I offer my humble obeisances unto the lotus feet of such a spiritual master, who is a bona fide representative of Shri Hari [Krishna].

(8) By the mercy of the spiritual master one receives the benediction of Krishna. Without the grace of the spiritual master, one cannot make any advancement. Therefore, I should always remember and praise the spiritual master. At least three times a day I should offer my respectful obeisances unto the lotus feet of my a spiritual master.

(9) That person who very attentively recites this *ashtakam* [eight verses]to Sri Gurudeva during the *brahma muhurta* is sure to achieve direct service to the lotus feet of Sri Krishna, the very life and soul of Vrindavana (Vrindavana-natha), upon attaining his *vastu-siddhi*, or pure spiritual form.

Chapter Four

Additional Prayers Sung During Mangala-Arati

THE PANCHA-TATTVA MAHA MANTRA

(Jaya) shri-krishna-chaitanya
prabhu nityananda
shri-advaita gadadhara
shrivasadi-gaura-bhakta-vrinda

I offer my obeisances unto the Supreme Lord, Shri Krishna Chaitanya Mahaprabhu, along with His associates, Lord Nityananda, Shri Advaita Acharya, Gadadhara, Shrivasa and all the devotees of the Lord. (This mantra is very important and is known as the Pancha-tattva Maha-mantra. In order to derive the full benefit of chanting the Hare Krishna maha-mantra, we must first take shelter of Shri Chaitanya Mahaprabhu, learn the Pancha-tattva mantra, and then chant the Hare Krishna maha-mantra. That will be very effective. So this mantra is sung in most *kirtanas* before singing Hare Krishna, as well as before chanting *japa*.)

THE HARE KRISHNA MAHA-MANTRA

Hare Krishna Hare Krishna
Krishna Krishna Hare Hare
Hare Rama Hare Rama
Rama Rama Hare Hare

Translation
"Oh Lord Krishna, Oh energy of the Lord, please engage me in Your devotional service." (This is a simple call to the Lord and His energies. It should be chanted exactly like a small child crying for it's mother. The transcendental sound vibration of this mantra is the essence of all the *Vedas* and non-different from Lord Krishna personally. In the temples, this mantra is sung during some portion of almost all *kirtanas*.)

PREMA-DHVANI OR PRANAM PRAYERS

(Someone says these prayers after the *arati*, while everyone joins in with the "Jaya" at the end of each line. This is a very basic rendition, while additional lines and obeisances to other personalities and holy places can be said as well.)

1. Jaya-nitya-lila-pravishta om Vishnu-pada paramahamsa parivrajakacharya ashtottara-shata Shri Srimad His Divine Grace Srila A. C. Bhaktivedanta Swami Maharaja Prabhupada ki jaya.

2. Jaya om Vishnu-pada paramahamsa parivrajakacharya ashtottara-shata Shri Srimad Bhaktisiddhanta Sarasvati Goswami Maharaja Prabhupada ki jaya.

3. Ananta-kotivaishnava-vrinda ki jaya.

4. Namacharya Haridasa Thakura ki jaya

5. Iskcon founder acharya Srila Prabhupada ki jaya.

6. Premse kaho Shri-Krishna-Caitanya, Prabhu Nityananda, jaya Advaita, Gadadhara, Shrivasadi-gaura-bhakta-vrinda ki jaya.

7. Shri-Shri-Radha-Krishna Gopa-Gopinatha, Shyama Kund, Radha Kund, Girigovardhana ki jaya.

8. Vrindavana-dhama ki jaya.

9. Mathura-dhama ki jaya.

10. Navadvipa-dhama ki jaya.

11. Jagannatha-puri dhama ki jaya.

12. Ganga-mayi ki jaya

13. Yamuna-mayi ki jaya.

14. Tulasi-devi ki jaya.

15. Bhakti-devi ki jaya.

16. Sankirtana-yajna ki jaya.

17. Brihad-mridanga ki jaya.

18. Samaveta-bhakta-vrinda ki jaya.

19. Gaura-premananda, Hari Hari bol,

20. All glories to the assembled devotees. (Hare Krishna) All glories to the assembled devotees. (Hare Krishna) All glories to Sri Guru and Gauranga.

Chapter Four

SHRI NRISIMHA PRANAM
(Obeisances to Lord Nrisimha, sung at the end of *arati*)

namaste narasimhaya
prahladahlada-dayine
hiranyakashipor vakshah-
shila-tanka-nakhalaye

ito nrisimhah parato nrisimho
yato yato yami tato nrisimhah
bahir nrisimho hridaye nrisimho
nrisimham adim sharanam prapadye

tave kara-kamala-vare nakham
adbhuta-shringam
dalita-hiranyakashipu-tanu-bhrigam
keshava-dhrita-narahari-rupa jaya jagadisha hare

Translation

I offer my obeisances to Lord Narasimha, who gives joy to Prahlada Maharaja and whose nails are like chisels on the stonelike chest of the demon Hiranyakashipu.

Lord Nrisimha is here and also there. Wherever I go Lord Nrisimha is there. He is in the heart and is outside as well. I surrender to Lord Nrisimha, the origin of all things and the supreme refuge.

O Keshava! O Lord of the universe! O Lord Hari, who have assumed the form of half-man, half-lion! All glories to You! Just as one can easily crush a wasp between one's fingernails, so in the same way the body of the wasp-like demon, Hiranyakashipu, has been ripped apart by the wonderful pointed nails on Your beautiful lotus hands. (This verse is from *Shri Dasavatara-stotra*, the *Gita-govinda*, written by Jayadeva Gosvami.)

TULASI-ARATI KIRTANA

vrindayai tulasi-devyai
priyayai keshavasya cha
vishnu-bhakti-prade devi
satyavatyai namo namaha

Translation

(This first mantra is when we offer obeisances to Shrimati Tulasi Devi. Srila Prabhupada explains that the Tulasi tree is a pure devotee of Krishna in the body of a plant. Worship of the Tulasi plant is very important in devotional service.) "I offer my repeated obeisances unto Vrinda, Shrimati Tulasi Devi, who is very dear to Lord Keshava. O goddess, you bestow devotional service to Lord Krishna and possess the highest truth."

The following is the song sung during the Tulasi *arati*:

namo namah tulasi krishna-preyasi namo namaha
radha-krishna-seva pabo ei abhilashi
ye tomara sharana loy, tara vancha purna hoy
kripa kori' koro tare brindavana-basi
mor ei abhilash bilas kunje dio vas
nayane heribo sada jugala-rupa-rashi
ei nivedana dharo sakhir anugata koro
seva-adhikara diye koro nija dasi
dina krishna-dase koy ei jena mora hoy
shri-radha-govinda-preme sada jena bhasi

Translation

O Tulasi, beloved of Krishna, I bow before you again and again. My desire is to obtain the service of Shri Shri Radha-Krishna.

Whoever takes shelter of you has his wishes fulfilled. Bestowing your mercy on him, you make him a resident of Vrindavana.

My desire is that you will also grant me a residence in the pleasure groves of Shri Vrindavana-dhama. Thus, within my vision I will always behold the beautiful pastimes of Radha and Krishna.

I beg you to make me a follower of the cowherd damsels of Vraja. Please give me the privilege of devotional service and make me your own maidservant.

This very fallen and lowly servant of Krishna prays, "May I always swim in the love of Shri Radha and Govinda."

After the *arati*, devotees circumambulate the Tulasi plant while singing the following prayer:

> yani kani cha papani
> brahma-hatyadikani cha
> tani tani pranashyanti
> pradakshina pade pade

"By the circumambulation of Shrimati Tulasi Devi all the sins that one may have committed are destroyed at every step, even the sin of killing a brahman."

THE TEN OFFENSES IN CHANTING THE HOLY NAMES
(The general order of prayers in many temples is that after the Tulasi *puja*, the ten offenses in chanting Hare Krishna *japa* are recited, usually together with whoever is at the morning program.)

1. To blaspheme the devotees who have dedicated their lives to the propagation of the holy names of the Lord.
2. To consider the names of the demigods like lord Shiva or lord Brahma to be equal to, or independent of, the name of Lord Vishnu.
3. To disobey the orders of the spiritual master.
4. To blaspheme the Vedic literature or literature in pursuance of the Vedic version.
5. To consider the glories of chanting Hare Krishna as imagination.
6. To give mundane interpretation of the holy name of the Lord.
7. To commit sinful activities on the strength of chanting the holy names of the Lord.

8. To consider the chanting of Hare Krishna as one of the auspicious, ritualistic activities which are offered in the *Vedas* as fruitive activities (*karma-kanda*).

9. To instruct a faithless person about the glories of the holy name.

10. To not have complete faith in the chanting of the holy names and to maintain material attachments even after understanding so many instructions on this matter. It is also offensive to be inattentive while chanting.

Anyone who claims to be a Vaishnava must carefully guard against these ten offenses in order to quickly achieve the desired success, Krishna Prema!

Now let us offer are respectful obeisances unto all the Vaishnavas, devotees of the Lord. They are just like desire trees who can fulfill the desires of everyone and they are full of compassion for the fallen conditioned souls.

SHRI VAISHNAVA PRANAM
(Obeisances to fellow devotees often said after the early *aratis* and before doing *japa*)

vancha-kalpatarubhyash cha
kripa-sindubhya eva cha
patitanam pavanabhyo
vaishnavebhyo namo namaha

Translation

I offer my respectful obeisances unto all the Vaishnavas, devotees of the Lord. They are just like desire trees who can fulfill the desires of everyone and they are full of compassion for the fallen conditioned souls.

Chapter Four

SRI SRI SHIKSHASHTAKA
by Lord Chaitanya Mahaprabhu

Lord Chaitanya Mahaprabhu did not do much writing, but was widely renowned as a scholar in His youth. Nonetheless, He did leave these eight verses known as *Sikshashtaka*. These explain the essence of His mission and the philosophy of devotional service to Lord Krishna. See the article on Lord Chaitanya to learn more about Him.

(1)
cheto-darpana-marjanam bhava-maha-davagni-nirvapanam
shreyah-kairava-chandrika-vitaranam vidya-vadhu-jivanam
anandambhudhi-vardhanam prati-padam purnamritasvadanam
sarvatma-snapanam param vijayate shri-krishna-sankirtanam

Glory to the Shri Krishna *sankirtana* (congregational chanting of the Lord's holy names), which cleanses the heart of all the dust accumulated for years and extinguishes the fire of conditional life, of repeated birth and death. That *sankirtana* movement is the prime benediction for humanity at large because it spreads the rays of the benediction moon. It is the life of all transcendental knowledge. It increases the ocean of transcendental bliss, and it enables us to fully taste the nectar for which we are always anxious.

(2)
namnam akari bahudha nija-sarva-shaktis
tatrarpita niyamitah smarane na kalaha
etadrishi tava kripa bhagavan mamapi
durdaivam idrisham ihajani nanuragahah

O my Lord, Your holy name alone can render all benediction to living beings, and thus You have hundreds and millions of names, like Krishna and Govinda. In these transcendental names, you have invested all Your transcendental energies. There are not even hard and fast rules for chanting these names. O my Lord, out of kindness You enable us to easily approach you by Your holy names, but I am so unfortunate that I have no attraction for them.

(3)
trinad api sunicena
taror api sahishnuna
amanina manadena
kirtaniyah sada harihi

One should chant the holy name of the Lord in a humble state of mind, thinking oneself lower than the straw in the street; one should be more tolerant than a tree, devoid of all sense of false prestige, and should be ready to offer all respect to others. In such a state of mind one can chant the holy name of the Lord constantly.

(4)
na dhanam na janam na sundarim
kavitam va jagad-isha kamaye
mama janmani janmanishvare
bhavatad bhaktir ahaituki tvayi

O almighty Lord, I have no desire to accumulate wealth, nor do I desire beautiful women, nor do I want any number of followers. I only want your causeless devotional service, birth after birth.

(5)
ayi nanda-tanuja kinkaram
patitam mam vishame bhavambudhau
kripaya tava pada-pankaja-
sthita-dhuli-sadrisham vichintaya

O son of Maharaja Nanda [Krishna], I am Your eternal servitor, yet somehow or other I have fallen into the ocean of birth and death. Please pick me up from this ocean of death and place me as one of the atoms at Your lotus feet.

(6)
nayanam galad-ashru-dharaya
vadanam gadgada-ruddhaya gira

pulakair nichitam vapuh kada
tava nama-grahane bhavishyati

O my Lord, when will my eyes be decorated with tears of love flowing constantly when I chant Your holy name? When will my voice choke up, and when will the hairs of my body stand on end at the recitation of Your name?

(7)
yugayitam nimeshena
chakshusha pravrishayitam
shunyayitam jagat sarvam
govinda-virahena me

O Govinda! Feeling Your separation, I am considering a moment to be like twelve years or more. Tears are flowing from my eyes like torrents of rain, and I am feeling all vacant in the world in Your absence.

(8)
ashlishya va pada-ratam pinashtu mam
adarshanan marma-hatam karotu va
yatha tatha va vidadhatu lampato
mat-prana-nathas tu sa eva naparaha

I know no one but Krishna as my Lord, and He shall remain so even if He handles me roughly by His embrace or makes me brokenhearted by not being present before me. He is completely free to do anything and everything, for He is always my worshipful Lord, unconditionally.

JAYA RADHA-MADHAVA
(Sung before morning class, written by Shrila Bhaktinoda Thakura)
jaya radha-madhava kunja-bihari
gopi-jana-vallabha giri-vara-dhari
yashoda-nandana braja-jana-ranjana
jamuna-tira-vana-chari

Translation

Krishna is the lover of Radha. He displays many amorous pastimes in the groves of Vrindavana, He is the lover of the cowherd maidens of Vraja, the holder of the great hill named Govardhana, the beloved son of Mother Yashoda, the delighter of the inhabitants of Vraja, and He wanders in the forests along the banks of the River Yamuna.

(Srila Prabhupada was very fond of this song and sang it just before his lectures. In Allahabad and Gorakhpur, Srila Prabhupada fell into a trance after singing the first two lines, and after some time he came back into external consciousness and said: "Now just chant Hare Krishna." Srila Prabhupada said that this song is "a picture of Vrindavana. Everything is there--Shrimati Radharani, Vrindavana, Govardhana, Yashoda, and all the cowherd boys.")

MANTRAS CHANTED BEFORE CLASS

Om namah bhagavate vasudevaya
"I offer my obeisances to the Supreme Personality of Godhead, Vasudeva."

narayanam namaskritya
naram chaiva narottamam
devim sarasvatim vyasam
tato jayam udirayet

"Before reciting this *Srimad-Bhagavatam*, which is the very means of conquest, one should offer respectful obeisances unto the Personality of Godhead, Narayana, unto Nara-narayana Rishi, the supermost human being, unto Mother Sarasvati, the goddess of learning, and unto Srila Vyasadeva, the author." (*Srimad-Bhagavatam* 1.2.4)

shrinvatam sva-kathah krsnah
punya-shravana-kirtanah
hridy antah stho hy abhadrani
vidhunoti suhrit satam

"Sri Krishna, the Personality of Godhead, who is the Paramatma in everyone's heart and the benefactor of the truthful devotee, cleanses desire for material enjoyment from the heart of the devotee who has developed the urge to hear His messages, which are in themselves virtuous when properly heard and chanted." (*Srimad-Bhagavatam* 1.2.17)

>nashta-prayeshu abhadreshu
>nityam bhagavata-sevaya
>bhagavaty uttama-shloke
>bhaktir bhavati naishthiki

"By regular attendance in classes on the *Bhagavatam* and by rendering service to the pure devotee, all that is troublesome to the heart is almost completely destroyed, and loving service unto the Personality of Godhead, who is praised with transcendental songs, is established as an irrevocable fact." (*Bhag.* 1.2.18)

MANTRAS CHANTED BEFORE CLASS COMMENTARY

Sri Guru Pranama

>Om ajnana-timirandhasya   jnananjana-shalakaya
>chakshur unmilitam yena   tasmai shri-guruve namaha

I was born in the darkest of ignorance, and my spiritual master opened my eyes with the torch of knowledge. I offer my respectful obeisances unto him.

Sri Rupa Pranama

>shri-chaitanya-mano 'bhishtam   sthapitam yena bhu-tale
>svayam rupah kada mahyam   dadati sva-padantikam

When will Srila Rupa Gosvami Prabhupada, who has established within this material world the mission to fulfill the desire of Lord Chaitanya, give me shelter under his lotus feet?

Mangalacarana

vande 'ham shri-guroh shri-yuta-pada-kamalam shri-gurun vaishnavams cha
shri-rupam sagrajatam saha-gana-raghunathanvitam tam sa-jivam
sadvaitam savadhutam parijana-sahitam krishna-chaitanya-devam
shri-radha-krishna-padan saha-gana-lalita-shri-vishakhanvitamsh cha

I offer my respectful obeisances unto the lotus feet of my spiritual master and unto the feet of all Vaishnavas. I offer my respectful obeisances unto the lotus feet of Shrila Rupa Gosvami along with his elder brother Sanatana Gosvami, as well as Raghunatha Dasa and Raghunatha Bhatta, Gopala Bhatta, and Shrila Jiva Gosvami. I offer my respectful obeisances to Lord Krishna Chaitanya and Lord Nityananda, along with Advaita Acharya, Gadadhara, Shrivasa, and other associates. I offer my respectful obeisances to Shrimati Radharani, and Shri Krishna along with Their associates, Shri Lalita and Vishakha.

Sri Krishna Pranama

he krishna karuna-sindho   dina bandho jagat pate
gopesha gopika-kanta   radha-kanta namo 'stu te

O my dear Krishna, You are the friend of the distressed and the source of creation. You are the master of the gopis and the lover of Radharani. I offer my respectful obeisances unto You.

Sri Radha Pranama

tapta-kanchana-gaurangi   radhe vrindavaneshvari
vrishabhanu-sute devi   pranamami hari-priye

I offer my respects to Radharani whose bodily complexion is like molten gold and who is the Queen of Vrindavana. You are the daughter of King Vrishabhanu, and You are very dear to Lord Krishna.

Sri Vaishnava Pranama

vancha-kalpatarubhyash cha   kripa-sindhubhya eva cha
patitanam pavanebhyo   vaishnavebhyo namo namaha

I offer my respectful obeisances unto all the Vaishnava devotees of the Lord who can fulfill the desires of everyone, just like desire trees, and who are full of compassion for the fallen souls.

Pancha-tattva Maha-mantra
shri krishna chaitanya prabhu nityananda
shri advaita gadadhara shrivasadi-gaura-bhakta-vrinda

I offer my obeisances to Shri Krishna Chaitanya, Prabhu Nityananda, Sri Advaita, Gadadhara, Shrivasa and all others in the line of devotion.

Hare Krishna, Hare Krishna, Krishna Krishna, Hare Hare
Hare Rama, Hare Rama, Rama Rama, Hare Hare

Additional Pranama Mantras
(These, along with the previous ones listed above, are often used during *pushpa abhisheka* ceremonies, that is when a shower of flowers are offered from the devotees)

Sri Bhaktisiddhanta Sarasvati Pranati
namo om vishnu-padaya krishna-preshthaya bhutale
shrimate bhaktisiddhanta-sarasvati namine

I offer my respectful obeisances unto His Divine Grace Bhaktisiddhanta Sarasvati, who is very dear to Lord Krishna, having taken shelter of His lotus feet.

shri-varshabhanavi-devi-dayitaya kripabdhaye
krishna-sambandha-vijnana-dayine prabhave namaha

I offer my respectful obeisances to Sri Varshabhanavi-devi-dayita dasa [another name of Srila Bhaktisiddhanta Sarasvati], who is favored by Srimati Radharani and who is the ocean of transcendental mercy and the deliverer of the science of Krishna.

madhuryojjvala-premadhya-sri-rupanuga-bhaktida-
sri-gaura-karuna-shakti-vigrahaya namo 'stu te

I offer my respectful obeisances unto you, the personified energy of Sri Chaitanya's mercy, who delivers devotional service which is enriched with conjugal love of Radha and Krishna, coming exactly in the line of revelation of Srila Rupa Goswami.

namas te gaura-vani-shri-murtaye dina-tarine
rupanuga-viruddhapasiddhanta-dhvanta-harine

I offer my respectful obeisances unto you, who are the personified teachings of Lord Chaitanya. You are the deliverer of the fallen souls. You do not tolerate any statement which is against the teachings of devotional service enunciated by Srila Rupa Goswami.

Srila Gaurakishora Pranati
namo gaura-kishoraya sakshad-vairagya-murtaye
vipralambha-rasambhode padambujaya te namaha

I offer my respectful obeisances unto Gaurakishora dasa Babaji Maharaja [the spiritual master of Bhaktisiddhanta Sarasvati], who is renunciation personified. He is always merged in a feeling of separation and intense love of Krishna.

Srila Bhaktivinoda Pranati
namo bhaktivinodaya sac-chid-ananda-namine
gaura-shakti-svarupaya rupanuga-varaya te

I offer my respectful obeisances unto Saccidananda Bhaktivinoda, who is transcendental energy of Chaitanya Mahaprabhu. He is a strict follower of the Gosvamis, headed by Srila Rupa.

Srila Jagannatha Pranati
gauravirbhava-bhumes tvam nirdeshta saj-jana-priyaha
vaishnava-sarvabhaumah sri-jagannathaya te namaha

I offer my respectful obeisances to Jagannatha dasa Babaji, who is respected by the entire Vaishnava community and who discovered the place where Lord Chaitanya appeared.

Sri Gauranga Pranama
namo maha-vadanyaya krishna-prema-pradaya te
krishnaya krishna-chaitanya-namne gaura-tvise namaha

O most munificent incarnation! You are Krishna Himself appearing as Sri Krishna Chaitanya Mahaprabhu. You have assumed the golden color of Srimati Radharani, and You are widely distributing pure love of Krishna. We offer our respectful obeisances unto You.

Sri Pancha-tattva Pranama
pancha-tattvatmakam krishnam bhakta-rupa-svarupakam
bhaktavataram bhaktakhyam namami bhakta-shaktikam

I offer my obeisances unto the Supreme Lord, Krishna, who is nondifferent from His features as a devotee, devotional incarnation, devotional manifestation, pure devotee, and devotional energy.

Krishna Pranam
namo brahmanya-devaya go-brahmana-hitaya cha
jagad-dhitaya krishnaya govindaya namo namaha

I offer my respectful obeisances to the Supreme Absolute Truth, Krishna, who is the well-wisher of the cows and the brahmanas as well as the living entities in general. I offer my repeated obeisances to Govinda, who is the pleasure reservoir for all the senses.

Sambandhadhideva Pranama
jayatam suratau pangor mama manda-mater gati
mat-sarvasva-padambhojau radha-madana-mohanau

Glory to the all-merciful Radha and Madana-mohana! I am lame and ill advised, yet they are my directors, and Their lotus feet are everything to me.

Abhidheyadhideva Pranama
divyad-vrindaranya-kalpa-drumadhaha
shrimad-ratnagara-simhasana-sthau
shrimad-radha-shrila-govinda-devau
preshthalibhih sevyamanau smarami

In a temple of jewels in Vrindavana, underneath a desire tree, Sri Sri Radha-Govinda, served by their most confidential associates, sit upon an effulgent throne. I offer my humble obeisances unto Them.

Prayojanadhideva Pranama
shriman rasa-rasarambhi vamshi-vata-tata-sthitaha
karshan venu-svanair gopir gopinathaha shriye 'stu naha

Sri Srila Gopinatha, who originated the transcendental mellow of the rasa dance, stands on the shore in Vamshivata and attracts the attention of the cowherd damsels with the sound of His celebrated flute. May they all confer upon us their benediction.

FROM THE BRAHMA-SAMHITA
(Sung during the greeting of the Deities)

govindam adi-purusham tam aham bhajami
govindam adi-purusham tam aham bhajami
govindam adi-purusham tam aham bhajami

venum kvanantam aravinda-dalayataksham
barhavatamsam asitambuda-sundarangam
kandarpa-koti-kamaniya-vishesha-shobham
govindam adi-purusham tam aham bhajami

Translation

I worship Govinda, the primeval Lord, who is adept at playing on His flute, whose eyes are like the petals of a blooming lotus, whose head is bedecked with a peacock's feather, whose figure of beauty is tinged with the hue of blue clouds, and whose unique loveliness charms millions of Cupids.

> angani yasya sakalendriya-vittimanti
> pashyanti panti kalayanti chiram jaganti
> ananda-chin-maya-sad-ujjvala-virgrahasya
> govindam adi-purusham tam aham bhajami

Translation

I worship Govinda, the primeval Lord, whose transcendental form is full of bliss, truth, and substantiality and thus emanates the most dazzling splendor. Each of the limbs of that transcendental figure possesses in itself the full-fledged functions of all the organs, and He eternally sees, maintains, and manifests the infinite universes, both spiritual and material.

SRI GURU-VANDANA

(Sung during Guru *puja*, worship of the spiritual master, by Shrila Narottama dasa Thakura)

(1)
shri-guru-charana-padma, kevala-bhakati-sadma
bando mui savadhana mate
jahara prasade bhai, e bhava toriya jai,
krishna-prapti hoy jaha ha'te

(2)
guru-mukha-padma-vakya, chittete koriya aikya
ar na koriho mane asha
shri-guru-charane rati, ei se uttama-gati
je prasade pure sarva asha

(3)
chakhu-dan dilo jei, janme janme prabhu sei
divya-jnan hride prokashito
prema-bhakti jaha hoite, avidya vinasha jate
vede gay jahara charito

(4)
shri-guru karuna-sindhu, adhama janara bandhu
lokanath lokera jivana
ha ha prabhu koro doya, deho more pada-chaya
ebe jasha ghushuk tribhavana

tuya pade loinu sarana
jaya jaya prabhupada! jaya jaya gurudeva!

Translation

(1) The lotus feet of our spiritual master are the only way by which we can attain pure devotional service. I bow to his lotus feet with great awe and reverence. By his grace one can cross the ocean of material suffering and obtain the mercy of Krishna.

(2) My only wish is to have my consciousness purified by the words emanating from his lotus mouth. Attachment to his lotus feet is the perfection that fulfills all desires.

(3) He opens my darkened eyes and fills my heart with transcendental knowledge. He is my Lord birth after birth. From him ecstatic prema emanates; by him ignorance is destroyed. The Vedic scriptures sing of his character.

(4) Our spiritual master is the ocean of mercy, the friend of the poor, and the lord and master of the devotees. O master! Be merciful unto me. Give me the shade of your lotus feet. Your fame is spread all over the three worlds. We take shelter of your lotus feet. You are the friend of the most fallen.

I take shelter at your lotus feet.
All glories to Srila Prabhupada! All glories to Gurudeva!

Chapter Four

SRI NAMA-KIRTANA
(Another nice song sung anytime, but often after greeting the deities, by Shrila Bhaktivinoda Thakura)

(1)
yashomati-nandana, braja-baro-nagara
gokula-ranjana kana
gopi-parana-dhana, madana-manohara
kaliya-damana-vidhana

(2)
amala harinam amiya-vilasa
vipina-purandara, navina nagara-bora
bamshi-badana suvasa

(3)
braja-jana-palana, asura-kula-nashana
nanda-godhana-rakhowala
govinda madhava, navanita-taskara
sundara nanda-gopala

(4)
jamuna-tata-chara, gopi-basana-hara
rasa-rasika kripamoya
shri-radha-vallabha, brindabana-natabara
bhakativinod-ashraya

Translation

(1) Lord Krishna is the beloved son of mother Yashoda; the transcendental lover in the land of Vraja; the delight of Gokula; Kana [a nickname of Krishna]; the wealth of the lives of the gopis. He steals the mind of even Cupid and punishes the Kaliya serpent.

(2) These pure, holy names of Lord Hari are full of sweet, nectarean pastimes. Krishna is the Lord of the twelve forests of Vraja. He is ever-youthful and is the best of lovers. He is always playing on a flute, and He is an excellent dresser.

(3) Krishna is the protector of the inhabitants of Vraja; the destroyer of various demoniac dynasties; the keeper and tender of Nanda Maharaja's cows; the giver of pleasure to the cows, land, and spiritual senses; the husband of the goddess of fortune; the butter thief; and the beautiful cowherd boy of Nanda Maharaja.

(4) Krishna wanders along the banks of the River Yamuna. He stole the garments of the young damsels of Vraja who were bathing there. He delights in the mellows of the rasa dance; He is very merciful; the lover and beloved of Shrimati Radharani; the great dancer of Vrindavana; and the shelter and only refuge of Thakura Bhaktivinoda.

Other Nice Songs

GOVINDA JAYA JAYA

govinda jaya jaya gopala jaya jaya
radha-ramana hari govinda jaya jaya

Translation
All glories to Lord Govinda (the giver of pleasure to the senses and cows) and Lord Gopala (the transcendental Cowherd Boy). All glories to Radha-Ramana (another name of Krishna), Hari (Lord Krishna who takes away the material attachments of the devotees) and Govinda.

PRAYER TO LORD CHAITANYA AND LORD NITYANANDA

nitai gouranga, nitai gouranga
jaya shachinandana, gaura hari

Translation
All glories to Lord Nityananda and Lord Chaitanya, the son of Shachi-devi, who is Krishna Himself with a golden hue.

Chapter Four

PRAYERS TO LORD JAGANNATHA

jagannatha swami nayana-patha-gami bhavatu me

Translation
May that Jagannatha Swami (Lord of the universe) be the object of my vision.

PRASADA-SEVAYA
(Sung before honoring the Lord's *prasada*--from *Gitavali*)

Sharira abidya-jal, jodendriya tahe kal,
jiva phele vishaya-sagore
ta'ra madhye jihwa ati, lobhamoy sudurmati,
ta'ke jeta kathina samsare

krishna baro doyamoy, koribare jihwa jay,
swa-prasad-anna dilo bhai
sei annamrita pao, radha-krishna-guna gao,
preme dako chaitanya-nitai

1. This material body is a network of ignorance, and the senses are one's deadly enemies, for they throw the soul into this ocean of material sense enjoyment. Among those senses the tongue is the most voracious and uncontrollable; it is very difficult to conquer the tongue in this world.

2. Lord Krishna is very merciful and has given us the remnants of His own food just to control the tongue. Now please accept that nectarean Krishna-prasada and sing the glories of Their Lordships Sri Sri Radha and Krishna, and in love call out "Chaitanya Nitai!"

GLORIFICATION OF THE LORD'S PRASADA
(from the *Mahabharata*)

maha-prasade govinde
nama-brahmani-vaishnava

svalpa-punya-vatam rajan
vishvaso naiva jayate

"O King, for those who have amassed very few pious activities, their faith in maha-prasada, in Sri Govinda, in the Holy Name and in the Vaishnava is never born [again]."

Additional Kirtanas

FROM "SHRI SHRI SHAD-GOSWAMY-ASHTAKA"
(Verse 2 is sung before reading *The Nectar of Devotion*)

Verse 1
krishnotkirtana-gana-nartana-parau premamritambho-nidhi
dhiradhira-jana-priyau priya-karau nirmatsarau pujitau
sri-caitanya-kripa-bharau bhuvi bhuvo bharavahantarakau
vande rupa-sanatanau raghu-yugau sri-jiva-gopalakau

I offer my respectful obeisances unto the six Gosvamis, namely Sri Rupa Gosvami, Sri Sanatana Gosvami, Sri Raghunatha Bhatta Gosvami, Sri Raghunatha dasa Gosvami, Sri Jiva Gosvami, and Sri Gopala Bhatta Gosvami, who are always engaged in chanting the holy name of Krishna and dancing. They are just like the ocean of love of God, and they are popular both with the gentle and with the ruffians, because they are not envious of anyone. Whatever they do, they are all-pleasing to everyone, and they are fully blessed by Lord Caitanya. Thus they are engaged in missionary activities meant to deliver all the conditioned souls in the material universe.

Verse 2
nana-sastra-vicaranaika-nipunau sad-dharma-samsthapakau
lokanam hita-karinau tri-bhuvane manyau saranyakarau
radha-krsna-padaravinda-bhajananandena mattalikau
vande rupa-sanatanau raghu-yugau sri-jiva-gopalakau

Chapter Four

I offer my respectful obeisances unto the six Gosvamis, namely Sri Rupa Gosvami, Sri Sanatana Gosvami, Sri Raghunatha Bhatta Gosvami, Sri Raghunatha dasa Gosvami, Sri Jiva Gosvami, and Sri Gopala Bhatta Gosvami, who are very expert in scrutinizingly studying all the revealed scriptures with the aim of establishing eternal religious principles for the benefit of all human beings. Thus they are honored all over the three worlds and they are worth taking shelter of because they are absorbed in the mood of the gopis and are engaged in the transcendental loving service of Radha and Krishna.

Verse 3
sri-gauranga-gunanuvarnana-vidhau sraddha-samrddhy-anvitau
papottapa-nikrntanau tanu-bhrtam govinda-ganamrtaih
anandambudhi-vardhanaika-nipunau kaivalya-nistarakau
vande rupa-sanatanau raghu-yugau sri-jiva-gopalakau

I offer my respectful obeisances unto the six Gosvamis, namely Sri Rupa Gosvami, Sri Sanatana Gosvami, Sri Raghunatha Bhatta Gosvami, Sri Raghunatha dasa Gosvami, Sri Jiva Gosvami, and Sri Gopala Bhatta Gosvami, who are very much enriched in understanding of Lord Chaitanya and who are thus expert in narrating His transcendental qualities. They can purify all conditioned souls from the reactions of their sinful activities by pouring upon them transcendental songs about Govinda. As such, they are very expert in increasing the limits of the ocean of transcendental bliss, and they are the saviors of the living entities from the devouring mouth of liberation.

Verse 4
tyaktva turnam asesa-mandala-pati-srenim sada tuccha-vat
bhutva dina-ganesakau karunaya kaupina-kanthasritau
gopi-bhava-rasamrtabdhi-lahari-kallola-magnau muhur
vande rupa-sanatanau raghu-yugau sri-jiva-gopalakau

I offer my respectful obeisances unto the six Gosvamis, namely Sri Rupa Gosvami, Sri Sanatana Gosvami, Sri Raghunatha Bhatta Gosvami, Sri Raghunatha dasa Gosvami, Sri Jiva Gosvami, and Sri

Gopala Bhatta Gosvami, who kicked off all association of aristocracy as insignificant. In order to deliver the poor conditioned souls, they accepted loincloths, treating themselves as mendicants, but they are always merged in the ecstatic ocean of the *gopis'* love for Krishna and bathe always and repeatedly in the waves of that ocean.

Verse 5

kujat-kokila-hamsa-sarasa-ganakirne mayurakule
nana-ratna-nibaddha-mula-vitapa-sri-yukta-vrndavane
radha-krsnam ahar-nisam prabhajatau jivarthadau yau muda
vande rupa-sanatanau raghu-yugau sri-jiva-gopalakau

    I offer my respectful obeisances unto the six Gosvamis, namely Sri Rupa Gosvami, Sri Sanatana Gosvami, Sri Raghunatha Bhatta Gosvami, Sri Raghunatha dasa Gosvami, Sri Jiva Gosvami, and Sri Gopala Bhatta Gosvami, who were always engaged in worshiping Radha-Krishna in the transcendental land of Vrindavana where there are beautiful trees full of fruits and flowers which have under their roots all valuable jewels. The Gosvamis are perfectly competent to bestow upon the living entities the greatest boon of the goal of life.

Verse 6

sankhya-purvaka-nama-gana-natibhih kalavasani-krtau
nidrahara-viharakadi-vijitau chatyanta-dinau cha yau
radha-krsna-guna-smrter madhurimanandena sammohitau
vande rupa-sanatanau raghu-yugau sri-jiva-gopalakau

    I offer my respectful obeisances unto the six Gosvamis, namely Sri Rupa Gosvami, Sri Sanatana Gosvami, Sri Raghunatha Bhatta Gosvami, Sri Raghunatha dasa Gosvami, Sri Jiva Gosvami, and Sri Gopala Bhatta Gosvami, who were engaged in chanting the holy names of the Lord and bowing down in a scheduled measurement. In this way they utilized their valuable lives and in executing these devotional activities they conquered over eating and sleeping and were always meek and humble enchanted by remembering the transcendental qualities of the Lord.

Chapter Four

Verse 7
radha-kunda-tate kalinda-tanaya-tire cha vamsivate
premonmada-vasad asesa-dasaya grastau pramattau sada
gayantau cha kada harer guna-varam bhavabhibhutau muda
vande rupa-sanatanau raghu-yugau sri-jiva-gopalakau

I offer my respectful obeisances unto the six Gosvamis, namely Sri Rupa Gosvami, Sri Sanatana Gosvami, Sri Raghunatha Bhatta Gosvami, Sri Raghunatha dasa Gosvami, Sri Jiva Gosvami, and Sri Gopala Bhatta Gosvami, who were sometimes on the bank of the Radha-kunda lake or the shores of the Yamuna and sometimes at Vamsivata. There they appeared just like madmen in the full ecstasy of love for Krishna, exhibiting different transcendental symptoms in their bodies, and they were merged in the ecstasy of Krishna consciousness.

Verse 8
he radhe vraja-devike ca lalite he nanda-suno kutah
sri-govardhana-kalpa-padapa-tale kalindi-vane kutah
ghosantav iti sarvato vraja-pure khedair maha-vihvalau
vande rupa-sanatanau raghu-yugau sri-jiva-gopalakau

I offer my respectful obeisances unto the six Gosvamis, namely Sri Rupa Gosvami, Sri Sanatana Gosvami, Sri Raghunatha Bhatta Gosvami, Sri Raghunatha dasa Gosvami, Sri Jiva Gosvami, and Sri Gopala Bhatta Gosvami, who were chanting very loudly everywhere in Vrindavana, shouting, "Queen of Vrindavana, Radharani! O Lalita! O son of Nanda Maharaja! Where are you all now? Are you just on the hill of Govardhana, or are you under the trees on the bank of the Yamuna? Where are you?" These were their moods in executing Krishna consciousness.

KIRTANA RECITED BEFORE READING "KRISHNA BOOK"

krishna krishna krishna krishna krishna krishna krishna he
krishna krishna krishna krishna krishna krishna krishna he

krishna krishna krishna krishna krishna krishna raksha mam
krishna krishna krishna krishna krishna krishna pahi mam
rama raghava rama raghava rama raghava raksha mam
krishna keshava krishna keshava krishna keshava pahi mam

O Lord Krishna, please protect me and maintain me. O Lord Rama, descendant of King Raghu, please protect me. O Krishna, O Keshava, killer of the Keshi demon, please maintain me.

NAMA-SANKIRTANA
By Srila Narottama dasa Thakura

1
hari harayenamah krishna yadavaya namaha
yadavaya madhavaya keshavaya namaha

2
gopala govinda rama shri-madhusudana
giridhari gopinatha madana-mohana

3
shri-chaitanya-nityananda shri-adwaita-sita
hari guru vaishnava bhagavata gita

4
shri-rupa-sanatana bhatta-raghunatha
shri-jiva gopala-bhatta dasa-raghunatha

5
ei chay gosair kori charana vandan
jaha hoite bighna-nash abhishta-puran

6
ei chay gosai jar-mui tar das
ta-sabara pada-renu mora pancha-gras

Chapter Four

7
tadera charana-sebi-bhakta-sane bas
janame janame hoy e abhilash

8
ei chay gosai jabe braje koila bas
radha-krishna-nitya-lila korila prakash

9
anande bolo hari bhaja brindaban
shri-guru-vaishnava-pade mayaiya man

10
shri-guru-vaishnava-pada-padma kori ash
narottama dasa kohe nama-sankirtana

1. O Lord Hari, O Lord Krishna, I offer my obeisances to You, who are known as Hari, Yadava, Madhava, and Keshava.

2. O Gopala, Govinda, Rama, Shri Madhusudana, Giridhari, Gopinatha, and Madana-mohana.

3. All glories to Shri Chaitanya and Nityananda. All glories to Shri Adwaita Acharya and His consort, Shri Sita Thakurani. All glories to Lord Hari, to the spiritual master, the Vaishnavas, *Srimad-Bhagavatam*, and *Srimad Bhagavad-gita*.

4. All glories to Shri Rupa Goswami, Sanatana Goswami, Raghunatha Bhatta Goswami, Shri Jiva Goswami, Gopala Bhatta Goswami, and Raghunatha Dasa Goswami.

5. I offer my obeisances to the feet of these Six Goswamis. Bowing to them destroys all obstacles to devotion and fulfills all spiritual desires.

6. I am the servant of that person who is a servant of these Six Goswamis. the dust of their lotus feet is my five kinds of foods.

7. This is my desire: that birth after birth I may live with those devotees who serve the lotus feet of these Six Goswamis.

8. When these Six Goswamis lived in Vraja, they revealed the lost holy places and explained the eternal pastimes of Radha & Krishna.

9. Just shout the names of Lord Hari in great ecstasy and worship the transcendental realm of Vrindavana while absorbing your mind in meditation upon the divine feet of the spiritual master and the Vaishnavas.

10. Desiring to serve the lotus feet of Shri Guru and the Vaishnavas, Narottama Dasa sings this *sankirtana* of the holy names of Lord Hari.

GAURA-ARATI
(The evening *arati* song, by Shrila Bhaktivinoda Thakura)

(kiba) jaya jaya gorachander aratiko shobha
jahnavi-tata-vane jaga-mana-lobha

(Refrain:) jaga-mana-lobha
gauranger arotik shobha
jaga-mana-lobha

dakhine nitaichand, bame gadadhara
nikate adwaita, shrinivasa chatra-dhara

bosiyache gorachand ratna-simhasane
arati koren brahma-adi devi-gane

narahari-adi kori' chamara dhulaya
sanjaya-mukunda-basu-ghosh-adi gaya

shanka baje ghanta baje karatala
madhura mridanga baje parama rasala

(Refrain:) madhur madhur madhur baje
shanka baje ghanta baje
madhur madhur madhur baje

(kiba) bahu-koti chandra jini' vadana ujjvala
gala-deshe bana-mala kore jhalamala

shiva-shuka-narada preme gada-gada
bhaktivinoda dekhe gorara sampada

(Repeat first verse of song)

Translation

All glories, all glories to the beautiful *arati* ceremony of Lord Chaitanya. This Gaura-arati is taking place in a grove on the banks of the Jahnavi [Ganges] and is attracting the minds of all living entities in the universe.

On Lord Chaitanya's right side is Lord Nityananda, and on His left side is Shri Gadadhara. Nearby stand Shri Advaita, and Shrivasa Thakura is holding an umbrella over Lord Chaitanya's head.

Lord Chaitanya has sat down on a jeweled throne, and the demigods, headed by Lord Brahma, perform the *arati* ceremony.

Narahari Sarakara and other associates of Lord Chaitanya fan Him with *chamaras*, and devotees headed by Sanjaya Pandita, Mukunda Datta, and Vasu Ghosha sing sweet *kirtana*.

Conchshells, bells, and *karatalas* resound, and the *mridangas* play very sweetly. This *kirtana* music is supremely sweet and relishable to hear.

The brilliance of Lord Chaitanya's face conquers millions upon millions of moons, and the garland of forest flowers around His neck shines.

Lord Shiva, Sukadeva Gosvami, and Narada Muni are all there, and their voices are choked with the ecstasy of transcendental love. Thus Thakura Bhaktivinoda envisions the glory of Lord Shri Chaitanya.

SHRI DAMODARASHTAKA
Sung every morning during the month of Kartika,
(October-November),
found in the *Padma Purana* of Krishna Dvaipayana Vyasa, spoken by Satyavrata Muni in a conversation with Narada Muni and Saunaka Rsi.

"In the month of Kartika one should worship Lord Damodara and daily recite the prayer known as Damodarastaka, which has been spoken by the sage Satyavrata and which attracts Lord Damodara." (*Sri Hari-bhakti-vilasa* 2.16.198)

(1)
namamisvaram sac-chid-ananda-rupam
lasat-kundalam gokule bhrajamanam
yasoda-bhiyolukhalad dhavamanam
paramrstam atyantato drutya gopya

(2)
rudantam muhur netra-yugmam mrjantam
karambhoja-yugmena satanka-netram
muhuh svasa-kampa-trirekhanka-kantha-
sthita-graivam damodaram bhakti-baddham

(3)
itidrk sva-lilabhir ananda-kunde
sva-ghosam nimajjantam akhyapayantam
tadiyesita-jnesu bhaktair jitatvam
punah prematas tam satavrtti vande

(4)
varam deva moksam na moksavadhim va
na chanyam vrne 'ham varesad apiha
idam te vapur natha gopala-balam
sada me manasy avirastam kim anyaih

(5)
idam te mukhambhojam atyanta-nilair
vrtam kuntalaih snigdha-raktais cha gopya
muhus cumbitam bimba-raktadharam me
manasy avirastam alam laksa-labhaih

(6)
namo deva damodarananta vishno
prasida prabho duhkha-jalabdhi-magnam
krpa-drsti-vrstyati-dinam batanu
grhanesa mam ajnam edhy aksi-drsyah

(7)
kuveratmajau baddha-murtyaiva yadvat
tvaya mocitau bhakti-bhajau krtau cha
tatha prema-bhaktim svakam me prayaccha
na mokse graho me 'sti damodareha

(8)
namas te 'stu damne sphurad-dipti-dhamne
tvadiyodarayatha visvasya dhamne
namo radhikayai tvadiya-priyayai
namo 'nanta-lilaya devaya tubhyam

Translation

(1) To the Supreme Lord, whose form is the embodiment of eternal existence, knowledge, and bliss, whose shark-shaped earrings are swinging to and fro, who is beautifully shining in the divine realm of Gokula, who [due to the offense of breaking the pot of yogurt that His mother was churning into butter and then stealing the butter that was kept hanging from a swing] is quickly running from the wooden grinding mortar in fear of mother Yasoda, but who has been caught from behind by her who ran after Him with greater speed - to that Supreme Lord, Sri Damodara, I offer my humble obeisances.

(2) [Seeing the whipping stick in His mother's hand,] He is crying and rubbing His eyes again and again with His two lotus hands. His eyes are filled with fear, and the necklace of pearls around His neck, which is marked with three lines like a conchshell, is shaking because of His quick breathing due to crying. To this Supreme Lord, Sri Damodara, whose belly is bound not with ropes but with His mother's pure love, I offer my humble obeisances.

(3) By such childhood pastimes as this He is drowning the

inhabitants of Gokula in pools of ecstasy, and is revealing to those devotees who are absorbed in knowledge of His supreme majesty and opulence that He is only conquered by devotees whose pure love is imbued with intimacy and is free from all conceptions of awe and reverence. With great love I again offer my obeisances to Lord Damodara hundreds and hundreds of times.

(4) O Lord, although You are able to give all kinds of benedictions, I do not pray to You for the boon of impersonal liberation, nor the highest liberation of eternal life in Vaikuntha, nor any other boon [which may be obtained by executing the nine processes of bhakti]. O Lord, I simply wish that this form of Yours as Bala Gopala in Vrndavana may ever be manifest in my heart, for what is the use to me of any other boon besides this?

(5) O Lord, Your lotus face, which is encircled by locks of soft black hair tinged with red, is kissed again and again by Mother Yasoda, and Your lips are reddish like the bimba fruit. May this beautiful vision of Your lotus face be ever manifest in my heart. Thousands and thousands of other benedictions are of no use to me.

(6) O Supreme Godhead, I offer my obeisances unto You. O Damodara! O Ananta! O Visnu! O master! O my Lord, be pleased upon me. By showering Your glance of mercy upon me, deliver this poor ignorant fool who is immersed in an ocean of worldly sorrows, and become visible to my eyes.

(7) O Lord Damodara, just as the two sons of Kuvera - Manigriva and Nalakuvara - were delivered from the curse of Narada and made into great devotees by You in Your form as a baby tied with rope to a wooden grinding mortar, in the same way, please give to me Your own *prema-bhakti*. I only long for this and have no desire for any kind of liberation.

(8) O Lord Damodara, I first of all offer my obeisances to the brilliantly effulgent rope which binds Your belly. I then offer my obeisances to Your belly, which is the abode of the entire universe. I humbly bow down to Your most beloved Srimati Radharani, and I offer all obeisances to You, the Supreme Lord, who displays unlimited pastimes.

Chapter Four

SAPARSHADA-BHAGAVAD-VIRAHA-JANITA-VILAPA
"Lamentation Due to Separation from the Lord and His Associates"
(Sung on the disappearance days of saints)

1
ye anila prema-dhana karuna prachura
heno prabhu kotha gela acharya-thakura

2
kaha mora svarupa rupa kaha sanatana
kaha dasa raghunatha patita-pavana

3
kaha mora bhatta-yuga kaha kaviraja
eka-kale kotha gela gora nata-raja

4
pashane kutibo matha anale pashibo
gauranga gunera nidhi kotha gele pabo

5
se-saba sangira sange ye koilo vilasa
se-sanga na paiya kande narottama dasa

Translation

1. He who brought the treasure of divine love and who was filled with compassion and mercy--where has such a personality as Shrinivasa Acharya gone?

2. Where are my Svarupa Damodara and Rupa Goswami? Where is Sanatana? Where is Raghunatha dasa, the savior of the fallen?

3. Where are my Raghunatha Bhatta and Gopala Bhatta, and where is Krishnadasa Kaviraja? Where did Lord Gauranga, the great dancer, suddenly go?

4. I will smash my head against the rock and enter into the fire. Where will I find Lord Gauranga, the reservoir of all wonderful qualities?

5. Being unable to obtain the association of Lord Gauranga accompanied by all of these devotees in whose association He performed His pastimes, Narottama Das simply weeps.

SHRI JAGANNATHASHTAKA
(Eight verses in glorification of Lord Jagannatha)

(1)
kadachit kalindi-tata-vipina-sangitaka-ravo
mudabhiri-nari-vadana-kamalasvada-madhupaha
rama-shambhu-brahmamara-pati-ganesharchita-pado
jagannathah swami nayana-patha-gami bhavatu me

(2)
bhuje savye venum shirasi shikhi-puccham kati-tate
dukulam netrante sahachara-kataksham vidadhate
sada shrimad-vrindavana-vasati-lila-paricayo
jagannathah swami nayana-patha-gami bhavatu me

(3)
mahambhodhes tire kanaka-rucire nila-shikhare
vasan prasadantah sahaja-balabhadrena balina
subhadra-madhya-sthah sakala-sura-sevavasara-do
jagannathah swami nayana-patha-gami bhavatu me

(4)
kripa-paravarah sajala-jalada-shreni-ruchiro
rama-vani-ramah sphurad-amala-pankeruha-mukhaha
surendrair aradhyah shruti-gana-shikha-gita-charito
jagannathah swami nayana-patha-gami bhavatu me

(5)
ratharudho gacchan pathi milita-bhudeva-patalaiha
stuti-pradurbhavam prati-padam upakarnya sa-dayaha
daya-sindhur bandhuh sakala jagatam sindhu-sutaya
jagannathah swami nayana-patha-gami bhavatu me

(6)
para-brahmapidah kuvalaya-dalotphulla-nayano
nivasi niladrau nihita-charano 'nanta-shirasi
rasanando radha-sarasa-vapur-alingana-sukho
jagannathah swami nayana-patha-gami bhavatu me

(7)
na vai yache rajyam na cha kanaka-manikya-vibhavam
na yache 'ham ramyam sakala jana-kamyam vara-vadhum
sada kale kale pramatha-patina gita-charito
jagannathah swami nayana-patha-gami bhavatu me

(8)
hara tvam samsaram druta-taram asaram sura-pate
hara tvam papanam vitatim aparam yadava-pate
aho dine 'nathe nihita-charano nishchitam idam
jagannathah swami nayana-patha-gami bhavatu me

Translation

(1) Sometimes in great happiness Lord Jagannatha makes a loud concert with His flute in the groves on the banks of the Yamuna. He is like a bumblebee tasting the beautiful lotus-like faces of the cowherd damsels of Vraja, and great personalities such as Lakshmi, Shiva, Brahma, Indra, and Ganesh worship His lotus feet. May that Jagannatha Swami be the object of my vision.

(2) In His left hand Lord Jagannatha holds a flute, on His head He wears peacock feathers, and on His hips He wears fine yellow silken cloth. From the corners of His eyes He bestows sidelong glances upon His loving devotees, and He always reveals Himself through His pastimes in His divine abode of Vrindavana. May that Jagannatha Swami be the object of my vision.

(3) On the shore of the great ocean, within a large palace atop the brilliant, golden Nilachala Hill, Lord Jagannatha resides with His powerful brother Balabhadra and His sister Subhadra, who stands between Them. May that Jagannatha Swami, who bestows the opportunity for devotional service upon all godly souls, be the object of

my vision.

(4) Lord Jagannatha is an ocean of mercy and is as beautiful as a row of blackish rain clouds. He is the storehouse of bliss for Lakshmi and Saraswati, and His face resembles a spotless, full-blown lotus. The best of demigods and sages worship Him, and the *Upanishads* sing His glories. May that Jagannatha Swami be the object of my vision.

(5) When Lord Jagannatha moves along the road on His Rathayatra car, at every step large assemblies of brahmanas loudly chant prayers and sing songs for His pleasure. Hearing their hymns, Lord Jagannatha becomes very favorably disposed toward them. He is the ocean of mercy and the true friend of all the worlds. May that Jagannatha Swami, along with His consort Lakshmi, who was born from the ocean of nectar, be the object of my vision.

(6) Lord Jagannatha, whose eyes resemble full-blown lotus petals, is the ornament of Lord Brahma's head. He resides on Nilachala Hill with His lotus feet placed on the heads of Anantadeva. Overwhelmed by the mellows of love, He joyfully embraces Srimati Radharani's body, which is like a cool pond. May that Jagannatha Swami be the object of my vision.

(7) I do not pray for a kingdom, nor for gold, rubies, or wealth. I do not ask for a beautiful wife, as desired by all men. I simply pray that Jagannatha Swami, whose glories Lord Shiva always sings, may be the constant object of my vision.

(8) O Lord of the demigods, please quickly remove this useless material existence I am undergoing. O Lord of the Yadus, please destroy this vast, shoreless ocean of sins. Ah, this is certain: Lord Jagannatha bestows His lotus feet upon those who feel themselves fallen and have no shelter in this world but Him. May that Jagannatha Swami be the object of my vision.

GURUDEVA
(By Srila Bhaktivinoda Thakura)

(1)
gurudev!
kripa-bindu diya, koro' ei dase

trinapekha ati hina
sakala sahane, bala diya koro'
nija-mane spriha-hina

(2)
sakale sammana, korite shakati
deho' natha jathajatha
tabe to' gaibo, hari-nama-sukhe,
aparadha ha'be hata

(3)
kabe heno kripa, labhiya e jana
kritartha hoibe, natha
shakti-buddhi-hina, ami ati dina
koro' more atma-satha

(4)
jogyata-vichare, kichu nahi pai
tomara karuna–sara
karuna na hoile, kandiya kandiya
prana no rakhibo ara

Translation

(1) Gurudeva! By a drop of your mercy make this servant of yours more humble than a blade of grass. Give me strength to bear all trials and troubles, and free me from all desires for personal honor.

(2) O lord and master! Invest me with the power to properly honor all living beings. Only then will I sing the holy name in great ecstasy and will all me offenses cease.

(3) O lord and master! When will this devotee be blessed by obtaining your mercy? I am low, fallen, and devoid of all strength and intelligence. Please make me your beloved servant.

(4) When I examine myself, I find nothing of value. Your mercy is therefore essential to me. If you are not merciful, I will constantly weep, and I will not maintain my life any longer.

SAVARANA-SRI-GAURA-PADA-PADME PRARTHANA

(A Prayer to the Lotus Feet of Sri Gauranga,
from *Prarthana* by Srila Narottama dasa Thakura)

(1)
shri-krishna-chaitanya prabhu doya koro more
toma bina ke doyalu jagat-samsare

(2)
patita-pavana-hetu tava avatara
mo sama patita prabhu na paibe ara

(3)
ha ha prabhu nityananda, premananda sukhi
kripabalokana koro ami boro duhkhi

(4)
doya koro sita-pati adwaita gosai
tava kripa-bale pai chaitanya-nitai

(5)
ha ha swarup, santana, rupa, raghunatha
bhatta-juga, shri-jiva ha prabhu lokanatha

(6)
doya koro shri-acharya prabhu shrinivasa
ramachandra-sanga mage narottama-dasa

Purport
by His Divine Grace
Srila A. C. Bhaktivedanta Swami Prabhupada

    This is a song composed by Narottama dasa Thakura. He prays to Lord Chaitanya, "My dear Lord, please be merciful to me, because who can be more merciful than Your Lordship within these three

Chapter Four

worlds?" Actually, this is a fact. Not only Narottama dasa Thakura, but Rupa Goswami also prayed to Lord Chaitanya in this way. At the time of the first meeting of Lord Chaitanya and Rupa Goswami at Prayag (Allahabad), Srila Rupa Goswami said, "My dear Lord, You are the most munificent of all incarnations, because You are distributing love of Krishna, Krishna consciousness."

When Krishna was personally present, He simply asked us to surrender, but He did not distribute Himself so easily. He made conditions—"First of all you surrender." But this incarnation, Lord Chaitanya, although Krishna Himself, makes no such condition. He simply distributes: "Take love of Krishna." Therefore, Lord Chaitanya is approved as the most munificent incarnation. Narottama dasa Thakura says, "Please be merciful to me. You are so magnanimous because You have seen the fallen souls of this age, and You are very much compassionate to them, but You should know also that I am the most fallen. No one is more greatly fallen than me." *Patita-pavana-hetu tava avatara*: "Your incarnation is just to reclaim the conditioned fallen souls, but I assure You that You will not find a greater fallen soul than me. Therefore, my claim is first."

Then he prays to Lord Nityananda. He says, *ha ha prabhu nityananda premananda-sukhi*: "My dear Lord Nityananda, You are always joyful in spiritual bliss. Since You always appear very happy, I have come to You because I am most unhappy. If You kindly put Your glance over me, I may also become happy." Then he prays to Advaita Prabhu: *Doya koro sita-pati adwaita gosai*. Advaita Prabhu's wife's name was Sita. Therefore He is sometimes addressed as sita-pati. Thus, Narottama dasa Thakura prays, "My dear Adwaita Prabhu, husband of Sita, You are so kind. Please be kind to me. It You are kind to me, naturally Lord Chaitanya and Nityananda will also be kind to me." Actually, Advaita Prabhu invited Lord Chaitanya to come down (and appear in this material world). When Advaita Prabhu saw that the fallen souls were all engaged simply in sense gratificatory processes, not understanding Krishna consciousness, He felt very much compassionate toward the fallen souls, and He also felt Himself incapable of claiming them all. He therefore prayed to Lord Krishna, "Please come Yourself. Without Your personal presence it is not possible to deliver these fallen souls." Thus, by His invitation, Lord Chaitanya appeared. Naturally, Narottama dasa Thakura prays to Advaita Prabhu, "If You will be kind to me, naturally Lord Chaitanya and Nityananda also will be kind to me."

Then he prays to the Goswamis: *ha ha swarup, santana, rupa, raghunatha*. Swarup refers to Swarupa Damodara, the personal secretary of Lord Chaitanya. He was always with Chaitanya Mahaprabhu and immediately arranged for whatever Chaitanya Mahaprabhu wanted. Two personal attendants, Svarupa Damodara and Govinda, were always constantly with Lord Chaitanya. Therefore, Narottama dasa Thakura also prays to Svarupa Damodara and then to the six Goswamis, the next disciples of Lord Chaitanya–Sri Rupa Goswami, Sri Sanatana Goswami, Sri Bhatta Raghunatha Goswami, Sri Gopal Bhatta Goswami, Sri Jiva Goswami, and Sri Raghunatha dasa Goswami. These six Goswamis were directly instructed by Lord Chaitanya to spread this movement of Krishna consciousness. Narottama dasa Thakura also prays for their mercy.

After the six Goswamis, the next *acharya* was Srinivas Acharya. Actually, Narottama dasa Thakura was in the disciplic succession after Srinivasa Acharya and was almost his contemporary, and Narottama dasa's personal friend was Ramachandra Chakravarti. Therefore he prays, "I always desire the company of Ramachandra." He desires a devotee's company. The whole process is that we should always pray for the mercy of the superior *acharyas* and keep company with pure devotees. Then it will be easier for us to advance in Krishna consciousness and receive the mercy of Lord Chaitanya and Lord Krishna. This is the sum and substance of this song sung by Narottama Dasa Thakura.

PART TWO

A DEEPER LOOK INTO THE BASICS

CHAPTER FIVE

On Chanting Hare Krishna

Although "Hare Krishna" has become a household word, practically nobody knows what it means. Is it merely a repetitious incantation designed to hypnotize its practitioners? Is it a form of escapism? Or is it a genuine meditation that can actually summon higher awareness? As recorded on his first LP in late 1966, Srila Prabhupāda illuminates the inner meaning of the Hare Krishna mantra as follows:

The transcendental vibration established by the chanting of Hare Krishna, Hare Krishna, Krishna Krishna, Hare Hare / Hare Rama, Hare Rama, Rama Rama, Hare Hare is the sublime method for reviving our transcendental consciousness. As living spiritual souls, we are all originally Krishna conscious entities, but due to our association with matter from time immemorial, our consciousness is now adulterated by the material atmosphere. The material atmosphere, in which we are now living, is called maya, or illusion. Maya means "that which is not." And what is this illusion? The illusion is that we are all trying to be lords of material nature, while actually we are under the grip of her stringent laws. When a servant artificially tries to imitate the all-powerful master, he is said to be in illusion. We are trying to exploit the resources of material nature, but actually we are becoming more and more entangled in her complexities. Therefore, although we are engaged in a hard struggle to conquer nature, we are ever more dependent on her. This illusory struggle against material nature can be stopped at once by revival of our eternal Krishna consciousness.

Hare Krishna, Hare Krishna, Krishna Krishna, Hare Hare is the transcendental process for reviving this original, pure consciousness. By chanting this transcendental vibration, we can cleanse away all misgivings within our hearts. The basic principle of all such misgivings is the false consciousness that I am the lord of all I survey.

Krishna consciousness is not an artificial imposition on the mind. This consciousness is the original, natural energy of the living entity. When we hear this transcendental vibration, this consciousness is revived. This simplest method of meditation is recommended for this age. By practical experience also, one can perceive that by chanting this maha-mantra, or the Great Chanting for Deliverance, one can at once feel a transcendental ecstasy coming through from the spiritual stratum. In the material concept of life we are busy in the matter of sense gratification, as if we were in the lower, animal stage. A little elevated from this status of sense gratification, one is engaged in mental speculation for the purpose of getting out of the material clutches. A little elevated from this speculative status, when one is intelligent enough, one tries to find out the supreme cause of all causes—within and without. And when one is factually on the plane of spiritual understanding, surpassing the stages of sense, mind, and intelligence, he is then on the transcendental plane.

This chanting of the Hare Krishna mantra is enacted from the spiritual platform, and thus this sound vibration surpasses all lower strata of consciousness—namely sensual, mental, and intellectual. There is no need, therefore, to understand the language of the mantra, nor is there any need for mental speculation, nor any intellectual adjustment for chanting this mahā-mantra. It is automatic, from the spiritual platform, and as such, anyone can take part in the chanting without any previous qualification.

In a more advanced stage, of course, one is not expected to commit offenses on the grounds of spiritual understanding. In the beginning, there may not be the presence of all transcendental ecstasies, which are eight in number. These are: (1) being stopped as though dumb, (2) perspiration, (3) standing up of hairs on the body, (4) dislocation of voice, (5) trembling, (6) fading of the body, (7) crying in ecstasy, and (8) trance. But there is no doubt that chanting for a while can take one immediately to the spiritual platform, and one shows the first symptom of this in the urge to dance along with the chanting of the mantra. We have seen this practically. Even a child can take part in the chanting and dancing. Of course, for one who is too entangled in material life, it takes a little more time to come to the standard point, but even such a materially engrossed man is raised to the spiritual platform very quickly. When the mantra is chanted by a pure devotee of the Lord in love, it has the greatest efficacy on hearers, and as such this chanting should be heard from the lips of a pure devotee of the Lord, so that immediate effects can be achieved. As far as possible, chanting from the lips of non-devotees should be avoided just as milk touched by the lips of a serpent has poisonous effects.

As Srila Prabhupada continues: The word Hara is the form of addressing the energy of the Lord, and the words Krishna and Rama are forms of addressing the Lord Himself. Both Krishna and Rama mean "the supreme pleasure," and Hara is the supreme pleasure energy of the Lord, changed to Hare in the vocative. The supreme pleasure energy of the Lord helps us to reach the Lord.

The material energy, called maya, is also one of the multi-energies of the Lord. And we, the living entities, are also the energy, marginal energy, of the Lord. The living entities are described as superior to material energy. When the superior energy is in contact with the inferior energy, an incompatible situation arises; but when the superior marginal energy is in contact with the superior energy, Hara, it is established in its happy, normal condition.

These three words, namely Hare, Krishna, and Rama, are the transcendental seeds of the maha-mantra. The chanting is a spiritual call for the Lord and His energy, to give protection to the conditioned soul. This chanting is exactly like the genuine cry of a child for its mother's presence. Mother Hara helps the devotee achieve the Lord Father's grace, and the Lord reveals Himself to the devotee who chants this mantra sincerely.

No other means of spiritual realization is as effective in this age of quarrel and hypocrisy as the chanting of the *maha-mantra*: Hare Krishna, Hare Krishna, Krishna Krishna, Hare Hare / Hare Rama, Hare Rama, Rama Rama, Hare Hare.

As it is explained in the *Srimad-Bhagavatam* (12.3.51): "My dear

King, although Kali-yuga is full of faults, there is still one good quality about this age. It is that simply by chanting the Hare Krishna *mahamantra*, one can become free from material bondage and be promoted to the transcendental kingdom."

HOW TO CHANT HARE KRISHNA

There are a few basic ways to chant mantras. The primary way that is prescribed in this age is through *kirtana*, or *sankirtana*, which is loud group or congregational chanting where a main singer leads the chanting and melody, while the rest of the group sings in refrain, following the leader. This can be done with the use of *mridunga* drums and *karatala* hand cymbals and other instruments. However, simple tunes are best so that it does not become complicated and everyone can join in. The more people that join in, the more powerful it becomes.

The most important mantra to chant in this age of Kali-yuga, as recommended in various Vedic literature, is the Hare Krishna mantra, which is a formula consisting of the Lord's names. A few such verse are as follows:

harer nama harer nama harer namaiva kevalam
kalau nasty eva nasty eva nasty eva gatir anyatha

"Chant the holy names, chant the holy names, chant the holy names, in this age of quarrel and confusion [Kali-yuga], there is no other way, there is no other way, there is no other way." (*Brihan-naradiya Purana*)

hare krishna hare krishna krishna krishna hare hare
hare rama hare rama rama rama hare hare
iti shodashakam namnam kali-kalmasha nashanam
natah parataropayah sarva-vedeshu drishyate

"These sixteen names composed of thirty-two syllables are the only means to counteract the evil effects of Kali-yuga. In all the *Vedas* it is seen that to cross the ocean of nescience, there is no alternative to the chanting of the holy name." (*Kalisantarana Upanishad*)

This indicates that for this age of Kali-yuga, chanting the holy names of Krishna is the *yuga-dharma*, or recommended process for spiritual advancement in this age.

The other primary way of chanting is through *japa*, or quiet chanting for one's own concentration and benefit. In *japa*, the names must be pronounced distinctly and accurately, and then you simply listen. That is the meditation. Sometimes people begin to mumble to the point that no one can understand what they are saying. If no one else can understand it, then how can Krishna hear His own names from this sort of chanting. And in our chanting, we should have the attitude that we are calling for Him to accept our service. And part of that service is to chant His names nicely and clearly. We should also make sure we chant the whole mantra, and not leave out words, nor talk while we are chanting *japa*, or reading while chanting. Our minds should be simply focused on the chanting for it to have deep effects on our consciousness.

The nice thing about chanting is that there are no hard and fast rules for chanting the Hare Krishna *maha-mantra*. One can chant anywhere, anytime, in any situation. In fact, the *Caitanya-caritamrita* describes that chanting the holy name at any time or place, even during sleep or while eating, brings one all perfection. (*Caitanya-caritamrita*, Antya-lila, 20.18)

However, there are different stages of chanting. The first stage of chanting is the offensive stage, when we often still hold on to our attachments, have little taste for chanting, and are working at clearing our mind of unwanted things. The second stage is offenseless chanting, after we have made a little progress and are starting to get a taste for the holy names. Then is the third or pure stage of chanting, which is when the chanting becomes extremely powerful. This is when we have a strong taste or attraction for the Lord's holy names, and can become absorbed in the hearing and chanting of them.

The proper way to chant is to give up all of our internal thoughts. The fact is, it is almost impossible to meditate on the void and empty our mind of all thinking. Our mind is always being pulled here and there by something. But the chanting process is easy because we simply concentrate on the mantra. However, our meditation on the mantra will be most effective if we can avoid the internal dialogue we always have within our mind. We should not be chanting while we make plans for the day, or while focusing our attention on other things. The *maha-mantra* is the Supreme in the incarnation of sound. Therefore, we must chant with complete respect and veneration. We must give the mantra our full attention, otherwise the chanting is considered offensive. The process is to simply chant and hear. That is all. If we can do that, then we will make rapid progress and quickly attain the second stage of chanting, which is the offenseless stage.

As one progresses through the second stage, a person begins to get a taste for the chanting, and begins to feel the nectar of joy and bliss within the names. As a person enters the third or pure stage of chanting, the layers of ignorance that keeps one from realizing their spiritual identity are peeled away. At the fullest point, one gains direct perception of their spiritual identity and relationship with God, and is immediately liberated while still in the material body. The Lord reveals Himself to such a sincere devotee and the devotee relishes the taste of transcendental life. As Srila Rupa Gosvami states in his *Sri Upadesamrita* (text 7), everything about Krishna is spiritually sweet, such as His names, qualities and activities. But one who suffers from the disease of ignorance cannot taste this sweetness. Yet by chanting the names everyday, a person can destroy this disease and relish the natural sweetness of Krishna's names.

The Hare Krishna mantra is said to contain everything for both material and spiritual well-being. So if one chants Hare Krishna with material desires, he can attain these, though that is not the goal. And if one wants *mukti*, or liberation from the material world, he can also get that. Then again if one chants the Hare Krishna *maha-mantra* understanding that Radha and Krishna are personally present there enjoying intimate pastimes in Vrindavana, then one can attain Their eternal loving service. Ultimately, the content of the mantra cannot be separated from the *sadhaka's* or practitioner's mentality. Both have a part to play at what will be attained through the use of it.

The essential state of mind that one should have while chanting the *maha-mantra* is described by Sri Chaitanya Mahaprabhu Himself in the third verse of His *Siksashtaka* prayers:

> One should chant the holy name of the Lord in a humble state of mind, thinking oneself lower than the straw in the street; one should be more tolerant than a tree, devoid of all sense of false prestige and should be ready to offer all respect to others. In such a state of mind one can chant the holy name of the Lord constantly.

The names of God come directly from the spiritual world, Vaikuntha, which means the place of no anxiety. Therefore, the more we are absorbed in *kuntha*, or anxiety caused by material pursuits, the longer it will take for us to reach the Vaikuntha platform. But the more we associate with the Vaikuntha vibration of the *maha-mantra*, the sooner we will progress to the stage of experiencing the ecstasy that comes from awakening our transcendental love for the Supreme. The *Caitanya-caritamrita* confirms that bodily transformations of spiritual ecstasy, such as trembling, perspiration, a faltering voice, and tears, may manifest when one's spiritual love for the Lord is actually awakened. (*Caitanya-caritamrita*, Adi-lila, 8.27)

To begin progressing on the path of chanting the *maha-mantra*, it is prescribed that the practitioner chant on beads called *japa-mala*, similar to a rosary. This consists of 108 beads with one extra head bead, which is larger than the others. This represents the 108 *Upanishads*, or, as described elsewhere, Krishna in the form of the head bead surrounded by 108 of His most advanced devotees, the *gopis* of Vrindavana.

You may be able to purchase a set of *japa* beads at certain import shops or temples. If you cannot find them anywhere, you can also make them. Simply go to a crafts shop and purchase 108 beads of the same size and one larger bead of your choice for the Krishna bead. Also get a length of durable nylon cord. String the 108 beads with a knot in between each one and bring the two ends of the cord through one hole of the Krishna bead and out the other side where you tie the two ends of the cord together in a firm knot. Then cut the remaining lengths of the cord so you have a small tassel. Now you have got your own set of beads for *japa* meditation, also called *japa-mala*.

It is also best to keep our beads in a bead bag, a cloth bag with a strap that goes around our neck and hangs over our stomach so we can easily access our beads when we want. This also helps keeps the beads clean. The bag should also be kept clean or washed or even replaced when necessary. The beads should never touch the floor.

One chants the Hare Krishna mantra once on each bead while holding the beads between your thumb and middle finger. Chant from the head bead all the way around the 108 beads. This is one round, or one *mala*. Then without chanting on the Krishna bead, turn the beads around in your hand, and go in the opposite direction and chant another round, chanting on each bead. One should set a certain amount of time each day, preferably in the morning, to peacefully sit down or walk and chant the particular number of rounds you have set for yourself. One may chant two rounds, four rounds, or whatever one can do.

For those who are serious, it is prescribed that they chant a total of at least sixteen rounds everyday. With a little practice, this normally takes about two hours. Initiated *bhaktas* need to chant at least 16 rounds. Two rounds will take about fifteen minutes. But one should set a fixed number of rounds to chant everyday. Then one can also spend some time reading *Bhagavad-gita* or *Srimad-Bhagavatam* to enhance his or her spiritual development. A daily program of chanting and reading will produce definite results very quickly.

As with any form of meditation, it is best to do your chanting in the early morning when it is quiet and peaceful, and before your mind starts with the activities of the day. However, you can do it anytime or even at a few different times, such as in the morning and again in the evening to put things back into perspective, especially if you have had a busy or difficult day.

When you are ready to use the mantra, it does not hurt to calm the mind through the basic steps of preparation for meditation that have already been described, such as sitting quietly and settling the mind, maybe do a few *pranayama* breathing techniques and so on. This is, after all, steps for preparing to attain deeper levels of awareness and consciousness, although this may not be necessary. Then take your *japa* beads and begin intently chanting the Hare Krishna mantra. When the mind is calm and focused, it especially will be able to concentrate on the vibrations of the mantra. As you chant it with your voice, it is received through the ear and considered by the intelligence. From there it goes deeper into the consciousness. Let no other thoughts enter the mind so that the mantra is all there is. Dive deep into the sound of your chanting and feel the vibration of the holy names and the divine energy they emit.

As you become regulated at this, doing it everyday, changes will begin to manifest in your consciousness that may be imperceptible at first, while other changes begin that will be noticeable from the start. You will often notice an internal energy within you that was not there before. Amongst other things, you may feel more sure of your own position and purpose in life, and a closer affinity with God and all beings. Of course, this is just the beginning, so if you do this regularly, deeper insights and realizations will occur as your consciousness acquires more clarity and purification.

This short description does not include that you could also get a real taste for the nectar within the Lord's holy names themselves as you can begin to perceive a reciprocation between yourself and the Lord in His names everytime you begin to chant. This takes on a whole different and deeper side of spiritual growth that more closely links one to God, which, after all, is the whole purpose of any sort of yoga or religion.

Illustrating how to hold the beads while chanting. Many times we use a cloth bead bag in which we keep and hold the beads.

CHAPTER SIX

The Pancha-Tattva Mantra

One of the other important mantras we chant and sing is that of the Pancha-tattva mantra, which is: *shri-krishna-chaitanya prabhu nityananda sri-advaita gadadhara srivasadi-gaura-bhakta-vrinda*. Sri Chaitanya Mahaprabhu, the most recent avatara of Lord Krishna, is always accompanied by His plenary expansion of Sri Nityananda Prabhu (an expansion of Lord Balarama, Lord Krishna's brother), Sri Advaita Prabhu (the expansion or incarnation of Maha-Vishnu), His internal potency Sri Gadadhara Prabhu, and His marginal potency of Srivasa Prabhu. When we see a painting of Them, Sri Chaitanya is in the midst of Them as the Supreme Personality of Godhead. Together, They are the Pancha-tattva, or God and His four main energies. Therefore, when we say this mantra, our obeisances to Him is complete.

It is also known that Sri Chaitanya does not accept any of our offenses. And you cannot make fast progress in bhakti-yoga when you are chanting the Hare Krishna *maha-mantra* offensively. So to help us avoid that condition, when we are chanting *japa* on our beads, before we chant each round of the *maha-mantra*, we first invoke the mercy of Lord Chaitanya by chanting this Pancha-tattva mantra.

Sri Chaitanya Mahaprabhu is known as *maha-vadanyavatara*, the most magnanimous incarnation, for He does not consider the offenses of the fallen souls. Therefore, we first take shelter of Him through this mantra Pancha-tattva mantra, and then chant the Hare Krishna *maha-mantra*. This becomes most effective.

WHO IS SRI CHAITANYA MAHAPRABHU

Sri Chaitanya Mahaprabhu (February 27, 1486 to 1534 A.D.) was born in Navadvipa, Bengal, on a full moon night during a lunar eclipse.

It is typical for people to bathe in the Ganges during an eclipse and chant the Lord's holy names for spiritual purification. So, everyone in the area was chanting the holy names when He was born. His parents, Jagannatha Misra and Sachidevi, gave Him the name of Vishvambhara, meaning the support of the universe, because astrologers had predicted His super human qualities and that He would deliver the people of the world. He was also nicknamed Nimai because He had been born under a nima tree.

During His childhood He exhibited extraordinary qualities, even having philosophical discussions with His mother. While growing, His brilliant intelligence began to become apparent. While still a child, He mastered Sanskrit and logic to the point of defeating local pundits, and established the truth of His spiritual and Vedic philosophy. He became so well known that many logicians of various religious and philosophical persuasions began to fear His presence and refused to debate with Him. Thus, Sri Chaitanya established the authority of the Vaishnava tradition through the process of debate and logic.

Then, when Sri Chaitanya went to Gaya on the pretext to perform ceremonies for the anniversary of His father's death, He received Vaishnava initiation from Ishvara Puri. Thereafter, He lost all interest in debate and simply absorbed Himself in chanting and singing the names of Lord Krishna in devotional ecstasy. Upon returning to Navadvipa, He gathered a following with whom He would engage in congregational singing of the Lord's holy names. Thus, He started the first *sankirtana* (congregational devotional singing) movement, and established the importance of chanting the names of God in this age as the most elevated of spiritual processes, and the prime means for liberation from material attachments.

At first, His chanting with people was for the few participants who were a part of His group, but then Sri Chaitanya ordered that the ecstasy of love of God be distributed to all people of the area. He gave no recognition for the privileges of caste, or for position, or type of philosophy a person had, or yogic asceticism. He only emphasized the devotional chanting of the Lord's holy names, using the Hare Krishna mantra (Hare Krishna, Hare Krishna, Krishna Krishna, Hare Hare / Hare Rama, Hare Rama, Rama Rama, Hare Hare) which can bring out the natural loving sentiments for God.

It was at the age of 24 when He shaved His head and took the order of sannyasa, the renounced stage of life, when He accepted the name of Krishna Chaitanya from Keshava Bharati during the initiation. He then spent four years traveling through South India, and also visited Vrindavana and Varanasi. During this time he also gave special instructions to Rupa and Sanatana Gosvamis, who then also spread the glories of the Divine Love for Radha and Krishna. They settled in Vrindavana where they spent their years in writing many books elaborating the instructions of Lord Chaitanya and the glories of bhakti for Radha and Krishna. They also revealed the places where Radha and Krishna performed many varied pastimes in that land of Vrindavana, which have remained special spots where devotees can become absorbed in the bliss of love of Sri Sri Radha and Krishna.

Lord Chaitanya spent His remaining years in Jagannatha Puri. During this time He was absorbed in ecstatic devotion to Krishna in the loving mood of Radharani, in which He would lose all external consciousness. He freely distributed the divine nectar of this love for Krishna to everyone and anyone, day and night. Even His presence or mere touch could transform everyone that came near Him into the same devotional mood. He remained like this until He finally left our vision at the age of 48.

Lord Chaitanya is considered and was established by Vedic scripture as the most recent incarnation of God. The Lord always descends to establish the codes of religion. This is confirmed in *Bhagavad-gita* (4.6-8) where Lord Krishna explains that although He is unborn and the Lord of all living beings, He still descends in His spiritual form in order to re-establish the proper religious principles and annihilate the miscreants whenever there is a decline of religion and a rise in irreligious activity.

Though there are many incarnations or *avataras* of God, all incarnations are known and predicted in the Vedic literature. Each *avatara* performs many wonderful pastimes. But in Kali-yuga, the Lord descends in the form of His own devotee as Sri Chaitanya in order to show the perfect example of how devotional service should be performed, and to stress the chanting of the Hare Krishna mantra for this age by inaugurating the process of the *sankirtana* movement (congregational chanting).

Predictions of the appearance of Lord Chaitanya can be found in many Vedic texts. One of the oldest prophecies concerning Sri Chaitanya's appearance in this world is found in the *Atharva Veda* verse, starting as: *ito 'ham krita-sannyaso 'vatarisyami*. In this verse the Supreme states: "I will descend as a sannyasi, a tall, fair, and saintly brahmana devotee, after four to five thousand years of Kali-yuga have passed. I will appear on earth near the Ganges shore and with all the signs of an exalted person, free from material desires. I will always chant the holy names of the Lord, and, thus, taste the sweetness of My own devotional service. Only other advanced devotees will understand Me."

Also, in a verse from the *Sama Veda*, starting as: *tathaham krita-sannyaso bhu-girbanah avatarisye*, the Supreme Being says that He will descend to earth as a brahmana-sannyasi at a place on the shore of the Ganges. Again and again He will chant the names of the Lord in the company of His associates to rescue the people who are devoured by sins in the age of Kali.

The *Mundaka Upanishad* (3.3) also relates the prophecy of Sri Chaitanya in a different way. It states, "When one realizes the golden form of Lord Gauranga, who is the ultimate actor and the source of the Supreme Brahman, he attains the highest knowledge. He transcends both pious and impious activities, becomes free from worldly bondage, and enters the divine abode of the Lord."

Another prophecy of the appearance of Sri Chaitanya is found in two verses in the *Bhavishya Purana*. It states:

ajayadhvamaja yadhvam na sansayah
kalau sankirtana rambhe bhavisyami saci sutah

"The Supreme Lord said: 'In Kali-yuga, I will appear as the son of Saci, and inaugurate the *sankirtana* movement. There is no doubt about this.'"

anandasru-kala-roma-harsa-purnam tapo-dhana
sarve mam eva draksyanti kalau sannyasa-rupinam

"O sage whose wealth is austerity, in the Kali-yuga everyone will see My form as a sannyasi, a form filled with tears of bliss and bodily hairs standing erect in ecstasy."

Another is from the *Svetasvatara Upanishad* (3.12):

*mahan praburvai purushah sattvasyaisha pravartakah
sunirmalamimam praptim ishano jyotiravyayaha*

"He is the most Benevolent Supreme Divinity [Mahaprabhu or the great master], as [through *sankirtana*] He graciously instigates [or bestows] intuitive wisdom in the *jiva* soul unto its fully developed cognition or purest attainment. This attainment of purest state or immortality is possible only by His grace as He is the Supreme Propeller and Imperishable Transcendental Enlightening Force."

How He is the "great master" or will "instigates intuitive wisdom" is described in another *Upanishad*. This is one of the lesser *Upanishads* known as the *Chaitanyopanishad*, or *Sri Caitanya Upanishad*. This comes from the ancient *Atharva Veda*. In this description there is not only the prediction of His appearance but a description of His life and purpose, and the reasons why His process of spiritual enlightenment is so powerful and effective in this age of Kali. The *Chaitanyopanishad* is a short text with only nineteen verses. All of them are very significant.

The *Sri Caitanya Upanishad* (texts 5-11) explains that one day when Pippalada asked his father, Lord Brahma, how the sinful living entities will be delivered in Kali-yuga and who should be the object of their worship and what mantra should they chant to be delivered, Brahma told him to listen carefully and he would describe what will take place in the age of Kali. Brahma said that the Supreme Lord Govinda, Krishna, will appear again in Kali-yuga as His own devotee in a two-armed form with a golden complexion in the area of Navadvipa along the Ganges. He will spread the system of devotional service and the chanting of the names of Krishna, especially in the form of the Hare Krishna *maha-mantra*; Hare Krishna, Hare Krishna, Krishna Krishna, Hare Hare / Hare Rama, Hare Rama, Rama Rama, Hare Hare.

Another prediction is from the *Vayu Purana*: "In the age of Kali

I shall descend as the son of Sachidevi to inaugurate the *sankirtana* movement." This is also confirmed in the *Srimad-Bhagavatam* (11.5.32) where it states: "In the age of Kali, intelligent persons perform congregational chanting to worship the incarnation of Godhead who constantly sings the names of Krishna. Although His complexion is not blackish [like that of Lord Krishna], He is Krishna Himself. He is accompanied by His associates, servants, weapons and confidential companions."

The great classic *Mahabharata* (Vishnu-sahasra-nama-stotra, 127.92.75) confirms that Sri Chaitanya Mahaprabhu is not different from Lord Sri Krishna: "The Supreme Lord has a golden complexion [when He appears as Lord Caitanya]. Indeed, His entire body, which is very nicely constituted, is like molten gold. Sandalwood pulp is smeared all over His body. He will take the fourth order of life [sannyasa] and will be very self-controlled. He will be distinguished from Mayavadi [impersonalist] sannyasis in that He will be fixed in devotional service and will propagate the *sankirtana* movement."

The *Caitanya-caritamrita* (Adi-lila, 3.19-20) also explains how the Supreme Lord Himself describes how He will appear as His own devotee to perform and teach devotional service by inaugurating the *sankirtana* movement, which is the religion for this age.

Another interesting story about the prediction of the appearance of Lord Chaitanya in Kali-yuga is related in a lengthy conversation between Murari Gupta and Damodara Pandita, two contemporaries of Sri Caitanya. It is found in the *Sri Caitanya Mangala*, a biography of Sri Chaitanya by Srila Locana Dasa Thakura. Among the many things they discuss are the symptoms and difficulties found in the age of Kali, how Lord Krishna appears on earth in this age, His confidential reasons for doing so, and how He revealed to Narada Muni His form as Lord Gauranga that He would accept while appearing on earth in this age. In this form He would distribute love of God to everyone He met by chanting the holy names. This conversation is very enlightening.

Within this conversation they further relate an incident recorded as the *Vishnu-Katyayani Samvada* of the *Padma Purana*. This is a conversation between Lord Vishnu and Katyayani (Parvati), Lord Shiva's wife. The story is that one time the great sage Narada Muni acquired the *maha-prasada*, personal food remnants, of Lord Narayana, Vishnu, and gave a morsel to his friend Lord Shiva. Shiva tasted it and he began to dance in ecstasy, to the point of disturbing the earth. When he was approached by Parvati about why he was dancing so, he explained what happened. However, she was unhappy and angry that he did not share any with her. Being devoted to Lord Vishnu and concerned for the spiritual well-being of all conditioned souls, she then vowed that if she should get the blessings of Lord Vishnu, she would see to it that the Lord's *maha-prasada* was distributed to everyone. Just then Lord Vishnu Himself appeared and conversed with her. He assured her that He would appear in the world as Sri Chaitanya Mahaprabhu in the age of Kali and would keep her promise and spread His mercy in the form of *maha-prasada*, food that has been offered to Him, and the chanting of His holy names to everyone, distributing His mercy everywhere.

Another book is the *Sri Hari-bhakti-vilasa* by Sanatana Gosvami. Sanatana lived about 500 years ago in Vrindavana, India and was a great scholar of the Vedic scripture. A portion of the book contains an anthology of an amazing assortment of verses from the Vedic texts which predict the appearance of Lord Chaitanya. Besides some of the quotes we have already cited, he includes verses from such texts as the *Chandogya Upanishad, Krishna Upanishad, Narada Purana, Kurma Purana, Garuda Purana, Devi Purana, Nrisimha Purana, Padma Purana, Brahma Purana, Agni Purana, Saura Purana, Matsya Purana, Vayu Purana, Markandeya Purana, Varaha Purana, Vamana Purana, Vishnu Purana, Skanda Purana, Upapuranas, Narayana-Samhita, Krishna-yamala, Brahma-yamala, Vishnu-yamala, Yoga-vasistha*, and the *Tantras*, such as *Urdhvamnaya-tantra, Kapila Tantra, Visvasara Tantra, Kularnava Tantra*, and others.

These and other predictions confirm the fact that Sri Chaitanya Mahaprabhu would appear to specifically propagate the chanting of the holy names. Furthermore, in the Fourth Chapter of the Antya-lila of the *Caitanya Bhagavata*, which is a biography of Sri Chaitanya Mahaprabhu written by Sri Vrindavan dasa Thakura who is said to be an incarnation of Srila Vyasadeva, Lord Chaitanya explains: "I have appeared on earth to propagate the congregational chanting of the holy names of God. In this way I will deliver the sinful material world. Those demons who never before accepted My authority and lordship will weep in joy by chanting My names. I will vigorously distribute devotional service, bhakti, which is sought after even by demigods, sages, and perfected beings, so that even the most abominable sinners will receive it. But those who, intoxicated with education, wealth, family background, and knowledge, criticize and offend My devotees, will be deprived of everything and will never know My true identity." Then Sri Chaitanya specifically states (Antya-lila 4.126): "I declare that My name will be preached in every town and village on this earth."

This verifies the fact that the chanting of the *maha-mantra* is the rare and special opportunity given by God for all to be relieved from the problems of the age of Kali and of material life in general. As confirmed in the *Caitanya-caritamrita* (Adi-lila, 3.77-78), it is Sri Krishna Chaitanya who inaugurates the congregational chanting of the holy names, which is the most sublime of all spiritual sacrifices. Intelligent people will worship Him through this means, while other foolish people will continue in the cycle of repeated birth and death in this material world.

In another place of the *Caitanya-caritamrita* (Antya-lila, 20.8-9), Sri Chaitanya specifically tells Svarupa Damodara and Ramananda Raya that chanting the holy names is the most practical way to attain salvation from material existence in this age, and anyone who is intelligent and takes up this process of worshiping Krishna will attain the direct shelter of Krishna.

He also strongly opposed the impersonalist philosophy of Shankaracharya and established the principle of *achintya-bhedabheda-tattva*. This specified that the Supreme and the individual soul are inconceivably and simultaneously one and different. This means that the Supreme and the individual *jiva* souls are the same in quality, being eternally spiritual, but always separate individually. The *jivas* are small and subject to being influenced by the material energy, while the Supreme is infinite and always above and beyond the material manifestation.

Sri Chaitanya also taught that the direct meaning of the Vedic *shastras* is that the living entities are to engage in devotional service, bhakti, to the Supreme, Bhagavan Sri Krishna. Through this practice there can develop a level of communication between God and the individual by which God will lovingly reveal Himself to those who become qualified. In this understanding the theistic philosophy of Vaishnavism reached its climax.

As previously explained, there is a system of self-realization especially recommended for each age. In the age of Kali, people are not attracted to spiritual pursuits and are often rebellious against anything that seems to restrict or stifle their freedom to do anything they want. Since in this age we are so easily distracted by so many things and our mind is always in a whirl, we need an easy path. Therefore, the Vedic *shastra* explains that God has given us an easy way to return to Him in this age. It is almost as if He has said, "Since you are My worst son, I give you the easiest process." The *Caitanya-caritamrita* (Adi-lila, 3.40) confirms this and says that the Supreme Being descends as Sri Chaitanya, with a golden complexion, to simply spread the glories of chanting the holy names, which is the only religious principle in this age of Kali. In this way, God Himself has given the method of chanting His holy names as the most effective means to reach His spiritual abode.

Sri Chaitanya Mahaprabhu did not become much involved in writing. In fact, He only wrote eight verses, the *Shikshastaka*, but His followers compiled extensive Sanskrit literature that documented His life and fully explained His teachings. For more complete descriptions and elaborations on His life, activities, and philosophy, as written by His close associates, such books are presently available through various outlets.

CHAPTER SEVEN

Greeting the Deities in the Temple

Seeing the deities in the temple is always a joy, especially when They are beautifully dressed in the morning. If you live at home, then you will see the deities whenever you reach the temple, or in your own home temple room. If you live in the temple ashrama, most temples have a specific time when the curtains are opened after the deities have been dressed, and when everyone can greet the deities and soak in Their beauty. Many Krishna temples, at least the Iskcon Krishna temples, open the curtains with the lovely music of the "Govinda" song, composed of a few verses from the *Brahma-samhita* with the refrain *Govindam adi-purusham tam aham bhajami*. This is Sanskrit which means "I worship Govinda, the primeval Lord."

Viewing the deities itself is a form of meditation on the goal of all meditation and yoga–the Supreme Person, the Absolute Truth, the Highest Reality, Cause and Source of everything that exists. But there is a process of this meditation on the deities. This is described in the *Srimad-Bhagavatam* (2.2.13) wherein it says, "The process of meditation should begin from the lotus feet of the Lord and progress to His smiling face. The meditation should be concentrate upon the lotus feet, then the calves, then the thighs, and in this way higher and higher. The more the mind becomes fixed upon the different parts of the limbs, one after another, the more the intelligence becomes purified."

The Supreme Lord is *sat-chit-ananda-vigraha*, which means the ultimate form of eternity, knowledge and bliss. Therefore, the more one concentrates on the transcendental spiritual form of the Lord as the deity, either on the lotus feet, the calves, the thighs, chest or smiling face, the more one becomes spiritually purified. That means the less one is attached to always thinking of how to satisfy the mind and senses. This is the process of purifying the intelligence and consciousness. Then one naturally contemplates the higher purposes of life and one's spiritual potential.

THE SIGNIFICANCE OF DEITIES AND DEITY WORSHIP

Deities play an important part in most temples of Krishna. But what is the significance of deities and deity worship? One thing to understand is that all the images or deities in the Vedic pantheon, as found in the temples, are made according to explicit details and instructions found in the Vedic texts. Then they are installed in the temple in an elaborate ceremony wherein the Divine personalities are called to appear in the form of the deity. Some of the deities you may see in various temples are demigods, while others, such as Krishna, Vishnu, or Ramachandra, are forms displaying various pastimes and *avataras* of the Supreme Being.

Some people, however, do not believe that God has a form. But many verses in the *Puranas* and particularly the *Brahma-samhita* establish that the Supreme Being does have specific forms according to His pastimes. These texts also describe His variegated features, which include His spiritual shape, appearance, beauty, characteristics, strength, intelligence, activities, etc. Therefore, it is considered that the authorized deities of the Supreme that are made according to these descriptions provide a view of the personal form of God.

Those who have no knowledge of God or His form will certainly consider the temple deities as idols. But this is because they think that the deities are simply the products of someone's imagination. Of course, there are those who say that God has no form, spiritual or material, or that there is no Supreme Being. Others think that since God must be formless, they can imagine or worship any material form as God, or they regard any image as merely an external representation of the Supreme. But images such as those of the demigods are not additional forms of an impersonal God, nor are they equal to God. All such people who think in the above mentioned ways have resorted to their own imagination to reach such conclusions and are, therefore, idolaters. Imaginary images and opinions of God that are formed by those who have not properly learned about, seen, or realized God are indeed idols, and those who accept such images or opinions are certainly idolaters. This is because these images or opinions are based on ignorance and are not a true likeness of the Supreme Being's personal form.

Nonetheless, God is described in the Vedic literature, which clearly explains that God is *sat-chit-ananda vigraha*, or the form of complete spiritual essence, full of eternity, knowledge, and bliss, and is not material in any way. Not only are such descriptions found in various Vedic texts, but many realized yogis and devotees have also directly perceived this as well. The Lord's body, soul, form, qualities, names, pastimes, etc., are all nondifferent and are of the same spiritual quality. This form of God is not an idol designed from someone's imagination, but is the true form, even if He should descend into this material creation. And since the spiritual nature of God is absolute, He is also nondifferent from His name. Thus, the name *Krishna* is an *avatara* or incarnation of Krishna in the form of sound. Similarly, His form in the temple is not merely a representation, but is also qualitatively the same as Krishna as the *archa-vigraha*, or the worshipable form.

Some people may question that if the deity is made from material elements, such as stone, marble, metal, wood, or paint, how can it be the spiritual form of God? The answer is given that since God is the source of all material and spiritual energies, material elements are also a form of God. Therefore, God can manifest as the deity in the temple, though made of stone or other elements, since He can transform what is spiritual into material energy, and material energy back into spiritual energy. Thus, the deity can easily be accepted as the Supreme since He can appear in any element as He chooses. In this way, even though we may be unqualified to see God, who is beyond the perceptibility of our material senses, the living beings in this material creation are allowed to see and approach the Supreme through His *archa-vigraha* form as the worshipable deity in the temple. This is considered His causeless mercy on the materially conditioned living beings. However, there are many stories in which the deity has acted in ways to show that He accepts our service and can interact with His devotees in many ways. And as we advance in our spiritual practice and sincerity, the same thing can happen to us, and already has with many.

In this way, the Supreme Being gives Himself to His devotees so they can become absorbed in serving, remembering and meditating on Him. Thus, the Supreme comes to dwell in the temple, and the temple becomes the spiritual abode on earth. In time, the body, mind and senses of the devotee become spiritualized by serving the deity, and the Supreme becomes fully manifest to him or her. Worshiping the deity of the Supreme and using one's senses in the process of bhakti-yoga, devotional service to the Supreme, provides a means for one's true essential spiritual nature to unfold. The devotee becomes spiritually realized and the deities reveal Their spiritual nature to the sincere souls according to their spiritual development. This can continue up to the level in which the Supreme Being in the form of the deity engages in a personal relationship and performs reciprocal, loving pastimes with the devotee, as has previously taken place with other advanced individuals.

At this stage, having *darshan* or seeing the deity is not simply a matter of looking at the deity in the temple, but to one who is spiritually realized it is a matter of experiencing the deity and entering into a personal, reciprocal relationship with the Supreme Personality in the form of the deity. At that stage, you may view the deity, but the deity also gazes at you, and then there is a spiritual exchange wherein the deity begins to reveal His personality to you. Krishna or the deity may also appear in one's dreams, often times to give some revelation or message for one's benefit. This is what separates those who are experienced from those who are not, or those who can delve into this spiritual exchange and those who may still be trying to figure it out. For those who have experienced such an exchange with the Supreme or His deity, at this stage the worship of the Supreme Being in the deity moves up to a whole different level, with no limits as to the spiritual love that can be shared between the devotee and the deity. This is one of the results of continuing on the path of bhakti-yoga.

CHAPTER EIGHT

Importance of Reading Devotional Texts

As we have explained, the morning is the best time for meditation and contemplation. This includes taking the time to read devotional texts. That is why in many temples there is time given in the morning to a reading or a class and discussion on a verse from an important devotional scripture. The class is usually set to last for about an hour wherein everyone sits and listens to the class, or adds comments to the discussion.

Two of the most important spiritual texts that give insight and advice to enhance our practice of bhakti-yoga is the *Bhagavad-gita* and the *Srimad-Bhagavatam*, also known as the *Bhagavata Purana*. Other books that have important instructions on the process of bhakti-yoga include the *Bhakti-rasamrita-sindhu* by Srila Rupa Goswami, or the translation by Srila Prabhupada called *The Nectar of Devotion*. Another is *The Teachings of Lord Chaitanya* which is the translation of a summary study of the *Caitanya-caritamrita* by Srila Bhaktivinoda Thakur. Another insightful book is Srila Rupa Goswami's *Sri Upadeshamrita*, or it's English translation called *The Nectar of Instruction* by Srila Prabhupada. There are other important books as well, which can be discussed later. In many Krishna temples they will have a class on *Bhagavad-gita* in the evening, and classes on the *Srimad-Bhagavatam* in the morning. There are so many different texts to choose from, why is the *Srimad-Bhagavatam* so important? The *Bhagavatam* itself explains its position and purpose with the following verses found within it:

"Completely rejecting all religious activities which are materially motivated, this *Bhagavata Purana* propounds the highest truth, which is understandable by those devotees who are fully pure in heart. The highest truth is reality distinguished from illusion for the welfare of all. Such truth uproots the threefold miseries. This beautiful *Bhagavatam*, compiled by the sage Vyasadeva, is sufficient in itself for God realization. What is the need of any other scripture? As soon as one attentively and submissively hears the message of *Bhagavatam*, by this culture of knowledge, the Supreme Lord is established within his heart." (*Bhag.* 1.1.2)

"This *Srimad-Bhagavatam* is the literary incarnation of God, and it is compiled by Srila Vyasadeva, the incarnation of God. It is meant for the ultimate good of all people, and it is all-successful, all-blissful and all-perfect." (*Bhag.* 1.3.40)

"This *Bhagavata Purana* is as brilliant as the sun, and it has arisen just after the departure of Lord Krishna to His own abode, accompanied by religion, knowledge, etc. Persons who have lost their vision due to the dense darkness of ignorance in the age of Kali shall get light from this *Purana*." (*Bhag.* 1.3.43)

"Those words which do not describe the glories of the Lord, who alone can sanctify the atmosphere of the whole universe, are considered by saintly persons to be like unto a place of pilgrimage for crows. Since the all-perfect persons are inhabitants of the transcendental abode, they do not derive any pleasure here." (*Bhag.*1.5.10)

"On the other hand, that literature which is full of descriptions of the transcendental glories of the name, fame, forms, pastimes, etc., of the unlimited Supreme Lord is a different creation, full of transcendental words directed toward bringing about a revolution in the impious lives of this world's misdirected civilization. Such transcendental literatures, even though imperfectly composed, are heard, sung and accepted by purified men who are thoroughly honest." (*Bhag.*1.5.11)

AS YOU READ AND STUDY WITH YOUR SPIRITUAL PRACTICE

As you practice your bhakti-yoga or devotional service, and then add regular reading and studying of the Vedic *shastra* and devotional texts, you will begin to see the importance of this spiritual path. It is like seeing through the spectacles of *shastra* as it is said. For those of us who wear glasses, we know we cannot see clearly without them. Similarly, we are all born in ignorance and cannot see clearly what is the purpose of life and this world without proper knowledge. Only by understanding the teachings of the spiritual master along with the knowledge provided in *shastra*, can we begin to see clearly who and what we are, how we got here, where we are going according to our actions and level of consciousness, and how to make the best use of this life and what we have. So as we continue on this path, our studying will broaden our perspective of what we are doing and the importance of spiritual knowledge and insight.

  As our perspective becomes clearer, it will also motivate us to keep going on this path. It is not that we need persuading to do it, but the realizations will begin to come naturally. We start to perceive the reality and purpose of life where others remain confused or unclear about why we are here, except to merely try to be happy on the sensual and mental platform. Sensual happiness itself always comes to and end, sometimes sooner than later, but at least at the time of death. Whereas spiritual life will continue to go on in some way, whether we achieve complete perfection by the end of this life, or whether we continue to progress in another life. As our study and practice continues, our understanding of this will also become more clear.

  The *Srimad-Bhagavatam* is a long, multi-volume book. Having it in your house is having the literary incarnation of God in your home. Do not become overwhelmed by its size, but read a little every day and make your way through it so that you can gradually and clearly acquire the knowledge within it. This is also a way of attaining advanced association.

CHAPTER NINE

Tulasi Devi: The Sacred Tree

We often see respect given to the Tulasi tree in most Krishna temples, especially in India. For some people, this may seem peculiar. So we should understand the importance of this plant. A verse in the *Skanda Purana* explains: "Tulasi is auspicious in all respects. Simply by seeing, simply by touching, simply by remembering, simply by praying to, simply by bowing before, simply by hearing about, or simply by sowing the tree, there is always auspiciousness. Anyone who comes in touch with the Tulasi tree in the above mentioned ways lives eternally in the Vaikuntha world." So let us explain more about the Tulasi tree.

Worship of the Tulasi tree is very important in bhakti-yoga. Tulasi is also Lord Krishna's favorite plant and He is fond of Tulasi leaves and buds. That is why they are offered with each preparation when food is presented to the deities. Many devotees also keep a Tulasi at their home.

In the morning, after *mangala arati*, all the assembled devotees attend the worship and circumambulation of Srimati Tulasi Devi. First the *bhaktas* offer obeisances to Tulasi Devi with the *tulasi-pranama* mantra. Then the song for Tulasi *puja* is sung while doing the Tulasi *arati*, the offering of incense, ghee lamp, and flowers. When the song is finished, the devotees circumambulate her four times and each devotee can offer a few drops of water to her, after which the devotees offer their obeisances again. The details of this are explained as follows;

HOW TO OFFER TULASI DEVI WORSHIP (PUJA)

The Tulasi *puja* is relatively simple, and anyone can learn how to do this. This consists of only three articles: incense, a ghee lamp, and flowers. Sooner or later, you will probably get an opportunity to offer

puja to Tulasi, so here are the steps that you need to know. First we do a simple *achamana* for purification, which is done as follows:
- Take the spoon from the water (*achamana*) cup and purify both hands by sprinkling water onto them.
- Place a spoon full of water into your right palm, chant om keshavaya namah, and sip.
- Again place a spoon full into your right palm, chant om narayanaya namah, and sip.
- One more spoon full into your right palm, chant om madhavaya namah, and sip.
- Then put a spoonful of water in your left hand and wash both hands.

Then we offer *puja* or worship to the Tulasi plant, first by offering the incense:
- Purify (sprinkle with a spoon full of water) the bell and the incense holder.
- Take a lighter or matches and light the incense.
- Pick up the bell in the left hand; ring the bell throughout the *puja*.
- Pick up the incense holder in the right hand and offer the incense to Tulasi by waving it in seven circles toward her whole form.
- Offer the incense to Srila Prabhupada (or the guru) in the same way and then to all the devotees by simply waving it in their direction.

Offering the ghee lamp:
- Purify the ghee lamp by putting a few drops of water on it with the spoon, but not on the ghee wick.
- Light it.
- Offer it to Tulasi: wave it four circles to the base, two to the middle, three to the top, and seven to the whole. Or simply seven circles to the whole plant.
- Then offer to Srila Prabhupada and then all the devotees by simply waving it in their direction.

Offering the Flowers:
- Purify the flowers by pouring a few drops on it with the spoon.
- Offer them to Tulasi with seven circles to the whole form.
- Place one at her base (optional).
- Offer them Srila Prabhupada and then all the devotees by waving them as before.
- Now the *puja* is complete. Now as the devotees circumambulate around Tulasi, you can serve the devotees by assisting them to purify their hands before watering Tulasi by using the spoon to put a few drops of water in their hand. Then they take the spoon from the second *achamana* cup to take a few drops of water and pour it into the pot. Then they can step aside and pay obeisances to Tulasi and continue singing the song. (You can find the songs and mantras for this in a previous chapter.)
- When everyone has watered Tulasi, you can take the *arati* try back to the *pujari* or priest room where such things are stored and clean it and store it for the next time.

Planting, watering, protecting, maintaining, circumambulating, seeing, bowing down to, praying to, and glorifying are all ways of serving and worshiping Tulasi and are highly beneficial. Caring for Tulasi at home is described in a later chapter.

THE IMPORTANCE OF THE TULASI PLANT

The Tulasi tree is a most important plant, and is often seen at numerous Vedic temples, especially those dedicated to Vishnu and Krishna. At such temples you are likely to find one or more in the courtyard wherein pilgrims circumambulate it, water it, or even offer prayers to it. Some temples will even have Tulasi groves, wherein you will see numerous Tulasi plants growing in a garden. Some temples will even have a special greenhouse just for taking care of Tulasi plants. At such temples, they may even prepare large garlands of Tulasi leaves and manjaris (the ends of the branches) for the deity of Lord Krishna to wear. It is said that Tulasi will not grow well where there is no devotion to the

Lord. In fact, how well Tulasi grows is said to be like a barometer that indicates how high the devotional attitude is of the devotee community around the temple.

Vaishnava devotees also use the wood to make neck beads and wear two or three strands of them around their necks signifying their devotion to the Lord. They also make their *japa mala* or chanting beads from wood of the Tulasi tree. Tulasi is considered to be a pure devotee of the Lord who has taken the form of a tree, and is very dear to Lord Vishnu. Lord Vishnu (Krishna) likes to wear garlands made of Tulasi leaves. Often sandalwood paste and Tulasi leaves are placed on the lotus feet of the deity of Lord Vishnu/Krishna. Therefore she is given the utmost respect. This is also why many devotees and Hindus in general also grow Tulasi in their homes. In this way, the Tulasi plant plays an important part in the spiritual life of many devotees. So what is the significance, history and legends behind this little tree?

To begin with, the Basil plant (Ocimum sanctum) is commonly called Tulasi (pronounced tulsi). In some accounts of the Puranic story of the Churning of the Ocean (*samudramathana*), the Tulasi is added to the list of articles which emerged from it, and is sacred to Krishna (according to Wilson's *Vishnu Purana* p, 67. n.8). It is also sacred to Lord Vishnu's consort Laksmi, and hence it is itself an object of worship.

The Tulasi plant also possesses curative properties and is said to be an antidote to snake-venom. It destroys mosquitoes and other pests and purifies the air. It even is said to ward off the messengers of Yama, the ruler of the dead, who will not enter a house containing a sprig of Tulasi. This is also one of the reasons why devotees wear the Tulasi as neck beads. When death occurs, the funeral pyre should be constructed of Tulasi, palasha, and sandal-wood.

There is further Puranic background for Tulasi attaining this spiritual importance. In fact, it is Mahalaksmi, wife of Visnu, who had taken the form of Tulasi. There is a story about it in the *Devi Bhagavata*. The *Puranic Encyclopedia* summarizes these legends as follows:

1) The curse of Sarasvati. Sarasvati, Ganga and Laksmi were all, in the beginning, wives of MahaVishnu. The Lord loved all the three

equally. But, as part of a pastime to bring about benefits to bhaktas in the material world, one day all the four were sitting together when Ganga sent lustful glances at Vishnu which was immediately noticed by both Sarasvati and Laksmi. Sarasvaii got angry and rising up caught hold of the hair of Ganga and dragged her to the ground. Laksmi then caught hold of Sarasvati to prevent further assault, but Sarasvati then poured all her rage on Laksmi and cursed her to be born as a plant on earth. Ganga devi could not bear this and she cursed Sarasvati to be born as a river on earth. Sarasvati retorted with a curse that Ganga also would be born as a river. When the whole tumult was over, Vishnu called Laksmi to his side and said, "Oh Devi, do not worry. Things have happened as predestined. You go and be born as the daughter of Dharmadhvaja and grow up there. From there by divine grace you will be transformed into a plant sacred enough to make all the three worlds pure. That plant will be named Tulasi. When you will be thus living as Tulasi, a demon named Sankhachuda with part of my virile strength will be born and he will marry you. Then you can come back to me. The holy river Padmavati will also be another form of your spirit."

2) The story of Dharmadhvaja. Who was this Dharmadhvaja to whom was born Mahalaksmi as a daughter? In times of old there was a Manu called Daksasavarni who was extremely virtuous and a part of Vishnu. Descending from Daksasavarni were Brahmasavarni, Dharmasavarni, Rudrasavarni, Devasavarni, Indrasavarni, Vrisadhvaja. This last named was a great devotee of Shiva and because of his great affection for this devotee, Shiva lived a whole period of a *deva-yuga* in the ashrama of Vrisadhvaja. King Vrisadhvaja by an edict prohibited the worship of any other deity than Shiva in his country. Even the worship of Mahalaksmi ordained by the *Vedas* during the month of Bhadra (September) became extinct. All *yagyas* (Vedic rituals) and worship of Vishnu came to a stop. Surya (the sun-god) got angry at this belittling of other gods than Shiva and cursed the King Vrisadhvaja that he would cease to be prosperous. Shiva did not like it and he went to punish Surya, holding his trident in his hand. Surya was frightened and he approached his father Kasyapa. Kasyapa and Surya went to Brahma and acquainted him with all details. Brahma also was helpless in the matter and so all three of them went to Mahavishnu. They prostrated before Vishnu and

told him everything. At that time Shiva also came there. Addressing all of them, Vishnu said, "Oh, Devas, within this half an hour, twenty-one yugas have passed by on the earth. He about whom you have come to speak to me is dead and gone. Even his son Rathadhvaja is dead. The latter has two sons named Dharmadhvaja and Kusadhvaja. They are dull and splendorless now because of the curse of Surya and are now worshipping Laksmi." Saying thus Vishnu disappeared.

3) Birth of Tulasi. Dharmadhvaja and Kusadhvaja did penance to propitiate Mahalaksmi. Kusadhvaja had a wife named Malavati. She bore a daughter named Vedavati. Sita, wife of Sri Rama, was a rebirth of this Vedavati.

King Dharmadhvaja had a wife named Madhavi. Maha-laksmi entered her womb as an embryo and after a hundred years Madhavi gave birth to a daughter. Even at the time of birth the child looked like a matured girl and was extremely pretty. She was therefore called Tulasi, meaning matchless. (Tula= match). This Tulasi, abandoning all worldly pleasures, went to Badarikashrama in the Himalayas and started doing penance there with the prayer that MahaVishnu should become her husband. She did penance for twenty-four thousand years sitting amidst fire in the hot season and sitting in water in the cold season and taking only fruits and water as food. Then she did penance for another thirty thousand years eating leaves only, another forty thousand years taking air only as food, and another ten thousand years without any food. At this stage Brahma appeared and asked her the object of her penance. She replied she wanted MahaVishnu to be her husband. Hearing this Brahma said thus: "Devi, you know the cowboy Sudama born of a part of Sri Krishna. That brilliant cowboy has now been born on earth, due to a curse of Radha, as a demon named Sankhachuda. He is matchlessly eminent and has once fallen in love with you seeing you at Goloka. You will become his wife and later you can become the wife of Narayana. At that time a part of your divine body will remain on earth as a plant named Tulasi. Tulasi will become the most sacred of all plants, dear to Vishnu, and all worship without using Tulasi leaves would be ineffective."

4) Marriage of Tulasi. Due to a curse of Radha, Sudama, the cowboy, was born on earth as a demon named Sankhachuda. He did

penance sitting at Badarikashrama and obtained the Vishnu Kavacha. Another object of his was to marry Tulasi. He obtained a boon from Brahma that his death would occur only when the Vishnu Kavacha was removed from his body and the chastity of his wife was lost. At that time Sankhachuda and Tulasi met each other in the forests and were married. Sankhachuda, brilliant and majestic, went about with Tulasi in amorous sports creating jealousy even among the devas. His arrogance gave innumerable troubles to the devas, and they along with Brahma and Shiva approached MahaVishnu for a remedy. Vishnu then sent Shiva with his spike to kill Sankhachuda, and he himself started to molest the chastity of his wife Tulasi. Sankhachuda took leave of Tulasi to go and fight with Shiva. When Tulasi was thus left alone, MahaVisnu in the form of Sankhachuda approached Tulasi and after some preliminary talks entered into sexual acts. Tulasi found some difference in the usual affairs and suspecting foul play jumped up to curse the impostor. At once MahaVishnu appeared in his true form and said, "You have been doing penance for a lone time to get me as your husband. Your husband Sankhachuda was the chief of my Parsadas, Sudama. It is time for him to go back to [the spiritual abode of] Goloka, getting himself released from the curse. By this time Shiva would have killed him and he would have gone to Goloka as Sudama. You can now abandon your body and come with me to Vaikuntha to enjoy life as my wife.

"Your body will decay and become a holy river named Gandaki; your hair will become the Tulasi plant, the leaves of which will be held sacred in all the three worlds."

Tulasi then changed herself into the form of Laksmi and went to Vaikuntha with MahaVishnu. (9th Skandha, *Devi Bhagavata*).

5) The greatness of Tulasi. Everything of the Tulasi plant, leaves, flowers, fruits, roots, twigs, skin and even the soil around her is holy. The soul of a dead one whose dead body is cremated using Tulasi twigs for firewood would attain a permanent place in Vishnuloka [the spiritual abode]. Even great sinners would be absolved of their sins if their dead bodies are cremated with Tulasi twigs [or are wearing Tulasi beads]. If at the time of death one thinks of God and mutters His name and if his dead body is later cremated with Tulasi twigs, he would have no rebirths. Even he who has done a crore of sins would attain *moksha* [liberation]

if at the time of cremating his dead body a piece of Tulasi twig is placed at the bottom of the funeral pyre. Just as all waters become pure by the union with Ganga water, all firewood is made pure by the addition of a small piece of Tulasi twig. If the dead body of one is cremated using Tulasi twigs alone, one's sins for a crore of Kalpa years [1 kalpa is 4,800,000 years] would be washed away. Yamadutas [the soldiers of Lord Yama, the king of death] would keep away from one whose dead body is cremated with Tulasi twigs and servants of Vishnu would come near. If a light is burnt for Vishnu with a Tulasi stick, it would be equal to burning several lakhs of lights for Vishnu. If one makes the Tulasi leaves into a paste and smears it on one's body and then worships Vishnu for one day, one would be getting the benefit of a hundred ordinary worships and also the benefit of doing a hundred godanas (gifts of cows). (Chapter 24, *Padma Purana*)

It is also accepted that if ever a person leaves his or her body while wearing Tulasi beads, either around the neck or elsewhere, it creates the same affect as described above as having one's cremation fire burnt using Tulasi.

A little home-grown Tulasi tree

CHAPTER TEN

Prasadam:
The Power of Sacred Food

On the spiritual path, those that are most inclined to lead a peaceful existence that respects the value of all life, and recognizes the spiritual essence in all beings, often adopt the vegetarian lifestyle. It is in accordance with the yogic principle of *ahimsa*, which is to observe nonviolence and abstain from injuring any being in any way. However, in the process of bhakti-yoga, devotion goes beyond simple vegetarianism, and food becomes a method of spiritual progress. In the Krishna temples, food is offered to the deities in a special sacrament, after which it becomes *prasadam*. This means the mercy of the Lord. Thus, the food we eat after it is offered to the Lord becomes a means for our purification and spiritual development.

Devotional service or bhakti-yoga is often described as a process of singing, dancing and feasting. But the feasting is done with spiritual food, Krishna *prasadam*.

In the *Bhagavad-gita* Lord Krishna says, "All that you do, all that you eat, all that you offer and give away, as well as all austerities that you may perform, should be done as an offering unto Me." So offering what we eat to the Lord is an integral part of bhakti-yoga and makes the food blessed with spiritual potencies. Then such food is called *prasadam*, or the mercy of the Lord.

The Lord also describes what He accepts as offerings: "If one offers Me with love and devotion a leaf, a flower, fruit or water, I will accept it." Thus, we can see that the Lord does not need anything, but if one offers fruits, grains, and vegetarian foods, He will accept it. The Lord does not accept foods like meat, fish or eggs, but only those that are pure and naturally available without harming others. So we offer what

Krishna likes, not those items which are distasteful to Him. We also do not use garlic, onions, or mushrooms when we prepare food for Krishna.

The Lord is fully satisfied in Himself. He is the creator of all so everything is already His. He supplies us with food through nature, but we give thanks to Him by offering it back in a mood of loving devotion. So if His devotee offers something with love, out of His causeless mercy Krishna accepts it. The Lord is never hungry for our food, but for the love and devotion we offer. And then He reciprocates with that love.

So on the spiritual path, eating food that is first offered to God is the ultimate perfection of a vegetarian diet. The Vedic literature explains that the purpose of human life is reawakening the soul's original relationship with God, and accepting *prasadam* is the way to help us reach that goal.

The food is meant to be cooked with the consciousness of love, knowing that it will be offered to Lord Krishna. In the spiritual world, Radharani cooks for Krishna and She never cooks the same preparation twice. The temple kitchen is understood to belong to Radharani.

The ingredients are selected with great care and must be fresh, clean and pure vegetarian. Also, in cooking for Krishna we do not taste the preparations while cooking. We leave the first taste for Krishna when it is offered.

After all the preparations are ready, we take a portion of each one and place it in bowls on a special plate and take it to the altar to offer it to the deities or pictures of Krishna.

Then the preparations are presented with special prayers as we ask that God accept our humble offering. The Lord accepts it with the most important part being the love with which it is offered. God does not need to eat, but it is our love for God which attracts Him to us and to accept our offering. Even if the most sumptuous banquet is offered to God but without devotion and love, Krishna will not be hungry to accept it. It is our love which catches the attention of Lord Krishna who is then inclined to accept our service.

After He glances over and tastes that loving offering of vegetarian preparations, He leaves the remnants for us to honor and relish. Krishna's potency is absorbed in that food. In this way, material substance becomes spiritualized, which then affects our body and mind in a similar way. This is His special mercy for us. Thus, the devotional process becomes an exchange of love between us and God, which includes food. And that food not only nourishes our body, but also purifies our consciousness.

By relishing the sacred food of Krishna *prasadam*, it purifies our heart and protects us from falling into illusion. In this way, the devotee imbibes the spiritual potency of Lord Krishna and becomes cleansed of sinful reactions by eating food that is first offered in sacrifice to God. We thus also become free from reincarnation, the continued cycle of life and death. This process prepares us for entering the spiritual world since the devotees there also relish eating in the company of Krishna.

Not only do we make advancement, but also all of the plants that are used in the preparations as an offering to God are also purified and reap spiritual benefit. However, we become implicated in karma if we cause the harm of any living being, even plants, if we use them for food without offering them to God. Thus *prasadam* also becomes the perfect yoga diet.

Therefore, the cooking, the offering, and then the respectful eating or honoring of this spiritualized food all become a part of the joyful process of devotional service to the Lord. Anyone can learn to do this and enjoy the happiness of experiencing *prasadam*. The Sunday love feast in the Hare Krishna temples is the opportunity in which everyone can participate in this opulence of Lord Krishna. So people are invited to attend as often as they like and make spiritual advancement simply by relishing Krishna *prasadam*. For those who stay in the temple ashrama, this becomes a regular daily part of their spiritual practice.

CHAPTER ELEVEN

Rules for Temple Etiquette

These are a few basic rules that should be followed while in the temple:

1. One should remove one's shoes before entering the temple room.

2. One should be dressed appropriately in conservative clothes that do not reveal too much skin, or one's midriff or too much of one's legs. One should always wear conservative clothes that keep the body comfortable but covered as well. In the West, clothes styles are often quite free and relaxed, but if it is too revealing it can be taken as disrespectful or even offensive to the deities or even the people who are there. So one should always try to dress in a most suitable and modest manner.

3. One should make a sound (like a knock on the door or ringing of the bell) and chant the name of the deities upon entering the temple room.

4. One should pay obeisances to the spiritual master upon entering or leaving the temple room, or to the deities.

5. One should not sit or pay obeisances with one's feet pointing toward the spiritual master or deities, or stand with one's back to Them.

6. One should not step over or touch one's feet to devotees or sacred paraphernalia such as *prasadam*, scriptures, chanting beads, etc.

7. One should not let sacred paraphernalia touch the ground, or bring them into the bathroom.

8. One should wear clean clothes and wash oneself after evacuating, before coming before the deities.

9. One should touch *prasadam* (sacred food) only with one's right hand, and should wash one's hands and mouth after eating, or before taking seconds on food.

10. One should avoid speaking about non-devotional topics while in front of the deities, and one should not argue or raise one's voice or become angry before Them, as this is offensive and a sign of immaturity.

11. One should also avoid belching or passing air in the temple room.

DANCING IN THE TEMPLE

Part of the process in the bhakti-yoga practice is dancing in the *kirtana*, especially in the Gaudiya tradition. Naturally, there is singing of *bhajans*, devotional songs, in quiet, meditative groups, and there is also singing songs in which the whole congregation participates, called *kirtana*. When the beat and spiritual bliss arouses people to move, then they can start dancing to the music and the chanting or singing.

However, this dancing should be conservative in nature. In other words, there is no intermingling of the men and women. It is not that kind of dancing. Usually you will see men on one side of the temple room and women on the other. And especially it is not meant to become overly wild to satisfy one's imaginary or artistic expression. People, for example, should not swing their backside too much, or their shoulders or chest in a provocative manner. This actually becomes distracting. I only mention this because some people come to the temple for the first time and begin to do the shimmy shake when dancing, which is not appropriate. In other words, when we dance we do it for the joy of satisfying the Lord. Not to please our own mind and senses. However, if guests start to dance in a provocative or overly wild style, devotees must be very careful in the way they correct them, if they do so at all, so their feelings are not hurt. They simply may not know the proper etiquette if they are at the temple for the first time.

When Srila Prabhupada came to America, he had a particular way of teaching his disciples how to dance. He had his disciples form a line behind him while he demonstrated a simple step. Holding his arms above his head, he would first swing his left foot forward across the right foot, and then bring it back again in a sweeping motion. Then he would bring his right foot over the left and bring it back again. With his arms upraised, Prabhupada would walk forward, swinging his body from side to side, left foot to the right, right foot to the left side, in time with the one-two-three rhythm of the *kirtana*. He demonstrated this in regular time, and in a slow, half-time rhythm. This was later called "the Swami step." And many devotees still dance in this simple manner, which anyone can do.

Some additional adaptations have developed since then. Sometimes the participants form two lines facing each other, and to the rhythm of the *kirtana*, they take one step towards each other, and one step back, sometimes with arms held in the air, and sometimes not. Or they start dancing in a circle, slowly running around those that are leading the *kirtana* in the center. Or sometimes in the middle of the circle there will be a central dancer who trades off with another, all taking turns in this way. Women can do these as well, and sometimes they also form a circle, holding hands and dancing together, moving toward the center, and then moving back. Other adaptations have also been done. But this is how everyone can dance in a conservative but joyful and fun manner together, while at the same time chanting along with the Hare Krishna mantra, or whatever devotional song is being sung.

Further details and instructions on the path of bhakti-yoga are more fully explained in the *Bhakti-rasamrita-sidhu* by Srila Rupa Goswami, or the summary called "The Nectar of Devotion" by Srila Prabhupada.

LEARNING THE INSTRUMENTS

In many activities within the temple room and before the deities, music and *bhajans* and *kirtanas* are a part of it. Therefore, devotees will be playing *kartalas* (small hand cymbals), *mridungas* (two-headed drums), harmoniums (keyboard), and other traditional instruments, such as the hand-held gong, etc. Traditional means that there is usually a traditional way of playing the instruments. This will often require training and practice. *Kartalas* are the easiest to play, just ringing them lightly together to three of the four beats in four/four time. Some songs are in different beats and will require more finesse. However, *kartalas* are meant to sound like the tinkling of the ankle bells of the dancing cowherd girls. So they are meant to sound like small bells. However, when the *kirtana* gets loud and exciting, then of course they are played more loudly as well. But it takes some training and experience to know how best to do this. When the *kartalas* are simply banged together, it can become abrasive to the ears, to the point you cannot properly hear the words the *kirtana* leader is singing. This is not proper, the instruments are only meant to accompany the singing in the *kirtana*, not dominate it. The chanting is always meant to take priority over the instruments. And when the instruments become too loud, they can actually damage the ears, causing a slight loss of hearing which increases as more people participate in such loud *kirtanas*. This is not how it is meant to be.

Mridunga drums are the same way, they can be played traditionally, which requires lessons and practice, or they can be played like banging a table top, loudly and without tradition. But when they are played with a traditional style, they can add a lot to the *kirtana* or *bhajan*, and everyone becomes attracted.

The point is that musical instruments are an integral part of the bhakti-yoga process with the *kirtanas* and *bhajans*. Therefore, *bhaktas* who want to play them should know what they are doing, and even get some training and certainly some practice to play them properly. It is always impressive to see and listen to a good *kirtana* group, with nice singing and instrument playing. It is a matter of having a refined consciousness and knowing that such activities are not meant only to inspire other devotees in their devotional service, but again it is done with the attempt to satisfy the Lord.

A typical set of *kartalas* used in *kirtanas* and group singing

CHAPTER TWELVE

Ekadasi: The Appearance and Purpose of This Special Day

Ekadasi is a special fast day that is followed twice a month by many bhakti-yogis. To help understand the purpose and importance of this day needs some explanation. *Eka* means "one," and *dasi* is the feminine form of the word *dasa*, which in this case means "ten." So Ekadasi is the eleventh day of both the dark and full moon of each month. On these days, *bhaktas* and devotees fast from beans and grains, and make an extra effort to increase their devotional service to Lord Sri Krishna. Such sacred fasting days will help any sincere soul achieve liberation from the world of birth and death. It is on this day of Ekadasi that helps one get a taste for renunciation from the illusory habit of always trying to gratify the temporary mind and senses.

On the day of the Ekadasi fast, one should also try to avoid strenuous physical labor if possible, and focus on performing devotional service, bhakti-yoga. Such service also means to increase one's chanting, such as chanting extra rounds of *japa* meditation. So other business can be left for later, or as much as possible on that day. Beans and grains may be cooked and offered for the deity, as usual, but for a bhakti-yogi, he or she avoids such things for the day, even if it is *maha-prasada*–food offered directly to the deity. Such *maha-prasada* can be saved for the next day. Then after fasting, at least from beans and grains for the day, there is usually a specified time in the morning the next day when it is advised to break the fast by taking grains.

It is also recommended that if you do eat, eat once in the day on Ekadasi. Fasting completely is even better, but many cannot do that, or should not do that for health reasons. And of course, one may drink the few drops of water when doing *achamana* for deity worship. However, doing our service and helping spread spiritual knowledge is a prime duty, which means if fasting is an austerity that impedes or hampers the more important duty of preaching, or spreading this spiritual knowledge, then a complete fast from food is not necessary, and a bhakti-yogi can eat one or even two meals in the day. Such meals are simple, such as only fruits and vegetable preparations. But if a devotee can meet his responsibilities and do all of his or her practices, then a complete fast can be done.

"Of all plants, the Tulasi is most dear to Me, and of all months, Kartika (October-November) is most dear, of all places of pilgrimage, My beloved Dwaraka is most dear, and of all days, Ekadasi is most dear." (*Padma Purana*, Uttara Khanda 112.3)

* * *

(The following was written in 1956 by Sri Navinacandra Cakravarti, a disciple of Srila Bhaktisiddhanta Sarasvati Thakura. There are many stories of Ekadasi in the *Puranas*, but most explain the material benefits and blessings one gets from observing Ekadasi. This article, based on the conversation between Srila Vyasadeva and Jaimini Rishi, gives the real spiritual reason for following the vow of observing Ekadasi as emphasized by Sri Chaitanya Mahaprabhu in the *Caitanya-caritamrita* and later by Srila Prabhupada.)

Many devotees are very inquisitive about the appearance of Sri Ekadasi and about her special characteristics. Therefore, we find in the 14th chapter of the *Padma Purana*, from the section entitled "Kriya-sagara-sara", a description of Ekadasi's importance.

Once the great sage Jaimini Rishi said to his spiritual master, "O Gurudeva! Previously, by your mercy, you described to me the history of the Ganga River, the benefits of worshiping Vishnu, the giving of grains in charity, the giving of water in charity, and the magnanimity of drinking water that has been used to wash the feet of the brahmanas. O best of sages, Sri Gurudeva, now, with great enthusiasm, I desire to hear of the benefits of fasting on Ekadasi and of the appearance of Ekadasi."

"O Gurudeva! When did Ekadasi take birth and from whom did

she appear? What are the rules of fasting on the day of Ekadasi? Please describe the benefits of following this vow and when it should be followed. Who is the utmost worshipable presiding deity of Sri Ekadasi? What are the faults in not observing Ekadasi properly? Please bestow your mercy upon me and tell about these subjects, as you are the only personality able to do so."

Srila Vyasadeva, upon hearing this inquiry from Jaimini Rishi, became situated in transcendental bliss. "O brahmana sage Jaimini! The results of following Ekadasi can be perfectly described by the Supreme Lord, Narayana, because Sri Narayana is the only personality capable of describing them in full. But I will give a very brief description in answer to your question."

"At the beginning of the material creation, the Supreme Lord created the moving and non-moving living entities within this world made of five gross material elements. Simultaneously, for the purpose of punishing the evil human beings, He created a personality whose form was the embodiment of the worst kinds of sin (Papa-purusha). The different limbs of this personality were constructed of various sinful activities. His head was made of the sin of murdering a brahmana, his two eyes were the form of drinking intoxicants, his mouth was made from the sin of stealing gold, his ears were the form of the sin of having illicit connection with the spiritual master's wife, his nose was of the sin of killing one's wife, his arms the form of the sin of killing a cow, his neck was made of the sin of stealing accumulated wealth, his chest of the sin of abortion, his lower chest of the sin of having sex with another's wife, his stomach of the sin of killings one's relatives, his navel of the sin of killing those who are dependent on him, his waist of the sin of egotistical self-appraisal, his thighs of the sin of offending the guru, his genitals of the sin of selling one's daughter, his buttocks of the sin of telling confidential matters, his feet of the sin of killing one's father, and his hair was the form of all sorts of less severe sinful activities. In this way, a horrible personality embodying all sinful activities and vices was created. His bodily color is black, and his eyes are yellow. He inflicts extreme misery upon sinful persons.

"The Supreme Personality of Godhead, Lord Vishnu, upon seeing this personality of sin began to think to Himself as follows: 'I am the creator of the miseries and happiness for the living entities. I am their master because I have created this personality of sin, who gives distress to all dishonest, deceitful and sinful persons. Now I must create someone who will control this personality'. At this time Sri Bhagavan created the personality of Yamaraja [the lord of death] and the different hellish planetary systems. Those living entities who are very sinful will be sent after death to Yamaraja, who will in turn, according to their sins, send them to an appropriate hellish region to suffer.

"After these adjustments had been made, the Supreme Lord, who is the giver of distress and happiness to the living entities, went to the house of Yamaraja, with the help of Garuda, the king of birds. When Yamaraja saw that Lord Vishnu had arrived, he immediately washed His feet and made an offering unto Him. He then had Him sit upon a golden throne. The Supreme Lord Vishnu became seated upon the throne, whereupon He heard very loud crying sounds from the southern direction. He became surprised by this and inquired of Yamaraja, 'From where is this loud crying coming?'

"Yamaraja in reply said, 'O Deva! The different living entities of the earthly planetary systems have fallen to the hellish regions. They are suffering extremely for their misdeeds. The horrible crying is because of suffering from the inflictions of their past bad actions.'

"After hearing this the Supreme Lord Vishnu went to the hellish region to the south. When the inhabitants saw who had come they began to cry even louder. The heart of the Supreme Lord Vishnu became filled with compassion. Lord Vishnu thought to Himself, 'I have created all this progeny, and it is because of Me that they are suffering.'"

Vyasadeva continued: "O Jaimini, just listen to what the Supreme Lord did next. After the merciful Supreme Lord thought over what He had previously considered, He suddenly manifested from His own form the deity of the lunar day Ekadasi. Afterward, the different sinful living entities began to follow the vow of Ekadasi and were then elevated quickly to the abode of Vaikuntha. O my child Jaimini, therefore the lunar day of Ekadasi is the selfsame form of the Supreme Lord, Vishnu, and the Supersoul within the heart of the living entities. Sri Ekadasi is the utmost pious activity and is situated as the head among all vows.

"Following the ascension of Sri Ekadasi, that personality

(Papa-purusha) who is the form of sinful activity gradually saw the influence that she, Ekadasi, had. Thus, he approached Lord Vishnu with doubts in his heart and began offering many prayers, whereupon Lord Vishnu became very pleased and said, 'I have become very pleased by your nice offerings. What boon is it that you want?'

"The Papa-purusha replied, "I am Your created progeny, and it is through me that you wanted distress given to the living entities who are very sinful. But now, by the influence of Sri Ekadasi, I have become all but destroyed. O Prabhu! After I die all of Your parts and parcels who have accepted material bodies will become liberated and return to the abode of Vaikuntha (the spiritual domain). If this liberation of all living entities takes place, then who will carry on Your activities? There will be no one to enact the pastimes in the earthly planetary systems! O Keshava! If you want these eternal pastimes to carry on, then You please save me from the fear of Ekadasi. No type of pious activity can bind me. But Ekadasi only, being Your own manifested form, can impede me. Out of fear of Sri Ekadasi I have fled and taken shelter of men; animals; insects; hills; trees; moving and non-moving living entities; rivers; oceans; forests; heavenly, earthly and hellish planetary systems; demigods; and the Gandharvas. I cannot find a place where I can be free from the fear of Sri Ekadasi. O my Master! I am a product of Your creation, so therefore very mercifully direct me to a place where I can reside fearlessly.'"

Vyasadeva then said to Jaimini, "After saying this, the embodiment of all sinful activities (Papa-purusha) fell down at the feet of the Supreme Lord Vishnu, who is the destroyer of all miseries and began to cry.

"After this, Lord Vishnu, observing the condition of the Papa-purusha, with laughter began to speak thus: 'O Papa-purusha, rise up! Don't lament any longer. Just listen, and I'll tell you where you can stay on the lunar day of Ekadasi. On the date of Sri Ekadasi, which is the benefactor of the three planetary systems, you can take shelter of foodstuffs in the form of grains. There is no reason to worry about this any more, because My form as Sri Ekadasi will no longer impede you.' After giving direction to the Papa-purusha, the Supreme Lord Vishnu disappeared and the Papa-purusha returned to the performance of his own activities.

"Therefore, those persons who are serious about the ultimate benefit of the soul will never eat grains on Ekadasi. According to the instructions of Lord Vishnu, every kind of sinful activity that can be found in the material world takes its residence in this place of (grains) foodstuff. Whoever follows Ekadasi is freed from all sins and never enters into the hellish regions. If one doesn't follow Ekadasi because of illusion, he is still considered the utmost sinner. For every mouthful of grain that is eaten by a resident of the earthly region (on Ekadasi), one receives the effect of killing millions of brahmanas. It is definitely necessary that one give up eating grains on Ekadasi. I very strongly say again and again, 'On Ekadasi, do not eat grains, do not eat grains, do not eat grains!' Whether one be a kshatriya, vaishya, shudra, or of any family, he should follow the lunar day of Ekadasi. From this the perfection of varna and ashrama will be attained. Especially since if one (even) by trickery follows Ekadasi, all his sins become destroyed and he very easily attains the supreme goal, the abode of Vaikuntha."

ADDITIONAL INFORMATION

From the above article and story we can understand that Ekadasi is a form of Lord Vishnu, and by observing the Ekadasi vow, it not only decreases the amount of sin (bad karma) we imbibe, but it also eats up sinful reactions to help pave our way back to the abode of Lord Vishnu, Vaikuntha. This is also why Ekadasi is called "The mother of devotion." It helps remove the obstacles on our path of devotional service to the Lord.

Ekadasi generally falls on the 11th day after the new moon, and the 11th day after the full moon. Eka means one and dasi is the feminine form of dasa, which means ten. Together it means eleven. Only occasionally may it fall on a different day. So it is on these days that devotees and devout Hindus will follow the vow of Ekadasi and not eat any beans or grains, or products with such substances in them. Thus, the diet is expected to be simple and plain as part of the mood of renunciation, and preferably only once in the day if possible. Other recommendations include that the food should be made of vegetables, fruit, water, milk products, nuts, sugar, and roots that are grown underground (except beet roots). Additional restrictions include spinach, eggplant, asafetida, and sea salt, but rock salt is alright.

Since there are 12 months in a year, with two Ekadasis in each month, there are 24 Ekadasis in each year. Each Ekadasi has a name, that are Utpanna, Mokshada, Saphala, Putrada, Shat-tila, Jaya, Vijaya, Amalaki, Papamochani, Kamada, Varuthini, Mohini, Apara, Nirjala, Yogini, Padma (Devashayani), Kamika, Putrada, Aja, Parivartini, Indira, Papankusha, Rama, and Haribodhini (Devotthani). Occasionally there are two extra Ekadasis that happen in a lunar leap year, which are Padmini and Parama.

Each Ekadasi day has particular benefits and blessings that one can attain by the performance of specific activities done on that day. By engaging in the extra study to learn what these are, one can derive even more benefit from each particular Ekadasi. Books devoted to Ekadasi are available that contain such information, so we will not include it here. However, reading the glories of each Ekadasi day, along with all the names of these days, will also achieve a similar goal of observing the Ekadasi vow. This also means that we are encouraged to increase our spiritual activities that day, which are centered around the chanting of the holy names of the Lord. Charity, especially to advanced devotees and preachers of the Vedic Dharma, or directly engaging in activities of Krishna's service, deity worship, chanting the *Purusha-sukta* hymns, or other spiritual activities on Ekadasi are also highly recommended and brings great spiritual benefits to the performer.

It is said that even if one mistakenly misses the observance of an Ekadasi, he or she may make up for it by observing it the very next day on Dvadasi, and then break one's fast from grains on the next day, Trayodasi. One may also observe the special fast on Nirjala Ekadasi. This is also called Bhima Ekadasi. This is because the Pandava brother known as Bhima was so strong and had such a voracious appetite that he could not observe Ekadasis twice a month. He could not fast because he was too hungry. So Lord Krishna told him to merely observe one Ekadasi a year, which is the Nirjala Ekadasi. *Nirjala* means no water. So he had to observe at least one Ekadasi a year, and on that day he had to abstain from not only beans and grains, but from all foods, even water. So devotees who miss an Ekadasi day often observe a complete fast from all food and liquids on the Nirjala Ekadasi, which is usually sometime in June, and thus possibly make up for whatever was missed. However, this is a very potent Ekadasi, so a complete fast on this day gives one who observes this many pious credits.

Sometimes there is a day called Mahadvadasi. This is when Ekadasi is astronomically combined with Dvadasi, or the twelfth day of the full moon or new moon lunar cycle. This is called a pure Ekadasi and the observance is often started the evening before Mahadvadasi and through the next day with the basic Ekadasi fast.

Breaking the Ekadasi fast on the next day with some foodstuffs made from grains is usually done two-and-a-half hours or shortly thereafter from the time of the sunrise.

In the *Caitanya-caritamrita* (Adi-lila, 15-9-10), Sri Chaitanya begs his mother to follow Ekadasi, as was expected of all His followers. And in the purport to this verse, Srila Prabhupada explains that even though devotees eat food cooked for and offered to Lord Vishnu, *prasada*, which is spiritually potent and free from all karma, even on Ekadasi a devotee does not eat even *maha-prasada* that has grains in it, even though it can be saved for the next day.

In this way, by the observance of the special Ekadasi day and its special fast, a person can accelerate their spiritual growth and awareness, and free themselves from negative karma that will only further bind them to the continuous rounds of birth and death.

OTHER SPECIAL DAYS AND FESTIVALS WE OBSERVE

Festivals are most joyous events in this tradition, and there are several that are especially important. Festivals are when the temple or the temple rooms in our homes can be nicely decorated with flower arrangements, the deities are also dressed with more flowers, and additional foodstuffs are prepared and offered to the deities. Celebrations include plays, dramas, musical presentations, and additional *kirtanas* and *japa* chanting. This may include a half-day fast followed by a feast, or on Krishna's appearance day it is a full day fast until after midnight when a feast is distributed. The most important thing is the increased hearing and chanting about the Lord. Some of these festivals include the following:

Gaura Purnima, the celebration of the appearance of Sri Chaitanya Mahaprabhu.

Rama-navami, the celebration of Lord Rama's appearance.

Nrisimha Chaturdasi, the celebration of the appearance of Lord Narasimha.

Rathayatra, the grand cart festival in the summer for Lord Jagannatha, Lord Balarama and Lady Subhadra.

Jhulana Yatra, the lovely festival when we put the little Radha-Krishna deities on a swing and every takes a turn at swinging Them

Lord Balarama's appearance day, when we celebrate His birthday.

Lord Krishna's Appearance day, known as Krishna Janmasthami, which is a grand festival when many people attend the temple programs that are especially arranged for this day, which goes on until midnight, the time when He first appeared as a baby in His *lila* or pastime.

Vyasa Puja, the celebration of the guru as the representative of Srila Vyasadeva, in which case we celebrate the appearance day of Srila Prabhupada on the day after Krishna Janmasthami.

Radhastami, this is the celebration of the appearance day of Srimati Radharani.

Govardhana Puja and Annakuta Mahotsava, another festival based on when Lord Krishna lifted Govardhan Hill. This is also when the temples and devotees take various foodstuffs and make a model of the hill, which is accepted as an expansion of Govardhana itself, which the devotees circumambulate, and which is later distributed as Krishna *prasada*.

Also the appearance and disappearance days of noteworthy saints. These are observed with various levels of celebration throughout the year, especially that of Srila Prabhupada which is observed with a half-day fast.

Chapter Twelve

CHATURMASYA

This is a period of four months in which bhakti-yogis often observe an additional dietary restriction. This is originally from the time when sannyasa monks would stop their traveling during the rainy season in India and then observe an additional vow of austerity during those months for their worship of Lord Krishna. This would be from July to October. This begins from the Shayana Ekadasi (in the month of Ashadha) to Uttara Ekadasi (in the month of Kartika).

So we may not be obligated to stop our activities and stay in one place for four months, but we may still be inclined to observe the dietary restrictions during Chaturmasya, which includes no eating of spinach during the first month, no yogurt during the second month, no milk during the third month, and no urad dahl during the fourth month.

After this period of Chaturmasya the sannyasis would again start their traveling and preaching and then would go back to their normal diet, at which time we can do the same.

CHAPTER THIRTEEN

The Nine Processes of Bhakti-yoga

We all find ourselves in the illusion of this world, and the purpose of yoga is to attain the realization of our spiritual identity as a spirit soul and our connection with the Supreme Soul, or the *jivatma* with Paramatma. The purpose of bhakti-yoga is to regain the perception and our connection with God as a loving servant of the Supreme. This is the atmosphere of the spiritual world, and if we humbly pursue the path of bhakti-yoga, we can enter back into that mood and atmosphere. In this way, the means brings us to the proper end. That is the end of all knowledge, or Vedanta, which in this case means to enter back into the spiritual domain and the activities that go on within the spiritual Vaikuntha planets and in Goloka Vrindavana, Lord Krishna's personal abode.

In this way, by learning how to make whatever we do into bhakti-yoga, our whole life, our activities, and where we live become spiritualized, a part of our service to the Supreme.

As Lord Krishna says in *Bhagavad-gita*:

> *sarva-dharman parityajya*
> *mam ekam sharanam vraja*
> *aham tvam sarva-papebhyo*
> *mokshayishyami ma shuchaha*

"Abandon all varieties of religion and just surrender unto Me. I shall deliver you from all sinful reactions. Do not fear."

This surrender is what attracts Krishna, and that is exactly the process of bhakti-yoga. It means that whatever else we may do, eventually we should give up all sorts of religious or yoga systems, and simply approach the Lord directly through love and devotion (*bhakti*) and He will guide us in the right direction for what we need to do to reach Him.

So when it comes to bhakti-yoga, or the art of engaging in the devotional service to the Lord, there are nine specific processes that allow us to practice this form of yoga. From these nine processes that are included in bhakti-yoga, we can expand them in many different ways that allow anyone to find a particular outlet, or even numerous forms of expression, that can be dovetailed and aligned with the bhakti-yoga process. This is explained in the *Srimad-Bhagavatam* (7.5.23-24):

> *shri-prahrada uvacha*
> *shravanam kirtanam vishnoh*
> *smaranam pada-sevanam*
> *archanam vandanam dasyam*
> *sakhyam atma-nivedanam*
>
> *iti pumsarpita vishnau*
> *bhaktish chen nava-lakshana*
> *kriyeta bhagavaty addha*
> *tan manye 'dhitam uttamam*

"Prahlada Maharaja said: Hearing and chanting about the transcendental holy name, form, qualities, paraphernalia and pastimes of Lord Vishnu, remembering them, serving the lotus feet of the Lord, offering the Lord respectful worship with sixteen types of paraphernalia, offering prayers to the Lord, becoming His servant, considering the Lord one's best friend, and surrendering everything unto Him (in other words, serving Him with the body, mind and words)–these nine processes are accepted as pure devotional service. One who has dedicated his life to the service of Krishna through any of these nine methods should be understood to be the most learned person, for he has acquired complete knowledge."

To briefly explain further, after receiving the Lord's teachings in the *Bhagavad-gita*, or the *Srimad-Bhagavatam*, hearing them is *sravanam*, which can be done in the form of reading books, listening to classes, hearing the devotional songs and *kirtanas*, or watching plays or dances that depict the pastimes of the Lord. This is the beginning stage of bhakti-yoga. Hearing is the means we begin to cleanse the materialistic thoughts and habits from our minds and activities. This also means there must be those who give the classes, sing the songs, perform the plays, write the plays, record the devotional music, produce the films or radio or television shows that offer such facility, or whatever else it takes. And this expands in so many ways through artistic expressions or technological knowledge to put such things together, all for the same purpose. This takes on the process of *kirtanam*, meaning to repeat the stories or the chanting and singing the devotional songs and mantras, and whatever it takes to do this.

Smaranam means remembering what we have heard and trying to understand the Supreme Lord more deeply. So we may take the time to study more about Him, such as reading the devotional and Vedic texts that relay information about His personality, pastimes, characteristics, etc. By understanding more about Him also brings us closer to Him, and helps fix our mind on this Absolute Reality. Besides the chanting of His holy names, this is the ultimate form of meditation.

Pada-sevanam means to engage in serving or worshiping the lotus feet of the Lord in various ways, according to time and circumstance. This is most easily done while serving the Lord in the temple. This again can be expanded to include so many activities that help ourselves or assists others to do this.

Archanam means to engage in the activities of worshiping the Lord in the temple, as in deity worship. But this also includes managing the temples so deity worship can go on nicely and where other people can attend to worship, helping put on festivals that evolve around the deities, such as the Jagannatha Ratha-yatra parade, or celebrating the appearance day of Lord Krishna, the Krishna Janmastami festival. All of this evolves around worshiping the Lord as the deities. So all this is included in *Archanam*.

Vandanam means to offer respectful worship of the Lord. *Vandanam* also means *namaskuru*–which is to offer prayers to the Lord. There is nothing more personal than to set one's ego aside and offer prayers to God, asking for blessings over difficulties, or expressing one's concern for others. God is always listening, whether you go before the deities in the temple, or simply have a talk with God while sitting alone outdoors somewhere. Many saints have books of prayers to God they have composed that show the varieties of prayers that can be offered and the many different moods in which the prayers were written.

Dasyam means to be accept oneself as an eternal servant of Krishna. This means that whatever we do can be dovetailed into a direct service for Krishna, or some tactic that helps us remember the Lord, or helps others remember God and the purpose of life, and so on. Or to simply work at our regular job or occupation to earn the money to help support the temple, or temple projects, or develop our own home temple room and worship of our home deities, and so on. This makes all of our activities into forms of service, or bhakti-yoga.

Sakyam means to be a well-wisher of Krishna, or to serve Him as a friend. This means to have a friendly attitude towards Lord Krishna, and to help in offering service to Him, and in assisting in whatever is connected with Him, such as trying to provide a nicer facility to expand His pastimes here in this world. This can include many things as well, such as helping with the service that is provided to the deity in the temple, or so many other things.

Atma-nivedanam means to offer everything to Krishna, as in one's body, mind or thought, and words, and whatever one may possess. This stage is reached when the devotee has no other interest but to serve and please the Lord.

So this shows that there is a wide variety of activities that can be included in the process of bhakti-yoga. It is not all isolated meditation or philosophical study, but it includes many things that we normally do. We only have to learn or be trained in how to engage in such activities with the right intention and consciousness, and the awareness of the Supreme Being, Krishna, and devotion to Him.

Not everyone can do all of these things, but that is not what it takes. You only have to pick one or two and do them properly according to the principles of bhakti-yoga. But these are all easy and consist of varieties of sweet activities that connect one with God, and that can change your life. Sincerely engaging in any of these nine processes is called *bhakti*, or devotion. The devotion with which one engages in these practices is the means by which one unites with the Supreme, and uniting with God is called yoga. Thus, this process is known as bhakti-yoga.

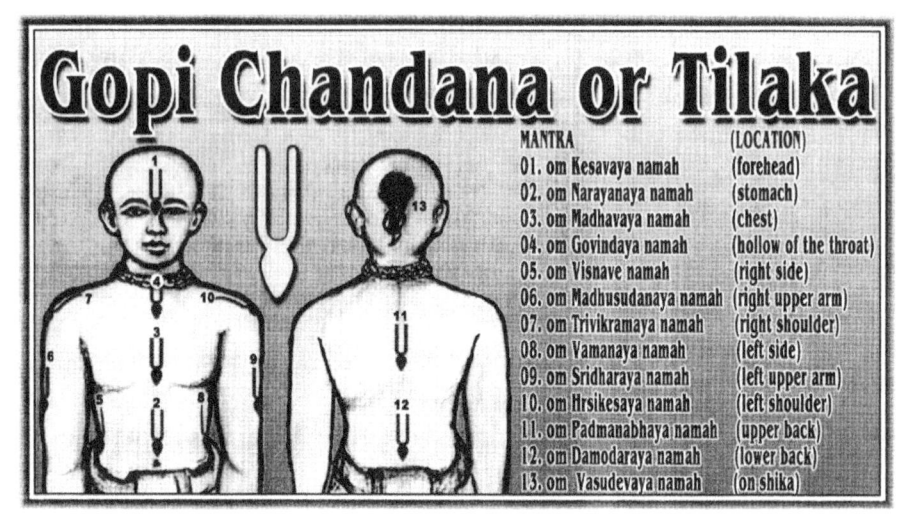

Gopi Chandana or Tilaka

MANTRA	(LOCATION)
01. om Kesavaya namah	(forehead)
02. om Narayanaya namah	(stomach)
03. om Madhavaya namah	(chest)
04. om Govindaya namah	(hollow of the throat)
05. om Visnave namah	(right side)
06. om Madhusudanaya namah	(right upper arm)
07. om Trivikramaya namah	(right shoulder)
08. om Vamanaya namah	(left side)
09. om Sridharaya namah	(left upper arm)
10. om Hrsikesaya namah	(left shoulder)
11. om Padmanabhaya namah	(upper back)
12. om Damodaraya namah	(lower back)
13. om Vasudevaya namah	(on shika)

A handy chart that shows the *tilaka* markings, how it looks and where to apply them, for those who want to put on *tilaka*.

CHAPTER FOURTEEN

A Few Additional Points to Understand

THE PURPOSE OF HAVING A GURU

In brief, a guru is a spiritual teacher who is knowledgeable in the Vedic scripture and the traditions, and can inspire and teach it to others so they can follow it in a practical manner. He or she is also experienced in the spiritual Truths, the goal of the Vedic path, and can show the way by example to those who enquire.

The word *guru* means one who is heavy with knowledge, not only cultivated knowledge acquired through personal training and practice, but also knowledge attained through personal experience and realizations of the spiritual perfection that is discussed in the Vedic scripture and by previous spiritual authorities. The word *guru* also means one who can deliver others from darkness. Such a qualified guru is one who should be approached with respect and served with humility and honor because such a guru who has seen the truth can give one knowledge and guidance for attaining the truth. Such a guru gives the second birth to a person into the spiritual understanding, beyond the common first biological birth one acquires from parents. Thus, a genuine guru can awaken a disciple to a new world of spiritual reality, a higher dimension. Such an awakening creates an eternal bond between the spiritual master and disciple.

WHAT IS "NAMASTE"

This is the popular greeting performed by pressing two hands together and holding them near the heart and bowing slightly while saying "Namaste." The whole act communicates to the world the spiritual significance that "You and I are one," or "I salute and worship the God within you, which is a mirror image of myself." It is also called *namaskar*, which is understood as salutations or prostration, and a way of paying homage to each other. Its spiritual significance is negating or reducing one's ego in the presence of another. The bowing of the head is a gracious form of extending friendship in love, respect and humility. Adding spiritual devotion to this gesture is done when we also add such sacred words as, "Namaste," "Hare Krishna," "Jai Sri Krishna," "Radhe Radhe," "Jai Sri Rama," "Hari Om," "Namo Narayana," "Om Shanti," etc. These words are actually paying respect to the Divine, and certain sayings are often preferred in particular places. Thus, the Namaste gesture with these words does not remain a superficial gesture but provides a deeper communication and meaning between one another.

WHY RED DOTS ARE WORN ON THE FOREHEAD

Sometimes you will find that many Hindu ladies wear red dots on their foreheads as a sign of being married, just as Christians wear wedding rings. It may be worn daily or on special occasions, or while going to the temple. This is called *kumkum*, and is often made from dyed rice flour. When men wear such dots, which are often applied with the finger tip, it is often because they have visited a temple, or are worshipers of Devi, in which case it is a sign of their devotion and that the body is a temple. (More is explained as follows.)

WHAT IS TILAKA OR FOREHEAD MARKS

The *tilaka* marks that may be seen on devotees and Hindu saints are usually in two forms: applied in a V shape in the center of the forehead, or as lines applied horizontally across the forehead. It will vary in design according to the sect of the person. A simple *tilaka* in the V shape may be white or dark, using *chandan* or clay from certain holy places, or sandalwood paste. These indicate that one is a Vaishnava, or worshiper of Vishnu and Krishna. Or it may have a red streak down the center that indicates that one is a worshiper of Lord Rama. Or it may be the three-lined sacred ash, called *bhasma*, streaked horizontally across the forehead that indicates one is a Shaivite, or worshiper of Shiva. A simple red dot is also worn by those who worship Devi. Other shapes and colors will indicate other purposes. Sometimes you may even see a holy man whose entire forehead is covered with *chandan* or *bhasma tilaka*.

Such marks may be applied as part of the morning ritual or custom with a mantra or prayer, or the *kumkum* or *chandan* are often offered by a temple priest to the guests who visit the temple after it has been offered to the temple deity. Among other things that it indicates is that it marks the body as a temple, a vehicle with the soul and Supersoul within. So it helps invoke a feeling of sanctity in the wearer, and reminds others of the spiritual significance of who we are. The *tilaka* also covers the spot between the eyebrows which is the seat of memory, thinking and the third eye, or spiritual center of consciousness, the Ajna Chakra. The *tilaka* is said to help activate that center. It is also said to help cool the forehead against heat generated from worry that may also cause headaches. Thus, it protects us from energy loss. However, the *tilaka* marks are also applied to other parts of the body, such as the arms, chest, and back, all of which are to indicate the sacredness of the soul within the body, or the holy aspect of the body when it is used in the service of the Lord.

WHY RING BELLS IN TEMPLES

When entering a temple, most of them have one or more bells hung from the ceiling. The devotee rings the bells as he or she enters, then proceeds for *darshan* to see the deities. The ring of the bell produces a sound similar to Om, the universal name of the Lord. This helps create an atmosphere of auspiciousness when entering the temple. This is also a reason why a bell is rung by a priest, *pujari*, while doing the *arati* ceremony. Ringing the bell, blowing the conch, and engaging in the *kirtanas* or singing holy songs, are all ways to worship the Lord and keep away all inauspicious and irrelevant noises and thoughts that might disturb or distract the worshipers from their devotions and inner peace.

THE SIGNIFICANCE OF THE ARATI CEREMONY

The *arati* ceremony is the offering of a ghee lamp to the deity or object of respect. These lamps usually have five or more flames on them. *Arati* is performed in the temples to the deities several times a day. It is also offered to special guests and holy saints. It is also accompanied with ringing a bell, singing or playing musical instruments.

In offering the lamp to the deity, it is held in the right hand and waved in a clockwise motion. It is a way of adding an intensity to the prayers and the image of the Lord. Besides, the aroma of the burning ghee is quite pleasing. Afterwards, the ghee lamp is passed around the room so that everyone can place their hands over the flame that has been offered to the deity, accepting it as holy remnants, *prasada*, and then touch the hands to the eyes or head. This is a gesture of accepting the light of knowledge, and the light which revealed the Lord. We use the lamp to light the form of the Lord who is in fact the source of all light. This was particularly significant before there was electricity and when temples were lit by lamps. The *arati* ceremony would especially provide light to various parts of the deity when the priest would wave the lamp in front of it. Some of the older temples in India are still like this today. We also accept this lamp as a symbol of lighting our own vision and thoughts with hopes that they may be divine and noble.

Sometimes camphor is also used in place of ghee. This also presents a pleasing scent. The ghee or camphor also represents our inherent tendencies that are being offered to the fire of knowledge, which reveals the form of the Lord and thus increases our mental and physical purity in service to the Lord.

THE REASON LAMPS ARE USED

In many homes and temples there are lamps that are lit. And many special functions start with the lighting of a lamp. Light symbolizes knowledge which keeps us free from the darkness of ignorance. Knowledge removes ignorance just as light removes darkness. Therefore, the lamp is lit and we bow to it as this knowledge is the greatest form of wealth. It is kept lit during special functions as a guide and witness to our thoughts and actions. Of course, now lamps are not as necessary with the use of electric bulbs, etc. But the lamp is the traditional instrument which represents our *vasanas* or negative inclinations, while the wick signifies our ego. As the lamp burns, it also represents the burning away of our bad habits and bodily ego. The flame burns upward, as knowledge also takes our views higher.

WHY A CONCH SHELL IS BLOWN

Whether in temples or in our household temple rooms, the conch shell is blown three times before the *arati* ceremony or *puja*, worship. It is kept on the altar as a symbol for Truth, *Dharma*, auspiciousness, and victory. It also was blown before a battle or after the victory of an army. Blowing the conch emanates the sound of Om, which contains all the knowledge of the *Vedas*. It is an auspicious sound and represents the truth behind the illusion. It also can purify the atmosphere, as well as the minds of those who hear it. It also represents *Dharma* or righteousness. So it is appropriate for it to be blown before the *arati* or *puja*. The sound of the conch draws one's attention to the presence of the Lord and the Vedic sound vibration. It thus drowns out the negative noises that may distract us from the sacred atmosphere or disturb our minds. This is also why sometimes devotees bow to the sound of the conch when it is blown.

The tradition relates that there was once a demon named Shankhasura who had defeated the devas (demigods) and stole the *Vedas* from them. He then hid at the bottom of the ocean. The devas prayed to Lord Vishnu for assistance. He incarnated as Matsya and killed the demon. The Lord blew one of the conch shells that hung from His ears and the Om resonated, from which the *Vedas* returned. For this reason the conch is also called *shankha* after Shankhasura. The Lord's conch shell is named Panchajanya.

WHY COCONUTS ARE OFFERED

One of the most common items that are offered to the deities in the temple by guests is the coconut. You will also see it being used to start special occasions, like weddings, festivals, etc., when it is offered and then broken. You may also see it sitting on top of a decorative pot with mango leaves. This is a representation of Lakshmi devi, the goddess of fortune, or sometimes Lord Shiva. The coconut is offered to the deity as a representation of the body (the coconut shell), mind (the white fruit) and soul (the milk). All these are offered to the deity, and then it is broken to let out the milk and fruit. This indicates the breaking of the ego. Then, after it is offered to the Lord, what remains is accepted as remnants from the Lord, as *prasada*. This represents a complete circle in which God accepts our offering of the body, mind and soul and gives back the mercy, *prasada*, of the Lord.

PURPOSE OF CIRCUMAMBULATING TEMPLES OR DEITIES

Another thing that you may see is when devotees circumambulate and go around the deities in the sanctum of a temple, or even around the temple itself, or around sacred places, like special hills or even holy towns. This is called *pradakshina*. This is a means of recognizing the center point of our lives, the center of the circular path we take in honor of the deities of the Lord, or something connected with Him. This is done in a clockwise manner to keep the deity on our right, which is the side of auspiciousness. So in a way, it is a reflection of going through life while keeping God in the center. Walking around holy sites is another way of undergoing austerities for spiritual merit. It is accepted that each step takes away some of our material karma, and thus helps us get free from the mundane affairs and worldly consciousness which causes us to undertake the actions which create our karma, which helps free us from further rounds of birth and death. Respect can be shown to our superiors or parents by circumambulating them three times as well. It is also said that circumambulating the temple is like circling the universe.

WHY THE LOTUS IS SACRED

The lotus, besides being India's national flower, is a symbol of truth, beauty and auspiciousness. The Lord is also compared with these principles and its beauty. You can easily find it in many parts of India adorning ponds and lakes. The lotus grows out of the water but rises above it. It remains beautiful and untainted regardless from where it grows. In this way, it shows that we too can remain unaffected by the world of trouble and doubt around us. The Vedic literature has numerous references to the beauty of the lotus, and it is a common architectural motif. Lord Vishnu and Goddess Lakshmi both carry a lotus in their hands. A lotus also emerged from the navel of Lord Vishnu during the process of universal creation, from which Brahma originated. Thus, the lotus also indicates the link between the Creator and the creation. So the lotus is highly regarded.

PURPOSE OF FASTING

Devotees sometimes fast on certain and special days. This sort of fasting is called *Upavaasa*, which means to stay near. This is in regard to staying near the Lord in mental disposition by spending more time in thought of God without using the time and energy in procuring items of food to prepare, cook and eat. Food does certain things to us according to its quality. Some of it will heighten our awareness while other types may indeed make our minds clouded and dull. So on special days, a devotee may save time and conserve energy by either eating very simple and light foods, or even by not eating at all. Thus, one's mind can remain alert and absorbed in thoughts of God, and not be pre-occupied thinking of what to eat.

On a more mundane level, it is also a way of giving the body and digestive system a break, and letting it get cleaned out. Fasting also helps bring control and discipline over the senses and calms our mind. However, fasting for some other reason based on ego or politics will not bring the same results. And one should not become unnecessarily weak by long fasts. This can become counterproductive in keeping the mind and senses equipoised for developing meditative spiritual awareness and love for God if we become too weak, or focused only on desiring food to eat. Lord Krishna advises us in the *Bhagavad-gita* that we should take the middle path of not eating too much nor too little, but to eat purely, simply and healthily for keeping body and soul together for spiritual purposes.

WHO MAY PRACTICE SANATANA-DHARMA

Since Sanatana-dharma or the Vedic process is a universal process and applicable to everyone regardless of time, place or circumstances, then naturally anyone can practice the principles of it. Anyone can and should be allowed to participate in the process. Furthermore, anyone who is looking for the ultimate spiritual truth is already one who is following the path of Sanatana-dharma. So you could say that anyone who is sincerely looking for such truth with an open mind is already on the spiritual path, at least on some level, and is thus also a Sanatana-dharmist, a follower of Sanatana-dharma.

The point is that there is one and only one God and one Absolute Truth. The very first of the Vedic books named the *Rig Veda* proclaims, *Ekam Sat, Viprah Bahudha Vadanti* (There is only one truth, only men describe it in different ways). So a Jew or a Christian or a Moslem or anyone who is in search of the Absolute Truth is automatically on the path of Sanatana-dharma to some degree. However, if they get stuck with accepting nothing more than their own local traditions, this may hamper their growth in understanding a broader range of the many aspects of the Supreme that are described in other scriptures, such as those in the Vedic literature. So a person's progress depends on how far he or she really wants to go in this lifetime, and how they approach various levels of knowledge to understand the Absolute Truth.

WHAT IS A SARI

A sari is the style of outfit that is worn by many women from India. It is a single piece of cloth, so one size fits all, that can be most beautiful and colorful that wraps around and covers the body completely. It may take a person a little practice putting it on after being shown how to wear one.

WHAT IS A DHOTI

This is for men, which is a single piece of cloth that is wrapped around the legs, tied and pleated at the waist in different ways, depending on the area of India in which it is done. It becomes a loose and comfortable piece of apparel, especially for the hot climate of South Asia. It is a traditional type of clothing that is still regularly worn in India. Combined with a shirt or what is called a kurta, it makes for a complete outfit.

WHY MANY DEVOTEES WEAR WHITE

In some yoga groups or ashramas many people wear white clothes. This is because it is a symbol for cleanliness, purity and peace. It is not a color that will agitate the mind. It is also a simple reminder of one's spiritual goal.

WHY MANY SWAMIS WEAR SAFFRON COLORED CLOTH

Saffron is often worn by those who have become spiritually advanced and materially renounced. Saffron is the sign of renunciation from many of the common comforts of the world. It represents a determined focus on one's spiritual goal of life. The color also gives peace and tranquility to the mind, which helps one on their spiritual journey and development.

The flags on Hindu temples, as well as the robes worn by our religious preachers, mostly Swamis and Sannyasis (religious and spiritually advanced individuals), are of saffron color. The persons wearing the saffron robes are those who have renounced married life. The color denotes the sun's light giving glow. The sun has a very prominent place in the Vedic literature as the source of energy that sustains life on earth. It acts as a reminder of the power of God, the act of selfless service and renunciation.

THE SIGNIFICANCE OF THE SHIKHA (TUFT OF HAIR)

Why do we see some priests and monks with a shaved head and a tuft of hair in the back? First of all, this tuft of hair is called a *shikha*. When long enough, it is tied in a knot at the crown-point (right above the suture) on the central top of the head. This point is given distinctive importance in the science of yoga and spirituality as the point of contact with the brain-center of intellectual and emotional sensitivity. It also indicates the body as a temple.

The *shikha* symbolizes the presence of discerning intellect, farsightedness, and the deity of knowledge upon our head. It is a flag of human culture. It reminds us of the religious principles of morality, righteousness, responsibility, and dutiful awareness.

This body is the fort of the individual self upon which the flag of the *shikha* is hoisted as the mark of the dignified values and virtues of humanity. The foreign invaders, the crusaders against the Vedic (Indian) culture had attempted to eliminate the roots of this divine culture by first cutting the *shikha* and removing the *sutra* (sacred thread) from the bodies of the followers of the Vedic religion. Thousands of innocent heads were cut off just for protesting against this attack. It was for protecting the glory of these universal emblems of human religion that Maharana Pratap, Vir Shivaji, Guru Govind Sigh, and other great martyrs of India had dedicated their noble lives. Today, we have forgotten their sacrifices that have helped keep the freedoms for us to continue with this Vedic culture.

The commencement of wearing of the *sutra* and tightening of the *shikha* at the time of initiation (*diksha*) into chanting the sacred Gayatri mantra is referred in the *shastras* as *dwijatva* -- the second birth, and the one who wears the sacred thread (*sutra*) and keeps the *shikha* is called a *dwija*, or twice-born brahmana. That means that regardless of whatever family line one has been born into, he has now attained his second birth as a brahmana.

The *shikha* also represents the *sirsa* (top) of the Gayatri mantra. It reminds the devotee of the subtle presence of the pure divine intelligence in the human mind. Tightening the hair knot right above the suture induces marvelous psychological benefits. It is said to help in harmonious blood circulation in the brain in normal conditions and augments alertness. As described in the yoga scriptures, it also lends support in increasing mental concentration and meditation. In terms of its sublime spiritual effects, the *shikha* works like an antenna in the outer domain of the *sahasrara chakra* (topmost extrasensory center) to link the individual consciousness with the cosmic consciousness in the elevated state of meditation on the Gayatri mantra.

THE MEANING OF THE SUTRA OR SACRED THREAD

The *sutra* is the name for the sacred thread that one uses while chanting the Gayatri mantra, also called *yagyopavit*, which is worn on the shoulder, usually hanging over the left shoulder and down across the chest around the right hip. This is given to an individual after the sacrament or initiation of *upnayana* or thread-ceremony.

The moral and social duties of human life are worn on our shoulders and kept attached to our hearts in symbolic form as the sacred thread of *yagyopavita* (*sutra*). It also hangs on our back. It has tied us from all sides, as a reminder of the moral disciplines and ethical duties as human beings.

In different *sampradayas* or schools of thought, spiritual lineages, the *yagyopavit* will have different numbers of threads, such as six threads and two knots, each joining three threads together, or nine threads and three knots. The knots are symbols of the three *granthis* (extrasensory roots of ultimate realizations) -- such as the Brahma-granthi, the Vishnu-granthi, and the Shiva-granthi. These also represent the segments of the Gayatri mantra that encode the sublime streams of manifestation of the omnipresent eternal sound of *Om*. The *yagyopavit* is like an image of the deity Gayatri. You enshrine the deity in the temple of your body by wearing it.

Wearing this sacred *sutra* on the shoulders, keeping it near the chest, should remind you of the duties, virtues, and principles that are taught and inspired through the words of the Gayatri mantra, which are industriousness, humility, austerity, orderliness, cooperation, wisdom, integrity of character, sense of responsibility, and courage.

These qualities open the door to a bright, happy and successful life. Inculcation of these qualities induces eminent transformation of personality. These are also the most desired virtues for social and global welfare and progress. The first five of these deal with behavior and deeds. Industriousness means constructive utilization of time and potentials with diligence and enthusiasm for the work in hand. Humility implies modesty, etiquette, and balanced and humble behavior with due respect for the self as well as for others. Austerity includes piety of mind and body. It also means adopting the principle of "simple living & high thinking" in daily life. You must note that foresighted, constructive and altruist use of the resources becomes possible by observing austerity in personal and spiritual life.

THE PURPOSE OF TOUCHING OUR HEAD TO THE FLOOR

When entering a temple, coming before the deity, or when seeing a great saint or devotee, many people will bow and touch their heads to the floor. This is called offering obeisances. Humility is an important quality in spiritual life, and bowing down in such a way is an outward expression of the desire to go beyond the ego. Lowering the head to the floor represents the surrender of self-importance and pride.

Sometimes you will also see a person stretch the whole body out on the floor. In Sanskrit this is called *dandavat*, falling like a *danda* or rod. This is considered the most humble way of showing respect for another.

WHAT ARE THE VEDIC TEXTS

Many times new *bhaktas*, or even experienced devotees, do not always understand how the many branches of Vedic literature fit together. This is something everyone on the Vedic path should understand. The Vedic texts start with *Shruti*. *Shruti* literally means "That which is heard." For a long period of time there was no Vedic literature. The other section of Vedic literature is called *Smriti*, which means that which is remembered, and usually consists of the later portions of the Vedic texts.

The Vedic spiritual knowledge was a vocal or oral tradition, and was passed down from person to person accordingly. The *Vedas* and *Upanishads* were in *Shruti* form for many, many years. In fact, the word *Upanishad* means "Upa (near), Ni (down), Shad (sit)." This means that the teachings of the *Upanishads* are conveyed from Guru to disciple, when the disciple sits very close to the guru.

The very first of the sacred books of Vedic culture, in fact the oldest books on earth, are called the *Vedas*. The word *veda* means knowledge. The word *veda* came from the root word *vid* meaning "to know." The *Vedas* are the very first scriptures of Vedic culture. *Vedas*, as described by the scriptures, were given by God. There are four Vedic *samhitas*, which are the *Rig Veda*, *Sama Veda*, *Atharva Veda*, and *Yajur Veda*. The Sanskrit word *samhita* means "put together." They contain wisdom that has been assembled to teach men the highest aspects of truths which can lead them to higher levels of existence, as well as to God. The *Vedas* also discuss rituals and ceremonies to attain self-realization as well as wisdom dealing with many other aspects of life. These four *samhitas* primarily contain the basic texts of hymns, formulas and chants to the various Vedic deities for the performance of rituals for the basic material needs of life.

To briefly described them, the *Rig Veda* -- *Veda* of Praise -- contains 10,522 verses in 1,017 hymns in ten books called *mandalas*. The *Rig Veda* is the oldest book in the world. The *Rig Veda* was around for many years before it was finally compiled in written form by Srila Vyasadeva. According to Bal Gangadhar Tilak and the Vedic tradition, it was written around 5000 BCE. The *Rig Veda* is older than Gilgamesh (2500 BCE) and the Old Testament.

In the *Rig Veda* there are 100 hymns addressed to Soma; 250 addressed to Indra; 200 hymns addressed to Agni; and many addressed to Surya. Few others are addressed to the Ushas, Aditi, Saraswati,

Varuna, and the Asvins. Lord Vishnu is not addressed so often therein because the *Vedas* focused more on appeasing the demigods for blessings to attain material facility rather than spiritual liberation.

The *Yajur Veda*, which is essentially the *Veda* of liturgy, contains some 3988 verses dealing with rules and regulations for conducting rituals and also offers various levels of wisdom and advice. It is based on the *Rig Veda* and consists of prose as well as verse. This *Veda* is indeed a priestly handbook, even describing the details of how to make an alter.

The *Sama Veda*, the *Veda* of chants, offers knowledge of music in 1549 verses. *Sama* means "melody." The classical Indian music originated from this *Veda*. This *Veda* is also connected with the *Rig Veda*. To some extent much of this *Veda* is a repetition of many *Rig Veda* verses sung in melodious format. Invocations of this *Veda* are primarily addressed to Soma (the Moon-god as well as the Soma drink); Agni (the fire god); and Indra (god of heaven). The *Chandogya Upanishad* came out of this *Veda*.

The *Atharva Veda* is said to be the knowledge given by the Sage Atharvana. It has around 6000 verses. Some state that sage Atharvana did not formulate this *Veda* but was merely the chief priest in the ceremonies associated with it. Atharvana who is mentioned in the *Rig Veda* was considered as the eldest son of Lord Brahma (God of creation). The *Atharva Veda* is also known as *Brahma Veda* because it is still used as a manual by Hindu Brahmana priests. Ayurveda is a part of *Atharva Veda*. A large number of *Upanishads* also came from the *Atharva Veda*.

Brahmanas are other Vedic books that provide descriptions as well as directions for the performance of rituals. The word originated from the Brahmana priests who conduct the Vedic rituals.

Aryanakas are additional books that contain mantras and interpretations of the Vedic rituals. These books are also known as "forest books" since they were used by saints who had retired to meditate in the forests.

The *Upanishads* are texts by different saints that reveal ultimate truths. Many of them are connected with certain *Vedas*. The *Upanishads* basically begin to explain the non-material aspect of the Absolute Truth and the oneness of Brahman. In this way, they do not really show that much about the personal nature of the Supreme Being. Thus, a person will not have much insight into the Supreme Being's personal form by studying only the *Upanishads*. However, some of them do go into introducing the fact that there is more to understand about God beyond the great Brahman.

The *Upanishads* also help explain the spiritual dimension of our real identity and our qualities which are the same as the spiritual Brahman, but are different in quantity. We are the infinitesimal whereas the Brahman and Bhagavan are the Infinite. Yet, if one does not complete the study of the Vedic literature, a misinterpretation of the *Upanishads* may lead one to think that this oneness of spiritual quality between ourselves or the *jiva* souls and the Brahman means that we are the same as Brahman, or that we are the same as God. But that is not accurate.

There are a total of 108 major *Upanishads*, and many more minor ones. The are 13 principle *Upanishads* which include: 1. *Isa Upanishad*, 2. *Kena Upanishad*, 3. *Katha Upanishad*, 4. *Prasna Upanishad*, 5. *Mundaka Upanishad*, 6. *Mandukya Upanishad*, 7. *Aitareya Upanishad*, 8. *Taittiriya Upanishad*, 9. *Chandogya Upanishad*, 10. *Brihadaranyaka Upanishad*, 11. *Kaushitaki Upanishad*, 12. *Shvetashvatara Upanishad*, and 13. *Maitri Upanishad*.

The *Vedanta Sutras* are another important book that also goes on to explain spiritual truths to the aspirant. But these are presented in codes, or *sutras*, that were meant to be explained by the spiritual master. So any edition of the *Vedanta Sutras* will mostly have large purports that help explain the meaning of the *sutras*. The basis of these explanations will depend on which school of thought in which the teacher has been trained. Thus, some will be more devotionally oriented, while others may be more inclined toward meditation on the impersonal Brahman. *Vedanta* essentially means the "End of the *Vedas*," or the end of all knowledge.

The *Itihasas* are the Vedic histories of the universe, known as the *Puranas*, which are a large and major portion of Vedic literature. The *Itihasas* also include the Vedic Epics, such as the *Ramayana* and the *Mahabharata*.

The *Ramayana* is the story of Lord Ramachandra, an incarnation of Lord Vishnu, and His princess Sita. It was written by Valmiki who wrote the whole *Ramayana* as the narration of a crying dove (who just lost her lover to a hunter's wicked arrow) to him. The original text was written in very stylish Sanskrit language. This beautiful poem consists of 24,000 couplets. The *Ramayana* is a story which projects the Vedic ideals of life. There are many versions of the *Ramayana*. The Hindi version was written by sage Tulsi Das. The Malayalam version (Kerala state) was written by Thuncheth Ezuthachan.

The story in brief is as follows: Jealousy of his step-mother exiled Rama into the jungles along with his wife Sita and brother Lakshmana. There poor Sita was kidnapped by Ravana, the demon-king of Sri Lanka. Rama went to rescue her with the aid of the monkey-king Sugriva. In a great battle, Rama annihilated Ravana and his army. Thereafter, Rama along with Sita and Lakshmana returned triumphantly to their kingdom. Rama is an example of the perfect husband and ruling king, Sita is the perfect wife, and Lakshmana is the perfect brother.

The *Ramayana* is a very cherished poem of the Hindus. The holy Deepavali festival is a celebration of victory of Rama over Ravana. Diwali or Deepavali is the "festival of lights" and is celebrated throughout India.

The *Mahabharata* is another of the world's great epics which consists of episodes, stories, dialogues, discourses, and sermons. It contains 110,000 couplets or 220,000 lines in 18 Parvas or sections. It is the longest poem in the world, again in Sanskrit. It is longer than Homer's Odyssey. It is the story of the Pandvas and Kauravas. The *Bhagavad-gita* is a chapter of the *Mahabharata*.

Apart from the 18 Parvas there is a section of poems in the form of an appendix with 16,375 verses which is known as Harivamsa Parva. So in total there are 19 Parvas, even though many saints do not consider the last Parva as important.

The *Bhagavad-gita*, which means the song of Bhagavan, or God, is a part of the *Mahabharata*, appearing in the middle of it. Many consider the *Bhagavad-gita* as the most important of the Vedic scriptures and the essence of the *Upanishads* and Vedic knowledge. Anyone interested in the most important of the Eastern philosophy should read the *Bhagavad-gita*. If all the *Upanishads* can be considered as cows, then the *Bhagavad-gita* can be considered as the milk.

The *Bhagavad-gita* consists of 18 chapters and over 700 verses. It discusses the main types of yogas, the means of self-realization. It is in the form of a very lively conversation between the warrior-prince Arjuna and his friend and charioteer Lord Krishna. This was spoken at the outset of the great *Mahabharata* war, in the middle of the battle field at Kuruksetra. This place can still be visited just three hours north of New Delhi. Just before the beginning of the war, Arjuna refused to fight when he found he had to kill thousands of his own kinsmen to be victorious in the war. Lord Krishna advised him on a very large variety of subjects in a question and answer format. At the end, Arjuna took Lord Krishna's advice and fought and won a very fierce war. The *Gita* has an answer to every problem a man may face in his life. It never commands anyone what to do. Instead it discusses pros and cons of every action and thought, leaving the decision up to the reader, just as Krishna left the decision of what to do up to Arjuna. Throughout the *Gita* you will not come across any line starting or ending with Thou Shalt Not. That is the reason why the *Gita* is the darling of millions of seekers of truth throughout the world.

There are many versions or translations of *Bhagavad-gita*. The very first English translation of the *Gita* was done by Charles Wilkins in 1785, with an introduction by Warren Hastings, the British Governor General of India. One of the most popular translations was done by Sir Edwin Arnold, under the title *The Song Celestial*. One of most descriptive and accurate translations of the *Gita* was done by His Grace A. C. Bhaktivedanta Swami Prabhupada of the International Society for Krishna Consciousness, called *The Bhagavad-gita As It Is*. Almost all saints in India have published their versions of the *Bhagavad-gita*, some of which arrive at various conclusions or viewpoints. So one does need to display some caution in picking which edition to read. Most intellectuals in the world go through the *Gita* at least once in their life time. Aldous Huxley wrote in his introduction of *The Song of God* by Swami Prabhavananda and Christopher Isherwood: "The *Bhagavad-gita* is perhaps the most systematic scriptural statement of the perennial philosophy." The *Gita* won the interest and admiration of great intellectuals such as Von Humboldt of Germany and Emerson of

America. It has also influenced many Western thinkers, such as Hagel and Schopenhauer.

Robert Oppenheimer, the very first Chairman of Atomic Energy Commission and father of the Atom bomb was a great admirer of the *Bhagavad-gita*. He learnt Sanskrit during the Manhattan Project to understand the true meaning of the *Gita*. He really shocked the world, when he quoted a couplet from the *Gita* (Chapter 11:12) after witnessing the first Atomic Explosion in the state of New Mexico, which reads, "If hundreds of thousands of suns rose up into the sky, they might resemble the effulgence of the Supreme Person in the universal form." Later when he addressed congress regarding the Atom Bomb he said the Atom Bomb reminded him of Lord Krishna who said in the *Bhagavad-gita*, "Time I am, the devourer of all."

The *Puranas* are the Vedic religious histories of the universe which expound various levels of the Vedic truths. They are divided into three sections. The six *Puranas* that are connected to Lord Vishnu and the mode of goodness or *sattva-guna* are: 1. *Vishnu Purana*, 2. *Narada Purana*, 3. *Srimad Bhagavata Purana*, 4. *Garuda Purana*, 5. *Padma Purana*, and 6. *Varaha Purana*.

The six *Puranas* that are primarily connected to Lord Brahma and *raja-guna* or the mode of passion are: 1. *Brahma Purana*, 2. *Brahmanda Purana*, 3. *Brahma-Vaivasvata Purana*, or the *Brahma-Vaivarta Purana*, 4. *Markandeya Purana*, 5. *Bhavishya Purana*, and 6. *Vamana Purana*.

The six *Puranas* that are connected to Lord Shiva and *tamo-guna* are: 1. *Matsya Purana*, 2. *Kurma Purana*, 3. *Linga Purana*, 4. *Vayu Purana*, 5. *Skanda Purana*, and 6. *Agni Purana*. Besides these, there are an additional 18 to 22 minor *Puranas*.

The 20 major *Puranas* include all the above as well as the *Shiva Purana* and the *Harivamsa Purana*. Of all *Puranas*, the *Srimad Bhagavata Purana* addressed to Lord Vishnu, and which discusses the detailed pastimes of Lord Krishna, is considered the most important. Traditionally it contains 18,000 stanzas in 12 cantos. It was written by Sage Badarayana, also known as VedaVyasa or Vyasadeva. Vyasadeva, after writing all of His previous Vedic books, said the *Bhagavatam* was His own commentary and conclusion of all Vedic thought. The greatest exponent of the *Srimad-Bhagavatam* is Sage Suka, the son of Sage VedaVyasa. This book was recited to King Pariksit by Sage Suka in one week before the death of the King by the bite of a serpent. This was after King Pariksit learned he was about to die and asked to hear the cream of all spiritual knowledge. So, much of the book is in dialogue form between King Pariksit and Sage Suka.

The *Srimad-Bhagavatam* consists of stories of all the *avataras* of Lord Vishnu. The 10th chapter of the book deals with the story of Lord Krishna in detail. The last chapter deals exclusively with the Kali-Yuga, the present age, and about the last *avatara* of Lord Vishnu, Kalki. There is also a vivid description of the Pralaya or the great deluge in the last chapter.

According to the *Bhagavata Purana*, the universe and creation came into existence because God in a pastime (*Lila*) willed to do so, and to manifest His inferior material energy. According to this scripture, there are nine different ways of exhibiting Bhakti or devotion to God, like listening to stories of God, meditating, serving and adoring his image and finally self-surrender. This book is an authority on Vaishnavism in Vedic culture and is a primary text to all Viashnavas (worshipers of Lord Vishnu and His *avataras*) including those of the Hare Krishna Movement.

The *Agamas* are another group of scriptures that worship God in particular forms, and describe detailed courses of discipline for the devotee. Like the *Upanishads*, there are many *Agamas*. They can be broadly divided into three sets, namely:
Vaishnava Agamas - worship God as Lord Vishnu;
Shaiva Agamas - worship God as Lord Shiva;
Shakti Agamas - worship God as Mother Goddess.

There are no *Agamas* for Lord Brahma (God of creation). Shaivites have 28 *Agamas* and 108 *Upa Agamas* (minor *Agamas*). Shaktas recognize 77 *Agamas*. There are many Vaishnava *Agamas* of which the *Pancharatra* is one of the most important. Each *Agama* consists of philosophy, mental discipline, rules for constructing temples, and religious practices.

The *Tantras* started during the Vedic age, which consist of cosmology, yogic exercises, etc. Tantra is very important and very vast.

The Sanskrit word *Tantra* means to expand. Tantrism researched into astronomy, astrology, palmistry, cosmology, as well as the knowledge of the chakras and the kundalini power, etc.

PART THREE

UNDERSTANDING A FEW BASICS OF THE PHILOSOPHY

CHAPTER FIFTEEN

Who am I?
The Vedic Description of the Soul

Who am I? What am I? Am I the body, mind or something more? These are the age old questions that every philosopher throughout the ages has tried to grasp and understand. After all, how will you know what to do in life if you do not even know who or what you are? However, the ancient Vedic literature of India has provided the clearest answers that have been found anywhere to answer these questions.

For example, the *Mundaka Upanishad* (3.1.9) explains that the living being is the soul, and that: "The soul is atomic in size and can be perceived by perfect intelligence. This atomic soul is situated within the heart, and spreads its influence all over the body of the embodied living entities. When the soul is purified from the contamination of the five kinds of material air, its spiritual influence is exhibited."

The *Chandogya Upanishad* (6.11.3) also states that although the body withers and dies when the self or soul leaves it, the living self does not die.

Further enlightenment is given in the *Srimad-Bhagavatam* (7.2.22) wherein it explains that the spirit soul has no death and is eternal and inexhaustible. He is completely different from the material body, but because of being misled by misuse of his slight independence, he is obliged to accept subtle and gross bodies created by the material energy and thus be subjected to so-called material happiness and distress.

The eternal nature of the self is also explained in *Bhagavad-gita* by Lord Sri Krishna where He specifically says that there was never a time when He did not exist, nor any of the living beings, including you. Nor shall any of us cease to be in the future. The embodied soul continually passes from boyhood to youth to old age in this body.

Similarly the soul enters another body at the time of death. But for one who is self-realized, there is no bewilderment through such a change.

It is further explained that we should know that which pervades the entire body by consciousness is indestructible. No one is able to destroy the imperishable soul. Only the material body of the eternal living entity is subject to destruction. . . For the soul there is never birth nor death. Nor, having once been, does he ever cease to be. He is unborn, undying and eternal. He is not slain when the body dies or is killed. . . As a person puts on new garments, giving up old ones, similarly, the soul accepts new material bodies, giving up the old and useless ones.

Certainly this knowledge can relieve anyone from the anxiety that comes from thinking our existence is finished at death. Spiritually, we do not die; yet, the body is used until it is no longer fit to continue. At that time, it may appear that we die, but that is not the case. The soul continues on its journey to another body according to its destiny.

The indestructibility of the soul is also explained. The individual soul is unbreakable and insoluble, and can be neither burned nor dried. The soul is everlasting, unchangeable, and eternally the same. Knowing this, we should not grieve for the temporary body.

So, the body dwindles and dies but the soul does not die: it simply changes bodies. Therefore, the body is like a shirt or coat that we wear for some time, and when it is worn out, we change it for a new one. Therefore, the Vedic literature, such as the *Chandogya Upanishad* (8.1.1), mentions that knowledge of the self within is what should be sought and understood by all. Realizing one's spiritual identity solves the problems and mysteries of life.

The more we realize our spiritual identity, the more we will see that we are beyond these temporary material bodies, and that our identity is not simply being a white body, or black, or yellow, or fat, skinny, intelligent, dumb, old, young, strong, weak, blind, etc. Real blindness means not being able to see through the temporary and superficial bodily conditions and into the real person within. Seeing reality means to recognize the spiritual nature of everyone.

The *Srimad-Bhagavatam* (11.28.35) explains that the soul is self-luminous, beyond birth and death, and unlimited by time or space and, therefore, beyond all change. The *Bhagavatam* (11.22.50) also points out that as one witnesses the birth and death of a tree and is separate from it, similarly the witness of the birth, death, and various activities of the body is within but separate from it.

The size of the soul is also described in the *Svetasvatara Upanishad* (5.9): "When the upper point of a hair is divided into one hundred parts and again each of such parts is further divided into one hundred parts, each such part is the measurement of the dimension of the spirit soul." So considering that the diameter of a typical hair is about three-thousandths of an inch wide, then to divide that into one hundreds parts, and then divide one of those parts again into one hundred parts means that it would be microscopic. And since it is spiritual and not made of material substance, to perceive the presence of the soul is not so easy. It is invisible to our material vision.

The *Katha Upanishad* relates that within the body, higher than the senses and the sense objects, exists the mind. More subtle than the mind is the intelligence, and higher and more subtle than the intellect is the self. That self is hidden in all beings and does not shine forth, but is seen by subtle seers through their sharp intellect.

From this we can understand that within the gross physical body, composed of various material elements, such as earth, air, water, etc., there is also the subtle body composed of the finer subtle elements of mind, intelligence and false ego. The psychic activities take place within the subtle body. It is also within the subtle body wherein exist the memories of past lives, however deep they may be. Yet, the living being has his spiritual form that is deeper than this subtlety, otherwise he could not have repeated births. A person actually sees his spiritual self as well as the presence of the Supreme Being when he perceives that both the gross and subtle bodies have nothing to do with the pure, spiritual self within. Therefore, it could be asked that since we are separate from the gross and subtle bodies, why do we so strongly identify with the material body? It is explained that though the material body is different from the soul, it is because of the ignorance due to material association that one falsely identifies oneself with the high and low bodily conditions.

It is further elaborated that only because of the mind and ego that we experience material happiness and distress. Yet, in actuality, the spirit soul is above such material existence and can never really be affected by material happiness and distress in any circumstance. A person who truly perceives this has nothing to fear from the material creation, or the appearance of births and deaths. Thus, he can attain real peace.

The *Chandogya Upanishad* (8.1.5-6) goes on to explain that the self is free from sin and old age, death and grief, hunger and thirst, lamentation and sadness, and all forms of bodily identification. It desires only what it ought to desire, and imagines nothing but what it ought to imagine. Those who depart from this life without having discovered the self and those true or spiritual desires have no freedom in all the worlds. But those who depart from here after realizing one's genuine spiritual identity and those spiritual inclinations have freedom in all the worlds.

So, to summarize, the soul is a particle of consciousness and bliss in its purified state of being. It is not material in any way. It is what departs from the body at the time of death and, in the subtle body, carries its mental impressions, desires and tendencies, along with the karmic results of its activities from one body to another. To understand and perceive this self, which is our genuine spiritual identity, is the real goal of life. Such a realization relieves one of further material existence. As it is explained, those who have purified their consciousness, becoming absorbed in spiritual knowledge and absolving any impurities in the mind, are liberated from karma that frees them from any future births. They are free from any more births in the material world and are delivered to the spiritual atmosphere. How to do this is the ultimate accomplishment of human existence.

When people ask how they can understand how God is eternal, and where did God come from, I answer that at first it is best to simply understand your own eternal nature, how the soul is eternal. Then you will have a little insight into how God is eternal. That is the primary goal of human existence, if one expects to accomplish the purpose of human life.

CHAPTER SIXTEEN

What Is Reincarnation

Reincarnation is called *samsara* in the classic Vedic texts of India. The word *samsara* is Sanskrit and means being bound to the cycle of repeated birth and death through numerous lifetimes. How this works is that those who are materially conditioned transmigrate through different bodies according to one's desires and past activities (or karma) and familiarities. Their desires, if materially motivated, requires a physical body to enable them to continue to work out their material longings in various conditions of life.

Generally, in the Eastern traditions it is considered that all forms of life or species have souls, which is the entity who reincarnates. Previous to when an entity is ready to incarnate as a human being on Earth, the soul may have gone through a whole series of lives in order to experience various levels of existence and consciousness. The principle is that an entity may actually progress through the different species of life, gradually working their way up until they reach the human form. Of course, the body is only the covering of the soul in which it appears. The living being will continually move upward in its cycles of reincarnation until it has experienced all the main varieties of existences that the material realm has to offer. This way the living being is fully experienced in working out material desires or longings in all kinds of forms by the time it reaches the human stage. Of course, not every being may have to go through all of this.

How reincarnation works is most elaborately described in the Vedic texts of India. The *Bhagavad-gita* (8.6) explains that whatever state of consciousness one attains when he or she quits this body, a similar state will be attained in the next life. This means that after the person has lived his or her life, the numerous variegated activities of the person forms an aggregated consciousness. All of our thoughts and actions throughout our life will collectively influence the state of being we are in at the time of death. This consciousness will determine what that person is thinking of at the end of one's life. This last thought and consciousness will then direct where that person will most likely go in the next life because this state of being carries over from this life into the next.

As it is further explained, the living entity in the material world carries the different levels of consciousness from one body to another in the same way the air carries aromas. In other words, we cannot see the aromas that the air carries, yet it can be perceived by the sense of smell. In a similar way, we cannot see the types of consciousness that the living being has developed, but it is carried from this body at the time of death and proceeds to another body in the next life to take up where it left off from the preceding existence. Of course, the next life may be in another physical body or in a subtle body in between births, or even in heavenly or hellish states of being.

After death, one continues the consciousness that was cultivated during life. It is our thought patterns that build the consciousness, which then directs us toward the required experience after death. One's state of consciousness or conception of life exists in the subtle body, which consists of mind, intelligence and false ego. The soul is covered by this subtle body, which exists within the gross material form. When the physical vehicle can no longer function, the subtle body and soul are forced out of it. Then, when the time is right, they are placed in another physical frame which properly accommodates the state of mind of the living entity. This is how the mental state which attracts the dying man determines how he begins his next life. If the dying man is absorbed in thoughts of material gain or sensual pleasures of wife, family, relatives, home, etc., then he must, at some point, get another material body to continue pursuing his worldly interests. After all, how can one satisfy his material desires without a material body?

For this reason, it is best that a person always cultivate pious activities and spiritual thoughts to help him or her enter a better life after death. If a person has tried to cut the knots of attachment to materialistic life, and engaged in spiritual activities, to the degree of advancement the person has made, he or she can go to a heavenly realm after death, or even reach the kingdom of God.

In any case, we can begin to understand that dying in the right consciousness in order to become free from the cycle of birth and death is an art that takes practice. We have to prepare for the moment of death so that we are not caught off guard or in an unsuitable state of mind. This is one of the purposes of yoga.

After what can be millions of births and deaths through many forms of life, trying to satisfy all of one's material desires, the soul may begin to get tired of these continuous attempts for happiness that often turn out to be so temporary. Then the person may turn toward finding spiritual meaning in life. In one's search for higher meaning, depending on the level of consciousness that a person develops, he or she can gradually enter higher and higher levels of development. Finally, if a person detects that he is actually not this body but a spiritual being within it, and reaches a spiritual level of consciousness, he can perfect his life so that he will enter the spiritual strata and no longer have to incarnate in the physical world. Thus, liberation is attained through Self-realization and the development of devotional service to God, which is the perfection of the spiritual path. Through human existence on Earth, the doorway to many other planes of existence is possible, including entrance into the spiritual world. It only depends on how we use this life.

The idea that a person has only one life to either become qualified to enter heaven or enter eternal damnation offers the soul no means of rehabilitation and only endless misery. This is not reasonable. The doctrine of reincarnation gives anyone ample scope to correct and re-educate himself in future births. An eternity in hell means that an infinite effect is produced by a finite cause, which is illogical. God has not created men to become nothing more than ever-lasting fuel to feed the fires of hell. Such a purpose in His creation would not come from an ever-loving God, but comes from the faulty ideas of man and his imperfect conceptions of God. After all, how many spotless men could there be in this world? Who has such a pure character to receive an immediate pass to heaven? The *Bhagavad-gita* explains that even the worst sinner can cross the ocean of birth and death by ascending the boat of transcendental knowledge. We simply have to be sincere in reaching that boat.

Furthermore, a person reaps the results of his sinful deeds for a limited amount of time. After being purged of one's sins, meaning suffering the painful reactions from one's bad activities, a person, knowing right from wrong, can have a fresh chance to freely work for his emancipation from further entanglement in material life. When he deserves and attains such freedom, the soul can enjoy perfect and eternal bliss in its devotional union with the Supreme Being. This is why it is always encouraged for one to strive for spiritual knowledge and the practice of enlightenment. By developing sincere and purified devotion for the Lord, one does not have to worry about one's future birth. Once a person has started this path of devotion, each life will take one closer to spiritual perfection, in whatever situation one finds him or herself.

So a person is encouraged to repent for one's sins or ill choices that were made while under the influence of lust, anger or greed, and cultivate forgiveness, purity and generosity. A person should also engage in charity, penance, meditation, *japa* (personal chanting of the Lord's holy names), *kirtan* (congregational singing of the Lord's holy names), and other spiritual practices, which destroy all sins and removes all doubts about spiritual knowledge. Then through steady practice one can gradually reach the spiritual world and be free from any further entanglement in reincarnation.

CHAPTER SEVENTEEN

What Is Karma

Karma is one of those topics that many people know a little about, but few understand the intricacies of it. To start with, Newton's third law of motion states that for every action there is an equal and opposite reaction. On the universal scale, this is the law of karma. The law of karma basically states that every action has a reaction and whatever you do to others will later return to you. Furthermore, ignorance of the law is no excuse. We are still accountable for everything we do, regardless of whether we understand it or not. Therefore, the best thing is to learn how it works.

If everyone understood the law of karma, we would all be living a happier life in a brighter world. Why? Because we could know how to adjust our lives so we would not be suffering the constant reactions of what we have done due to the false aims of life.

According to Vedic literature, karma is the law of cause and effect. For every action there is a cause as well as a reaction. Karma is produced by performing fruitive activities for bodily or mental development. One may perform pious activities that will produce good reactions or good karma for future enjoyment. Or one may perform selfish or what some call sinful activities that produce bad karma and future suffering. This follows a person wherever he or she goes in this life or future lives. Such karma, as well as the type of consciousness a person develops, establishes reactions that one must experience.

The *Svetashvatara Upanishad* (5.12) explains that the living being, the *jiva* soul, acquires many gross physical and subtle bodies due to the actions he performs, as is motivated by the material qualities to which he obtains. These bodies that are acquired continue to be a source of illusion as long as he is ignorant of his real identity.

The *Brihadaranyaka Upanishad* (4.45) further clarifies that as the *atma* or soul in the gross and subtle bodies acts, so thereby he obtains different conditions. By acting saintly he becomes a saint, and by acting immorally he becomes subject to the karmic consequences. In this way, he accrues piety or the burden of impiety accordingly.

Similarly, it is stated that as a man sows, so shall he reap. Therefore, as people live their present life, they cultivate a particular type of consciousness by their thoughts and activities, which may be good or bad. This creates a person's karma.

This karma will direct us into a body that is most appropriate for the reactions that we need to endure, or the lessons we need to learn. Thus, the cause of our existence comes from the activities of our previous lives. Since everything is based on a cause, it is one's karma that will determine one's situation, such as race, color, sex, or area of the world in which one will appear, or whether one is born in a rich or poor family, or be healthy or unhealthy, etc., etc.

So when the living beings take birth again, they get a certain kind of body that is most suitable for the type of consciousness they have developed. Therefore, according to the *Padma Purana*, there are 8,400,000 species of life, each offering a particular class of body for whatever kind of desires and consciousness the living being may have in this world. In this way, the living entity is the son of his past and the father of his future. Thus, he is presently affected by his previous life's activities and creates his future existence by the actions he performs in this life. A person will reincarnate into various forms of bodies that are most suitable for the living entity's consciousness, desires, and for what he deserves. So the living being inevitably continues in this cycle of birth and death and the consequences for his various good or bad activities as long as he is materially motivated.

What creates good or bad karma is also the nature of the intent behind the action. If one uses things selfishly or out of anger, greed, hate, revenge, etc., then the nature of the act is of darkness. One will incur bad karma from it that will later manifest as reversals in life, painful events, disease or accidents. While things that are done for the benefit of others, or out of kindness and love, with no thought of return, or for worshiping God, are all acts of goodness and piety, which will bring upliftment or good fortune to you. However, if you do something bad that happens because of an accident or a mistake, without the intent to do any harm to others, the karma is not so heavy. Maybe you were meant to be an instrument in someone else's karma, which is also yours. It will take into consideration your motivation. Yet the greater the intent or awareness of doing something wrong, the greater the degree of negative reaction there will be. So it is all based on the intent behind the action.

However, we should understand that, essentially, karma is for correcting a person, and not for mere retribution of past deeds. The universe is based on compassion. Everyone has certain lessons and ways in which he must develop, and the law of karma actually directs one in a manner to do that. Nonetheless, one is not condemned to stay in this cycle of repeated birth and death forever. There is a way out. In the human form one can acquire the knowledge of spiritual realization and attain release from karma and further rounds of birth and death. This is considered to be the most important achievement one can accomplish in life. This is why every religious process in the world encourages people who want freedom from earthly existence not to hanker for material attachments or sensual enjoyments which bind them to this world, but to work towards what can free them from further cycles of birth and death.

All karma can be negated when one truly aspires to understand or realize the higher purpose in life and spiritual truth. When one reaches that point, his life can be truly spiritual which gives eternal freedom from change. By striving for the Absolute Truth, or for serving God in devotional service, especially in bhakti-yoga, a person can reach the stage in which he is completely relieved of all karmic obstacles or responsibilities. Lord Krishna says in *Bhagavad-gita* (18.66): "Abandon all varieties of religion and just surrender unto Me. I shall deliver you from all sinful reaction. Do not fear."

Without being trained in this spiritual science, it is very difficult to understand how the living being leaves his body or what kind of body he will get in the future, or why there are various species of life which accommodate all the living entities' innumerable levels of consciousness. As related in the *Bhagavad-gita*, those who are spiritually ignorant cannot understand how a living entity can depart the body at the time of death, nor can they understand what kind of body he or she will enjoy while under the influence of the modes of nature. However, one who has been trained in knowledge can perceive this.

Thus, we encourage everyone to understand the law of karma more completely and how one can engage in the devotional service of the Lord in order to become free of all good or bad karma and develop a purely spiritualized consciousness. This is real freedom and liberation from all material limitations by which one can reach the spiritual strata.

CHAPTER EIGHTEEN

Who is Krishna

Many people may ask, "Who is Krishna?" There are numerous Vedic references that can be used to provide the proper explanations.

To begin with, it is the Vedic literature that most clearly reveals the nature and identity of the Absolute Truth or Supreme Personality. One such reference is the first and second verses of the *Vedanta Sutras*. The first verse states simply that, "Now one should enquire into the Brahman." This means that now that you have attained a human body, you should use your intelligence to discover what is really spiritual and what is the Absolute Truth. In no other form of life does the living being have such an opportunity. The second verse begins to explain what is this Absolute Truth: "He from whom everything originates is the Absolute." Thus, as it refers to "He", the source of all that exists, the ultimate point of creation is a person.

The *Rig Veda* (1.154.4-5) continues: "Him whose three places are filled with sweetness and imperishable joy, who verily alone upholds the threefold, the earth, the heaven, and all living beings. May I attain to His well-loved mansion where men devoted to God are happy. For there springs the well of honey in Vishnu's highest step."

As explained in the *Caitanya-caritamrita* (Adi. 2.106), Lord Krishna is the original primeval Lord, the source of all other expansions. All the revealed scriptures accept Sri Krishna as the Supreme Lord. Furthermore (*Cc*.Adi 2.24-26), it goes on to relate that Lord Krishna Himself is the one undivided Absolute Truth and ultimate reality. He manifests in three features, namely the Brahman (all-pervading spiritual energy), Paramatma (Supersoul in all beings) and Bhagavan (the Supreme Personality). The *Svetashvatara Upanishad* (5.4) also relates that the Supreme Being, Lord Krishna, is worshipable by everyone, the one adorable God, repository of all goodness, ruler of all creatures, born from the womb [in His pastime of Lord Krishna], for He is eternally present in all living beings [as Supersoul]. Furthermore, it states (3.8), "I have realized this transcendental Personality of Godhead who shines most brilliantly like the sun beyond all darkness. Only by realizing Him one goes beyond the cycle of birth and deaths. Absolutely there is no other means to get God-realization."

The *Svetashvatara Upanishad* (5.6) further elaborates that Lord Krishna is the topmost of all the gods. "He is the most esoteric aspect hidden in the *Upanishads* which form the essence of the *Vedas*. Brahma knows Him as the source of himself as well as the *Vedas*. The gods like Shiva and the seers of the ancient, like Vamadeva *rishi* realizing Him, ever became dovetailed in His service and therefore they naturally became immortal." And in (6.7) it continues: "Let us take our final resort at Him who is the Transcendent and the only adorable Lord of the universe, who is the highest deity over all the deities, the Supreme Ruler of all rulers–Him let us know as the Paramount Divinity."

The *GopalaTapani Upanishad*, which is about Gopala or Krishna, is quite clear on this point, and naturally has numerous verses that explain the nature of the Absolute Truth and Lord Krishna. A few of such verses include the following: "Brahma with his full awareness emphatically said, 'Sri Krishna is the Supreme Divinity. (1.3) He who meditates on Sri Krishna, serves Him with unalloyed devotion and [makes His transcendental senses gratified by engaging one's own spiritual senses in] rendering service to Him–all of them become immortal and attain the perfection of life. (1.10) Sri Krishna is that Supreme Divinity as the Paramount Eternal Reality among all other sentient beings and the Fountain-source of consciousness to all conscious beings. He is the only reality without a second but as a Supersoul dwelling in the cave of the hearts of all beings He rewards them in accordance with their respective actions in life. Those men of intuitive wisdom who serve Him with loving devotion surely attain the highest perfection of life. Whereas those who do not do so never gain this highest beatitude of their lives. (1.22) ... This Sri Krishna who is most dear to you all is the cause of all causes. He is the efficient cause of the creation of the universe as well as the superintending force for propelling the *jiva* souls. Therefore, although He is the enjoyer as well as the Lord of all sacrifices, He is ever *atmarama*, self-satisfied." (2.17)

So, summarily, as it is explained and concluded in a variety of Vedic texts, Lord Krishna is the Supreme Personality of Godhead. In other words, as it is said in Sanskrit, *krsnas tu bhagavan svayam* (*Bhagavata Purana* 1.3.28), Krishna is the source of all other incarnations and forms of God. He is the ultimate and end of all truth and philosophical enquiry, the goal or end result of Vedanta. He is the all-attractive personality and source of all pleasure for which we are always hankering. He is the origin from which everything else manifests. He is the unlimited source of all power, wealth, fame, beauty, wisdom, and renunciation. Thus, no one is greater than Him. Since Krishna is the source of all living beings, He is also considered the Supreme Father and source of all worlds. He is shown with a blue or blackish complexion. This represents absolute, pure consciousness, which also is unconditional love. Krishna is the embodiment of love. He is also *sat-chit-ananda vigraha*, which means the form of eternal knowledge and bliss, for which we are all seeking.

The reason why the Lord is called "Krishna" is explained in a book known as the *Sri Caitanya Upanishad*, which is connected with the *Atharva Veda*. In verse twelve it is explained: "These three names of the Supreme Lord (Hari, Krishna and Rama) may be explained in the following way: (1) 'Hari' means 'He who unties [*harati*] the knot of material desire in the hearts of the living entities'; (2) 'Krishna' is divided into two syllables 'krish' and 'na'. 'Krish' means 'He who attracts the minds of all living entities', and 'na' means 'the supreme transcendental pleasure'. These two syllables combine to become the name 'Krishna'; and (3) 'Rama' means 'He who delights [*ramayati*] all living entities', and it also means 'He who is full of transcendental bliss'. The *maha-mantra* consists of the repetition of these names of the Supreme Lord." In this way, Krishna's names represent His character and qualities, which, in this case, means the greatest and all attractive transcendental pleasure.

So, as we further our investigation of the identity of Sri Krishna in the Vedic literature, we find that they are full of descriptions of Lord Krishna as the Supreme Being. These actually can help us understand the nature of God regardless of which religion we may affiliate ourselves with. So it is encouraged for anyone to study these Vedic texts to increase one's understanding of God and spiritual reality.

If we are expected to understand God, then who better to explain His qualities and characteristics than Himself? So in the *Bhagavad-gita*, Krishna provides the Self-revelatory truth about His position in His explanations to Arjuna. There are numerous verses in this regard, of which the following are but a few: "And when you have thus learned the truth, you will know that all living beings are but part of Me--and that they are in Me, and are Mine. (4.35) The sages, knowing Me to be the ultimate purpose of all sacrifices and austerities, the Supreme Lord of all planets and demigods, and the benefactor and well-wisher of all living entities, attain peace from the pangs of material miseries. (5.29) Of all that is material and all that is spiritual in this world, know for certain that I am both its origin and dissolution." (7.6)

"I am the source of all spiritual and material worlds. Everything emanates from Me. The wise who perfectly know this engage in My devotional service and worship Me with all their hearts." (*Bg.*10:8)

Going on to the *Srimad-Bhagavatam*, Lord Krishna specifically explains that before, during, and after the creation, there is always Himself that exists. "Brahma it is I, the Personality of Godhead, who was existing before the creation, when there was nothing but Myself. Nor was there the material nature, the cause of this creation. That which you see now is also I, the Personality of Godhead, and after annihilation what remains will also be I, the Supreme Lord." (*Bhag.*2.9.33)

The *Brahma-samhita* (5.40) explains how the Brahman is but Sri Krishna's physical brilliance: "I worship Govinda, the primeval Lord who is endowed with great power. The glowing effulgence of His transcendental form is the impersonal Brahman, which is absolute, complete and unlimited, and which displays the varieties of countless planets with their different opulences in millions and millions of universes."

So, from the small amount of Vedic evidence that is supplied herein, it is clear that Lord Krishna's name, form, pastimes, etc., exist eternally in the spiritual dimension and are never affected by even a tinge of the material energy. Thus, He can appear as often and whenever He likes as He is, or in any form He chooses within this material manifestation. He is completely and totally spiritual for He is the Absolute Truth. As the *Vedanta Sutras* explain, the Absolute Truth is He from whom all else manifests. Thus, the Absolute Truth is the ultimate person known as Sri Krishna. And by knowing His characteristics and learning how to engage in devotional service to Him, we can reach His abode and enter into His pastimes and activities in the spiritual world.

Lord Krishna in the forests of His spiritual abode, on the banks of the Yamuna River with some of His favorite friends, the cow and peacock

CHAPTER NINETEEN

Why Be Vegetarian

On the spiritual path, there are several reasons why a person is recommended to be vegetarian. One primary reason is that we need to see the spiritual nature within all living beings, and that includes the animals and other creatures as well. Universal brotherhood means nonviolence to both humans and animals. It consists of understanding that animals also have souls. They are alive, conscious, and feel pain. And these are the indications of the presence of consciousness, which is the symptom of the soul. Even the Bible (*Genesis* 1.21; 1.24; 1.30; 2.7; and in many other places) refers to both animals and people as *nefesh chayah*, living souls. Those who eat meat, however, because of their desires to eat animals or see them as a source of food for one's stomach, are not so easily able to understand the spiritual nature of all beings. After all, if you know that all living entities are spiritual in essence, and that all living beings that are conscious show the symptoms of the soul within, then how can you kill them unnecessarily? Any living creature is also the same as we are in the respect that it is also a child of the same father, a part of the same Supreme Being. Thus, the killing of animals shows a great lack in spiritual awareness.

Many portions of the Vedic literature describe how the Supreme Being is the maintainer of innumerable living entities, humans as well as the animals, and is alive in the heart of every living being. Only those with spiritual consciousness can see the same Supreme Being in His expansion as Supersoul within every creature. To be kind and spiritual toward humans and be a killer or enemy toward animals is not a balanced philosophy, and exhibits one's spiritual ignorance.

The next reason for being vegetarian is to consider the amount of fear and suffering that animals experience in the slaughter industry. There are countless stories of how in fear cows cry, scream, and sometimes fall down dead while inside or even before they are taken into the slaughter house. Or how the veins of dead pigs are so big that it shows they have practically exploded from the fear the pig felt and the adrenalin that was produced while it was being led to slaughter. This certainly causes an immense amount of violence to permeate the atmosphere, which goes out and falls back on us in some form. Furthermore, the adrenalin and fear in the animal also produces toxins which then permeate the body of these animals, which meat-eaters ingest. People who consume such things cannot help but be effected by it. It causes tensions within them individually, which then spreads in their relations with others.

The ancient Vedic text of the *Manu-samhita* (5.45-8) says, "He who injures innoxious beings from a wish to give himself pleasure never finds happiness, neither living nor dead. He who does not seek to cause the suffering of bonds and death to living creatures, but desires the good of all beings, obtains endless bliss. . . Meat can never be obtained without injury to living creatures, and injury to sentient beings is detrimental to the attainment of heavenly bliss; let him therefore shun the use of meat."

The Bible (*Romans* 14.21) also says, "It is neither good to eat flesh, nor to drink wine." Another biblical commandment (*Exodus* 23.5) instructs us to help animals in pain, even if they belong to an enemy.

The Buddhist scripture (*Sutta-Nipata* 393) also advises: "Let him not destroy or cause to be destroyed any life at all, or sanction the acts of those who do so. Let him refrain from even hurting any creature, both those that are strong and those that tremble in the world." It is also said in the Buddhist scripture, the *Mahaparinirvana Sutra*, "The eating of meat extinguishes the seed of great compassion."

For Jews, the Talmud (*Avodah Zorah* 18B) forbids the association with hunters, not to mention engaging in hunting.

In the New Testament Jesus preferred mercy over sacrifice (*Matthew* 9.13; 12.7) and was opposed to the buying and selling of animals for sacrifice (*Matthew* 21.12-14; *Mark* 11.15; *John* 2.14-15). One of the missions of Jesus was to do away with animal sacrifice and cruelty to animals (*Hebrews* 10.5-10).

We especially find in *Isaiah* where Jesus scorns the slaughter and bloodshed of humans and animals. He declares (1.15) that God does not hear the prayers of animal killers: "But your iniquities have separated you and your God. And your sins have hid His face from you, so that He does not hear. For your hands are stained with blood. . . Their feet run to evil and they hasten to shed innocent blood. . . they know not the ways of peace." Isaiah also laments that he saw, "Joy and merrymaking, slaughtering of cattle and killing of sheep, eating of meat and drinking of wine, as you thought, 'let us eat and drink, for tomorrow we die.'" (22.13)

It is also established in the Bible (*Isaiah* 66.3), "He that killeth an ox is as if he slew a man." In this regard St. Basil (320-379 A.D.) taught, "The steam of meat darkens the light of the spirit. One can hardly have virtue if one enjoys meat meals and feasts."

Thus, we should find alternatives to killing animals to satisfy our appetites, especially when there are plenty of other healthy foods available. Otherwise, there must be reactions to such violence. We cannot expect peace in the world if we go on unnecessarily killing so many millions of animals for meat consumption or through abuse.

The third factor for being vegetarian is karma. As Newton's third law of motion relates, for every action there must be an equal and opposite reaction. On the universal scale this is called the law of karma, meaning what goes around comes around. This affects every individual, as well as communities and countries. As the nation sows, so shall it reap. This is something we should take very seriously, especially in our attempt to bring peace, harmony, and unity into the world. If so much violence is produced by the killing of animals, where do you think the reactions to this violence goes? It comes back to us in so many ways, such as the form of neighborhood and community crime, and on up to world wars. Violence breeds violence. Therefore, this will continue unless we know how to change.

Isaac Bashevis Singer, who won the Nobel Prize in Literature, asked, "How can we pray to God for mercy if we ourselves have no mercy? How can we speak of rights and justice if we take an innocent creature and shed its blood?" He went on to say, "I personally believe that as long as human beings will go shedding the blood of animals, there will never be any peace."

In conclusion, we can mention the March 10, 1966 issue of *L'Osservatore della Domenica*, the Vatican weekly newspaper, in which Msgr. Ferdinando Lambruschini wrote: "Man's conduct with regard to animals should be regulated by right reason, which prohibits the infliction of purposeless pain and suffering on them. To ill treat them, and make them suffer without reason, is an act of deplorable cruelty to be condemned from a Christian point of view. To make them suffer for one's own pleasure is an exhibition of sadism which every moralist must denounce."

Eating animals for the pleasure of one's tongue when there are plenty of other foods available certainly fits into this form of sadism. It stands to reason that this is counterproductive to any peace and unity or spiritual progress we wish to make. It is one of the things we need to consider seriously if we want to improve ourselves or the world. So here are a few reasons why a genuinely spiritual person will choose to be vegetarian.

BEYOND VEGETARIANISM

In the process of bhakti-yoga, devotion goes beyond simple vegetarianism, and food becomes a means of spiritual progress. In the *Bhagavad-gita* Lord Krishna says, "All that you do, all that you eat, all that you offer and give away, as well as all austerities that you may perform, should be done as an offering unto Me." So offering what we eat to the Lord is an integral part of bhakti-yoga and makes the food blessed with spiritual potencies. Then such food is called *prasadam*, or the mercy of the Lord.

The Lord also describes what He accepts as offerings: "If one offers Me with love and devotion a leaf, a flower, fruit or water, I will accept it." Thus, we can see that the Lord accepts fruits, grains, and vegetarian foods. The Lord does not accept foods like meat, fish or eggs, but only those that are pure and naturally available without harming others.

So on the spiritual path eating food that is first offered to God is the ultimate perfection of a vegetarian diet. The Vedic literature explains that the purpose of human life is reawakening the soul's original relationship with God, and accepting *prasadam* is the way to help us reach that goal.

On the spiritual path those who are the most inclined to lead a peaceful existence that respects the value of all life often adopt the vegetarian lifestyle. For some people this is a very big step. This is in accordance with the yogic principle of *ahimsa*, which is to observe nonviolence and abstain from injuring any being in any way. However, many people ask what about the plants that are killed in the process of cooking vegetarian foods. Don't they suffer? And don't we get reactions for that?

The basic law of nature is that every living being lives off the weaker living entities. But there is a way of living so that we all can benefit, that we all make spiritual development. And this spiritual lifestyle is a way in which that can happen. The way this works is in the process of bhakti-yoga, wherein devotion goes beyond simple vegetarianism, and food becomes a method of spiritual progress for both those who prepare and eat the food, and those living beings that are used in the preparations.

For example, in the Krishna temples, food is offered to the deities in a special sacrament, after which it becomes *prasadam*. This means the mercy of the Lord. Thus, the food we eat after it is offered to the Lord becomes more than just a means of nutritional sustenance, but it becomes a means for our purification and spiritual development.

The Lord does not need anything, but if one offers fruits, grains, and vegetarian foods, He will accept it. So, we offer what Lord Krishna likes, not those items which are distasteful to Him. We also do not use garlic, onions, or mushrooms when we prepare food for Krishna, for these are considered to invoke passion or are from impure sources, which similarly affect our consciousness. Foods for Krishna should be in the mode of goodness, *sattvic* foods which when we accept as *prasadam* also elevate our own consciousness.

The food is meant to be cooked with the consciousness of love, knowing that it will be offered to Lord Krishna first, and only after that distributed to ourselves or guests to take. The ingredients are selected with great care and must be fresh, clean and pure vegetarian. Also, in cooking for Krishna we do not taste the preparations while cooking. We leave the first taste for Krishna when it is offered to Him.

After all the preparations are ready, we take a portion of each one and place it in bowls on a special plate that is used for this purpose only and take it to the altar to offer it to the deities or pictures of Krishna.

Then the preparations are presented with special prayers as we ask that God accept our humble offering. The most important part of the offering is the love with which it is given, and then the Lord accepts it. God does not need to eat, but it is our love for God which attracts Him to us and to accept our offering. Even if the most sumptuous banquet is offered to God but without devotion and love, Krishna will not be hungry to accept it. It is our love, our devotion and bhakti, which catches the attention of Lord Krishna who is then inclined to accept our service.

After He glances over and tastes the loving offering of vegetarian preparations, He leaves the remnants of the food offerings for us to honor and relish. Krishna's potency is absorbed in that food. In this way, material substance becomes spiritualized, which then affects our body and mind in a similar and most positive and elevating way. This is His special mercy for us. Thus, the devotional process becomes an exchange of love between us and God, which includes food. And that food not only nourishes our body, but also spiritualizes our mind and consciousness.

By relishing the sacred food of Krishna *prasadam*, it purifies our heart and protects us from falling into illusion. In this way, the devotee imbibes the spiritual potency of Lord Krishna and becomes cleansed of sinful reactions by eating food that is first offered in sacrifice to God. We thus also become free from reincarnation, the continued cycle of birth and death. This process prepares us for entering the spiritual world since the devotees there also relish eating in the company of Lord Krishna.

However, what does this do for the plants that are offered? They are also living beings. In this process, not only do we make advancement, but all of the plants that are used in the preparations as an offering to God are also purified and reap spiritual benefit. They are used and offered to God and thus make progress in the same way we do. That is why this is beyond mere vegetarianism in which we may live more simply and nonviolently, but in this process everything we use in the service of the Lord becomes spiritualized.

If we merely cook for ourselves, we become implicated in karma or the reactions if we cause the harm of any living being, even plants. The vegetarian lifestyle surely causes less karma than the unnecessary slaughtering of innocent animals. However, the system of first offering food to the Lord and then taking *prasadam* becomes the perfect yoga diet and frees us from such karma.

Therefore, the cooking, the offering, and then the respectful eating or honoring of this spiritualized food all become a part of the joyful process of devotional service to the Lord. Anyone can learn to do this and enjoy the happiness of experiencing the potency of Krishna *prasadam*.

A special plate filled with many preparations to be offered to the deities. After is is offered, it is distributed amongst the devotees as the spiritually powerful food called Krishna *prasadam*.

CHAPTER TWENTY

Vedic Culture: As Relevant Today As Ever

By investigating the knowledge and viewpoints in the many topics found in Vedic culture we can certainly see that the practice and utilization of this Vedic knowledge can indeed assist us in many ways, even in these modern times. In regard to all the trouble we presently see in this world, maybe it is time to look at things through a different and deeper view to find the answers and directions that are so needed. The knowledge and understandings of this great Vedic culture may indeed be what will help us see through the fog of confusion that seems to envelope so much of society.

What we find in Vedic culture are areas of study, progress and expression that are as relevant today for human advancement as they were hundreds or thousands of years ago. India and its Vedic culture has contributed much to the world, such as its music, beautiful forms of art and architecture, martial arts, astronomy, holistic medicine in Ayurveda, and the mathematical system based on the number ten, along with its yoga systems and philosophy. In the United States, yoga has exploded into a three billion dollar industry. A recent survey (at the time of this writing) showed more than 16.5 million people, or nearly 8 percent of the United States, is practicing yoga.

Vedic mathematics is another example of its contribution to world progress. It is an ancient development that continues to play an important part in modern society. Without the advancements in math that had been established by Vedic culture as far back as 2500 BCE and passed along to others, such as the Greeks and Romans, we would not have many of the developments and inventions that we enjoy today. The Greek alphabet, for example, was a great hindrance to calculating. The

Egyptians also did not have a numerical system suitable for large calculations. For the number 986 they had to use 23 symbols. The Romans also were in want of a system of mathematical calculations. Only after they adopted the Indian system that was called "Arabic numerals" did they find what they needed.

The numeral script from India is said to have evolved from the Brahmi numerals. This spread to Arabia through traders and merchants, and from there up into Europe and elsewhere. It became known as the Arabic numerals, yet the Arabians had called them "Indian figures" (*Al-Arqan-Al-Hindu*) and the system of math was known as *hindisat*, or the Indian art.

The difference was that Vedic mathematics had developed the system of tens, hundreds, thousands, etc., and the basis of carrying the remainder of one column of numbers over to the next. This made for easy calculations of large numbers that was nearly impossible in other systems, as found with the Greeks, Romans, Egyptians, and even Chinese. The Vedic system had also invented the zero, which has been called one of the greatest developments in the history of mathematics.

Vedic culture already had an established mathematical system that had been recorded in the *Shulba Sutras*. These are known to date back to at least the 8th century BCE.

The *Shulba Sutras* were actually a portion of a larger text on mathematics known as the *Kalpa Sutras*. These and the Vedic mathematicians were recognized for their developments in arithmetic and algebra. Indians were the first to use letters of the alphabet to represent unknowns. But they were especially known for what they could do in geometry. In fact, geometrical instruments had been found in the Indus Valley dating back to 2500 BCE. Furthermore, what became known as the Pythagorean theorem was already existing in the *Baudhayana*, the earliest of the *Shulba Sutras* before the 8th century BCE. This was presented by Pythagoras around 540 BCE after he discovered it in his travels to India. So this shows the advanced nature of the Vedic civilization.

The Vedic system of math, as explained in the *sutras*, also reduced the number of steps in calculations to merely a few that otherwise required many steps by conventional methods. Thus, this ancient science is still worthy of study today.

A well-developed medical system was in existence well before the 1st century CE. Ayurveda is the Vedic system of holistic medicine. It has become quite popular in the West and is continuing to gain ground and acceptance. The word "Ayurveda," translated from Sanskrit, is composed of two words, '*Ayus*' which means life and '*Veda*' which denotes knowledge. So Ayurveda is the knowledge of healthy living and is not only the treatment of diseases. Ayurveda has twin objectives-- maintaining the health of the healthy, and cure illnesses of the diseased. The exact origin of Ayurveda is lost in the mists of antiquity. Since Panini is placed at 7th century BCE and Ayurveda depicts non-Paninian Sanskrit grammar, it is logical to place Ayurveda between at least the 6th–10th century BCE, if not earlier.

Jyotish is the Vedic form of astrology, which is an ancient science and is also being accepted and gaining popularity in the West. Vedic Astrology is meant to help the individual better find his or her way through life. It is to assist in discovering one's highest proclivities, personality, character, qualities, and traits and what may be one's best direction for a career and other things. Thus a person will least likely waste one's time in unfulfilling activities, professions or pursuits.

Gemology is an important field in today's market. But when we speak of Vedic gemology, we do not mean that it is merely for judging the value of a gem. The Vedic purpose in gemology is to determine the best type of quality gem for a person to wear. Thus, Vedic gemology worked in conjunction with Ayurveda and Jyotish to establish the best gem a person should wear for health and positive influence.

Vastu is the Vedic science of architectural and home arrangement. It made its way through the orient and became known as Feng Shui, which has become popular in the West. However, Vastu is a particular science that deals with the flow of energy through a house or building for the highest benefits for those living or working there. It is not enough to merely arrange a house so it looks nice or that there is a good flow of energy through it. But there is much that depends on the directions in which things are facing or which parts of the building accommodate certain activities.

Vedic art is another ancient development that still holds much appreciation in modern times. Art in the Vedic tradition was never a mere representation of an artist's imagination. It was always a vehicle to convey higher truths and principles, levels of reality that may exist beyond our sense perception. It was always used to bring us to a higher purpose of existence and awareness. In this way, it was always sacred and beheld the sacred. Still today it is used to allow others to enter into a transcendental experience.

Vedic paintings or symbols are unique in that they can deliver the same spiritual energy, vibration and insight that it represents. In other words, through the meditation and devotional mood of the artist, the art becomes a manifestation of the higher reality. In this way, the painting or symbol becomes the doorway to the spiritual essence contained within. They are like windows into the spiritual world. Through that window we can have the experience of *darshan* of the Divine or divinities, God or His associates. *Darshan* is not merely seeing the Divine but it is also entering into the exchange of seeing and being seen by the Divine.

As with art, dance in India was not merely an expression of an artist's emotional mindset or imagination, but was meant to be an interpretation or conveyance of higher spiritual principles or pastimes of the Divine. In fact, in the Vedic pantheon Shiva is known as Nataraja, the king of dancers. Shiva's dance was also not without a more significant purpose. His dance was based on the rhythm of cosmic energy that pervades the universe, and the destruction of the illusory energy by which all souls are given the opportunity for release from the illusion to attain liberation, *moksha*.

In this way, traditional Indian dance is highly spiritual and often accompanies important religious rituals and holy days and festivals. Vedic dance goes back to prehistoric times. Bharata Muni wrote his *Natya Shastra*, science of drama and dance, over 2000 years ago. In it he explains that it was Lord Brahma, the secondary engineer of the universal creation, who brought dance (*natya*) and drama to the people of Earth millions of years ago, shortly after the Earth was created.

Now dance has evolved into a tradition involving various schools and styles but with strict discipline. It is not uncommon that Indian families will have their daughters spend at least several years or more in such study and practice. In Vedic dance, there is a precise method of postures, facial and hand gestures (*mudras*), and movements, along with footwork that must be learned and synchronized to the beat and music in order to convey specific meanings, moods and stories to the audience. Many temples, especially in South India, were known for maintaining large groups of dancers that performed at festivals and religious functions.

When the dance is performed according to the spiritual standards, which some view as similar to the practice of yoga, even the dancers can invoke a high degree of spirituality in their own consciousness and bring unity between their inner selves and God. Then the transcendental atmosphere can manifest and draw the Divine to appear in the performers on stage. Thus, the environment becomes transformed and the audience may also experience *darshan* of the Divine and experience an inspiring upliftment in their own consciousness. In this way, the dance is divine beauty in motion. Or it is a way of invoking the spiritual dimension into our midst. Few other forms of dance attempt to do this.

So, as we can see, Vedic culture and its many areas of knowledge and devotional expression are still as relevant today as it was thousands of years ago. And humanity can benefit from it by introspection and in spiritual as well as material development as it did in the past.

The power and relevancy of Vedic culture are found in the number of tools it has always provided in order for humanity to reach its highest potentials, both as individuals who are searching for their own fulfillment and spiritual awakening, and as a society that can function in harmony with nature and cooperation amongst themselves.

PART FOUR

PRACTICING BHAKTI-YOGA AT HOME

CHAPTER TWENTY-ONE

Establishing a Home Altar

As I explained earlier, most people are no longer joining an ashrama to live full time as they did in the 1960s, although many people do stay in an ashrama for a time to get the experience. But most people have their own homes, or apartments, or a career with a family, or are students preparing for life. Nonetheless, a life without spiritual development is a life without reaching your fullest potential. So, many people are adding a spiritual structure to their lives, such as we find with bhakti-yoga.

You can still have your occupation and career and be a yogi or spiritual practitioner at the same time. After all, the rent or house payments, along with the utilities all have to be paid, and if you have children and dependents, you have to be responsible. But you can also spend some of that money for spiritual purposes, or give regular donations for supporting projects at the temple and things like that so that your work also becomes a part of devotional service. Or you can volunteer spare time to engage in services at the temple, or even purchase spiritual books to give to interested friends or to distribute to others.

Of course, it can be easier to focus and concentrate full time on your spiritual life while living in an ashrama, especially amongst other *bhaktas* or devotees who are doing the same, but you can still also make your home into a temple or ashrama. You can apply the format as presented in this book, and also study the teachings of Lord Krishna in the *Bhagavad-gita* and other books, and follow the guidance of your spiritual master if you have accepted one. You can follow the principles as outlined earlier in this book, and in this way, you can learn and advance as much as anyone, if you take it seriously.

If you are staying at home, one of the first things that we may want to do is to establish an area of our house or even a room that is allocated for our prayers, meditation, reading, and even *pujas* or worship. Then we can keep that area sacred, if possible, and put up nice photos or pictures of such things as the local deities, or Lord Krishna, or our spiritual master, or even holy places in India. Keeping it clean is also important so that it has a special atmosphere in it that allows us to get away from everything else, and become composed with thoughts of our spiritual identity and connection with God.

Having a separate room for your temple is much better than merely having a place on a shelf or cupboard somewhere. It provides the space where the whole atmosphere is dedicated to your spiritual development and the care for your altar or deities if you have Them. Then everything within the room is kept clean and dedicated solely for this purpose.

The ultimate goal of the Vedic process, and of bhakti-yoga in particular, is to re-establish our innate loving relationship with God. We do this by cultivating devotion (*bhakti*) toward Him. This is our meditation, which is the basis of all our activities. And one of the most effective means of devotional meditation is known as *puja*, or directly serving or worshiping God by making offerings to Him on the altar, or by simply meditating on His form as displayed in the pictures on the altar and on the walls of our home temple room.

After establishing our meditation area, the next thing that is nice to do is to set up an altar as well. So how do we do that?

The altar can be elaborate or very simple, depending on how we want it. It all depends on our ability and the facilities we have to work with, meaning the size of our home or apartment and our financial condition. An altar can be made by using a book shelf, or specially assembled with custom built cabinets, and shelves with nice steps for all the paraphernalia and pictures, and with drawers for placing special plates, incense, or even clothes for the deities, if we have Them. You may also want to have a nice altar cloth, something pretty but functional where you can place water cups for the pictures or deities, a small altar bell, incense holder, flower vases for fresh flowers, and things like that. But there are some basic things that you will want on the altar as well.

One thing is to have a photo of your spiritual master if you are initiated, or the guru for whom you are aspiring to take initiation. In my case, I have a photo of Srila Prabhupada, and also small photos of the line of the previous five gurus in our lineage or *parampara*. These photos are on the lower shelves, while the higher ones are for the deities or Their photos.

Then you will want a print of Lord Chaitanya and His four associates, called the Pancha-tattva. Lord Chaitanya is the most recent avatara of Lord Krishna in His form as His own devotee. He is the form of God, an *avatara* of Lord Krishna, who especially established the importance of *sankirtana*, group chanting of the Hare Krishna mantra. He is considered most merciful in the way He spread the process of attaining love of God, bhakti-yoga, for the benefit of everyone. Or you may want a photo of Lord Chaitanya and His brother Lord Nityananda, who are called Gaura-Nitai together, who are Krishna and Balarama. (Lord Chaitanya is also called Gaura or Gauranga because of His golden complexion.)

Then you will also need a print of Sri Sri Radha-Krishna or a photo of the local temple deities. Keep this picture in the center of your altar. Lord Krishna is, of course, the Supreme Personality in His most loving form, and Srimati Radharani is the spiritual potency of the Lord who is devotional service personified. Devotees take shelter of Her to be blessed to learn more about devotional service, or bhakti-yoga.

You may also want a photo of the deities of Lord Jagannatha, Lord Baladeva and Subhadra, which are deities that many temples have. Lord Jagannatha is Lord Krishna, Baladeva is Krishna's brother Balaram, and Subhadra is Their sister.

If you are prepared and ready, you may even want to have your own deities (*murtis*) of your favorite form of the Lord, such as Gaura-Nitai or Sri Sri Radha-Krishna. This takes a little more endeavor in serving Them, but again you can make it simple or elaborate. At home, you can decide on what kind of standard is most suitable for you. You do not have to be overly elaborate like the way things are done at the temple, unless you wish to do so. The thing is once you establish a standard, you want to keep it that way and attend to the deities or the pictures on your altar everyday.

Now that you have your altar, the next step is what to do with it.

TAKING CARE OF YOUR ALTAR

To take care of your altar, or the deities if you have them, every morning you should first be bathed and clean before going into the temple room or doing *puja*. Then knock on the temple room door or ring a little bell to announce your entrance, then go in the temple room, offer your obeisances by kneeling down and placing your head to the floor, and then do *achamana* for purification (this is explained later). Then clean the altar, refill the water cups while accepting the previously offered water as *prasada*, putting it in a separate container so you can drink it later, then remove any wilted flowers from the vases, and replace the flowers with fresh flowers when you can.

Offering obeisances or bowing down to one's guru when entering or leaving his presence is mandatory by saying his *pranam mantra*. We also offer obeisances when entering or leaving the temple room. When seeing sannyasis for the first time in the day, they should also be offered obeisances. But it is generally accepted that, except for one's guru, obeisances should not be offered to other devotees in front of the deities in the temple when the deity altar curtains are open, you can save that for later. But if the altar curtains are closed, obeisances are fine.

Try to be as punctual as possible at your home, but at the temple punctuality is key, everything should go on like clockwork, the same time for the same activities everyday.

When you have prepared the altar and temple room, when it is time to do the worship, while either sitting in front of your altar or standing before it, you want to first close your eyes, and take a few deep breaths and center yourself, be at peace and be open to God's grace as you prepare to offer Him something. Then you can light some incense and offer it to the pictures with your right hand in a circular movement while ringing your little altar bell with your left hand. Then place the incense in the holder. If you wish to do a full *arati* or *puja*, then a separate chapter will cover that. You can sing a devotional song or the Hare Krishna mantra while offering the pictures incense. You can also offer a ghee lamp (a *deep*) if you wish as well, and then a few fragrant flowers.

After the *puja* is over, you may again place your hands in the *namaste* gesture and offer your obeisances to the photos or deities on your altar. You can then recite a few mantras for respect to the deities as listed in a previous chapter on devotional songs and mantras. Or you can also use the following, first offering respects to your guru, and then to the deities:

> *Om ajnana-timirandhasya*
> *jnananjana-shalakaya*
> *chakshur unmilitam yena*
> *tasmai shri-guruve namaha*

"I offer my respectful obeisances to my spiritual teacher, who has opened my eyes with the torchlight of knowledge, which were blinded by the darkness of ignorance."

> *he krishna karuna-sindho*
> *dina bandho jagat pate*
> *gopesha gopika-kanta*
> *radha-kanta namo 'stu te*

"Oh Krishna, ocean of mercy, You are the friend of the distressed and the source of creation. You are the master of the cowherdmen and the lover of the *gopis*, especially Radha. I offer my respectful obeisances unto You."

> *tapta-kanchana-gaurangi*
> *radhe vrindavaneshvari*
> *vrishabhanu-sute devi*
> *pranamami hari-priye*

"I offer my respects to Radharani whose bodily complexion is like molten gold and who is the Queen of Vrindavana. You are the daughter of King Vrishabhanu, and You are very dear to Lord Krishna."

After the altar has been prepared and the *puja* has been done, however simple it may be, then it is time to start your meditation and

Chapter Twenty-One 181

japa chanting of the Hare Krishna mantra on beads. Or, when you have the time, you can perform a morning program, starting with a full *mangala arati*, and then on with the other elements of the program as outlined earlier, or whatever you can do. Remember, while at home you can decide on the standard you can keep, with the hope of raising it later on as you grow spiritually, or doing more on those days when you have the time, or even going to the local Krishna temple to follow the program there when days permit. At the temple, the deity worship is done in its complete form by the resident *pujaris* or priests.

Above is a home altar with large deities of Gaura-Nitai, and higher up are small Jagannatha, Balarama and Subhadra, and on the top shelf is Sri Sri Radha Krishna. Other deities of Krishna on are the side, and pictures of Srila Prabhupada and the parampara are on lower shelves, and many pictures of other deities and prints of Radha Krishna are on the walls.

CHAPTER TWENTY-TWO

The Basic Arati Procedure

Now that we have taught a few simple ways of taking care of your altar and doing *puja* at home, here is a more complete way of doing it, as it is done in the temple. This is supplied for those who may be ready or are interested in it. So if you wish to one day be qualified to do the *arati* at the temple, you can learn and practice it at home in the way it is described here. If you are already in the temple ashrama, then someone is likely to show you what to do along the same lines as described herein. However, every temple may have slight differences or adjustments in the way they do things, though it is better when a common standard is kept. So you would likely learn the procedure that is used at your local temple by one of the *pujaris* there.

Remember, as you learn to do these procedures, it will become like second nature as you become familiar with them. Also, if you are doing deity worship at home in a simple manner, do these as best you can. You may need to get instruction from those who are more familiar, and you may not have to be quite so particular in all of these steps. However, learning deity worship in the temple, where the deities have been ritually installed, then it is best to know and follow the procedures very carefully. So in the temple, the water in the cup on the altar may already be consecrated and you do not have to do this, but here we provide the basic instructions so you will know what to do.

CONSECRATING WATER FOR PURIFICATION (SAMANYA-ARGHYA)

Water is an important element in worship. Not only does it physically purify many items, but when consecrated by deity *mantra*, which is non-different from the deity, it gains spiritual potency. The water thus consecrated will be used for *prokshana* (sprinkling for purification) on the place, the articles, and oneself, and for the purpose of doing *achamana*. This process is common to all types of worship (*puja*), and the various *puja* manuals give similar methods for making the *samanya-arghya*, or pure water prepared in a simple way for general use. The priest or *pujari* normally establishes *samanya-arghya* at the start of the daily worship for use during the *pujas* that follow. To do this, the description is as follows for this procedure:

ESTABLISHING GENERAL ARGHYA WATER (SAMANYA-ARGHYA-STHAPANA)

Establish *samanya-arghya* before starting the worship. You will use this consecrated water for purifying the items used for worship by taking the spoon from the little water pot or cup and sprinkling a few drops on each item, like the incense, ghee lamp, etc. Fresh *samanya-arghya* water should be established at least twice a day, morning and afternoon.

To do this, set an empty water container or little pot or cup (called *pancha-patra*) in place and fill it with fresh water. After pouring a few drops of water from the *achamana-patra* or a spouted water pot onto the fingers of your right hand, purify the *pancha-patra* by *prokshana*, done like this:

• Chanting **om astraya phat**, sprinkle water on the *pancha-patra*. Invoke the Ganga River and other holy rivers by showing the *ankusha-mudra*, which means to place the middle finger of your right hand, as it protrudes from the others, just on the surface of the water in the pot, and if you are *brahmana* initiated have your *brahmana* thread wrapped around your thumb, and then chant:

gange cha yamune chaiva godavari sarasvati
narmade sindho kaveri jale 'smin sannidhim kuru

"May water from the holy rivers Ganga, Yamuna, Godavari, Sarasvate, Narmada, Sindhu, and Kaveri kindly be present."

• Now invoke the *bija*-syllable *om* into the water, chanting it eight times silently while holding the *bijakshara-mudra*, which means to bring your hands together and holding them horizontally over the *pancha-patra* (water pot) with the left hand on top of the right hand, while chanting *om*. Now the water in the little pot is considered to hold the waters from the sacred rivers and is ready for use.

DOING THE ACHAMANA PROCEDURE

Whenever we go on the altar or do anything in connection with the deities, and after making sure we are clean and wearing clean devotional clothes, such as a sari for women and dhoti for men, then we also do *achamana* for an additional purification. This takes only a few minutes, after which we can continue to take care of the deities or do the *arati* ceremony. So now take a few drops of water from the *pancha-patra* (water pot) and place them in the palm of your right hand. Then do as follows, sipping the water from the *brahma-tirtha* of your hand, which is the lower edge of your palm, next to the wrist.

• Chant **om keshavaya namaha** and sip water from the *brahma-tirtha* of your right hand.
• Chant **om narayanaya namaha** and sip water from the *brahma-tirtha* of your right hand.
• Chant **om madhavaya namaha** and sip water from the *brahma-tirtha* of your right hand.

The above is the "simple *achamana*," which is done quite often before doing pujas or when you take care of your home altar, but to do a full *achamana* continues as follows:

• Chant **om govindaya namaha** and sprinkle water (meaning nbo more than about three drops) on your right hand.
• Chant **om vishnave namaha** and sprinkle water on your left hand.
• Chant **om madhusudanaya namaha** and touch your right cheek with the fingers of your right hand.
• Chant **om trivikramaya namaha** and touch your left cheek with the

fingers of your right hand.
• Chant *om vamanaya namaha* and wipe above your upper lip with the base of your right thumb.
• Chant *om shridharaya namaha* and wipe below your lower lip with the base of your right thumb.
• Chant *om hrishikeshaya namaha* and sprinkle water on both hands.
• Chant *om padmanabhaya namaha* and sprinkle water on both of your feet.
• Chant *om damodaraya namaha* and sprinkle water on the top of your head.

While chanting the following *mantras*, then perform these hand motions:
• Chant *om vasudevaya namaha* and touch your upper and lower lips with the tips of the fingers of your right hand.
• Chant *om sankarshanaya namaha* and touch your right nostril with your right thumb and forefinger.
• Chant *om pradyumnaya namaha* and touch your left nostril with your right thumb and forefinger.
• Chant *om aniruddhaya namaha* and touch your right eye with your right thumb and ring finger.
• Chant *om purushottamaya namaha* and touch your left eye with your right thumb and ring finger.
• Chant *om adhokshajaya namaha* and touch your right ear with your right thumb and forefinger.
• Chant *om nrishimaya namaha* and touch your left ear with your right thumb and forefinger.
• Chant *om achyutaya namaha* and touch your navel with your right thumb and little finger.
• Chant *om janardanaya namaha* and touch your heart with the palm of your right hand.
• Chant *om upendraya namaha* and touch your head with all the fingertips of your right hand.
• Chant *om haraye namaha* and touch your right upper arm with the fingertips of your left hand.
• Chant *om krishnaya namaha* and touch your left upper arm with the fingertips of your right hand.

Now chant the following *mantra* from the *Rig Veda* while showing the *pranama-mudra* (palms together in front of your heart):

(om) tad vishno paramam padam
sada pashyanti surayaha
diviva chakshur-atatam
tad vipraso vipanyavo
jagrivam sah samindhate
vishnor yat paramam padam

"Just as those with ordinary vision see the sun's rays in the sky, so the wise and learned devotees always see the supreme abode of Lord Vishnu. Because those highly praiseworthy and spiritually awake *brahmanas* can see that abode, they can also reveal it to others." [*Rig Veda Samhita*]

DOING THE ARATI CEREMONY

Arati means to wave auspicious items in front of the deity or person to dispel inauspicious influences or elements, as a means of protection or upliftment. After doing *achamana* and purifying oneself, you assemble the necessary items to offer.

We now prepare the *arati* tray with the following items:
1. A blowing conch,
2. A cup (usually brass) and small spoon with fresh water,
3. Incense, usually three sticks,
4. A ghee lamp with five wicks, or at least with one wick,
5. A conch shell for offering water, with an extra cup to hold the water,
6. A small handkerchief, clean and nicely folded, usually cotton,
7. A small plate with a few flowers,
8. A chamara or yak tail fan, (which, along with the peacock fan, are kept on the altar or on the Vyasasana, the seat of the guru, representative of Srila Vyasadeva)
9. A peacock feather fan,
10. A bell (that is rung during the ceremony with the left hand),

11. Do not forget some matches or a lighter to light the incense and ghee wicks.

A *dhupa arati* is a shorter version of the *arati* ceremony wherein only incense, flowers and a *chamara* fan are offered, usually a few times a day in the temple.

Now we take the tray into the temple room or onto the deity altar, ringing the bell as you enter the altar. First pay respects to the deities and then proceed.
1. Blow the big conch shell three times to announce the start of the *arati*, and then open the altar curtains.
2. Place three drops of water on your hand and on each item before you offer it.
3. First light the incense, and as you offer the incense first to your guru, chant:

> *vanaspati-rasotpanno*
> *gandhatye gandha uttamaha*
> *aghreyah sarva-devanam*
> *dhupo 'yam pratigrihyatam*

Translation: "O Lord, please accept this incense, which is very sweet smelling for all the demigods. It provides the best of all aromas, being endowed with the fragrance produced from the sap of the king of trees."

When making an offering, always offer first to the guru, and then he offers to his guru, and it goes like this on up the line of the *parampara* until it reaches Lord Krishna. The guru also engages us in the worship of the deities by his instruction and by his grace. So we always offer everything to the guru first, and then we proceed to offer the items or food to the deities.
Then ring the bell in your left hand while offering the items with your right hand. Then as you offer the incense to Guru (your own guru first, then to Srila Prabhupada), you also chant the *mula* mantra, which is *aim gurave namah*.

To offer the incense: you offer it seven times (circles) around the whole body.

Then offer the incense to Srila Bhaktisiddhanta in the same way (if his deity is there), but using the *parama-guru mula* mantra, which is: *om parama-guruve namaha*.

Then offer it to Lord Nityananda, Lord Chaitanya, then to Srimati Radharani, and Lord Krishna, then to Lord Balarama, Lord Jagannatha, and to Lady Subhadra, and then to Sri Nathji and Bal Gopala, then turn and offer it as *prasada* to all the assembled devotees using three simple circles, or return to the front of Sri Sri Radha-Krishna, and offer the incense three times to the Tulasi on the altar, and then turn to offer it to the room full of assembled devotees. (This is specific to certain temples. The last steps may differ according to the situation or which deities are there.)

While first offering the incense (and each additional item thereafter) to each deity, you chant the *mula* mantra to each Deity, which are the following:

Lord Nityananda: *klim deva-jahnavi-vallabhaya namah*
Lord Chaitanya: *klim gauraya namaha*
Srimati Radharani: *srim ram radhikayai namaha*
Lord Krishna: *klim krishnaya namaha*
Lord Balarama: *om namo bhagavate vasudevaya*
Lord Jagannatha: *om gopijana-vallabhaya namaha*

For deities like Sri Nathji and Bal Gopala, you can use the Krishna *mula* mantra.

Use these mantras every time you offer an item to the particular deity. If your temple does not have all of these deities, then adopt the procedure to the deities you do have.

Now, when offering the noon *Rajabhoga arati*, next offer the camphor lamp. Offer the lamp to guru and then to each deity four times to the feet, twice to the waist, three times to the head, seven times to the whole body, ending by offering it to the room full of devotees, and leave the lamp near the front of the altar so someone can carry it around to everyone, first starting with Srila Prabhupada on the Vyasasana, and then to the senior devotees and all others.

4. Then offer the ghee lamp. As you first offer the ghee lamp to guru, chant this mantra for offering:

> *sva-prakasho maha-tejaha*
> *sarvatas timirapahaha*
> *sa bahyabhyantara-jyotir*
> *dipo 'yam pratigrihyatam*

Translation: "O Lord, please accept this lamp, whose light shines both inside and out, who is self-effulgent, possesses great effulgence and takes away the darkness on all sides."

Then using the same *mula* mantras for guru and each deity as described above, offer the lamp to each deity four times to the feet, twice to the waist, three times to the head, seven times to the whole body, as described above, ending by offering it to the room full of devotees as *prasada*, and leave the lamp near the front of the altar so someone can carry it around to everyone as before. One of the devotees can take the lamp and offer it to the other devotees in the temple room, starting with the guru (Srila Prabhupada) first by simply briefly holding the lamp in front of the *murti*, and then taking it to the other devotees in order of seniority. (In traditional Vishnu temples the lamp is taken first to Garuda in the back of the temple room.)

5. Then pour some of the water into the small conch and offer the conch of water seven times above the head to each deity. (Some of the newer manuals say to offer it three times above the head and seven times to the whole body.) Then, when finished with each deity, pour a little of the water back into the cup. When finished for all deities, put the cup near the front of the altar so someone can sprinkle it on the devotees, starting with the deity of Srila Prabhupada on the Vyasasana.

6. Then offer the cloth napkin seven times to the whole body.

7. Then offer the flower in seven circles around the whole body. Then put it near the front of the altar so someone can take it amongst the devotees so they can smell it, starting with Srila Prabhupada on the Vyasasana.

8. Then offer the *chamara* fan, fanning seven times to the whole body, again offering it to the room of devotees at the end.

9. Then offer the peacock fan seven times to the whole body to each deity, again offering it to the room of devotees at the end. (The peacock fan is not offered in the winter when it gets cold, usually from October to April.)

10. Then blow the big conch shell to announce the end of the *arati*.

11. Then loudly chant the *pranam mantras* at the end, unless someone else does it.

12. Then with joined hands softly offer the *pranam* prayers to your guru and Their Lordships.

When it is the early *mangala-arati*, after the *arati* and the conch is blown to end it, the scented oil is offered to the deities. Take a cotton swab or Q-tip that has the scented oil on it and offer it to the face of each deity so They can smell it. Then it is offered to the devotees as *prasada*. Generally, during the Nrisimha prayers, a devotee takes it around to others who accept it by rubbing it on the back of their right hand or wrist, and can then smell its fragrance. Natural oils only are used, not the cheap artificial or alcohol based oils.

13. Now take the tray of *arati* items to the *pujari* room and wash all items and tray and put them away for the next *arati*. Then also go back to the altar and clean it with a damp cloth as necessary.

14. Then you can sing the Narasimha prayers, unless someone else sings them, and after that close the curtains to the altar.

This is the basic process for doing the *arati* ceremony. If this is in the temple, after the *arati*, depending on the time of day, the curtains to the deity altar may be left open so any visitors can have *darshan* of the deities. At other times, the curtains may be closed so the deities can be prepared for being dressed. This happens either in the early morning or late evening, or when They are prepared for taking rest at noon or late evening. All of that can be discussed elsewhere.

Punctuality is key in doing the *arati*, especially at the temple. If the *arati* is supposed to start at 12 noon, then it should start at that time every day, not earlier or later, and then last about 25 minutes, with the deity curtains closed 30 minutes after the start, with a few minutes to clean the altar. It should not go on shorter or longer than that. The priest must know how to time this. A *dhupa* or short *arati* is about ten minutes.

MANTRAS FOR OBTAINING FORGIVENESS FOR ONE'S OFFENSES

If you want, after your *puja* or altar service, you can chant these lovely mantras for the forgiveness of any offenses you may have unknowingly made in your service to the deities. I remember I would always chant these at the end of my day's service in the evening.

> *mantra-hinam kriya-hinam*
> *bhakti-hinam janardana*
> *yat pujitam maya deva*
> *paripurnam tad astu me*

"O my Lord, O Janardana, whatever little *puja* or worship that has been performed by me, although it is without devotion, without proper mantras, and without the proper performance, please let that become complete."

> *yad-dattam bhakti-matrena*
> *patram pushpam phalam jalam*
> *aveditam nivedyan tu*
> *tad grihananukampaya*

"What has been offered with devotion, the leaf, the flower, the water, the fruit, the foodstuff, which has been offered, please, out of Your causeless mercy, accept it."

> *vidhi-hinam mantra-hinam*
> *yat kinchid upapaditam*
> *kriya-mantra-vihinam va*
> *tat sarvam kshantum arhasi*

"Whatever has happened without the proper chanting of the mantra, or without following the proper procedure, kindly forgive all that."

> *ajnanad athava jnanad*
> *ashubham yan maya kritam*
> *kshantum arhasi tat sarvam*
> *dasyenaiva grihana mam*
>
> *sthitih seva gatir yatra*
> *smritish chinta stutir vachaha*
> *bhuyat sarvatmana vishno*
> *madiyam tvayi cheshtitam*

"Whatever inauspicious things I have done out of ignorance or unknowingly, please forgive that, and accept me as your insignificant servant. Let my normal condition be service, let my movement be holy pilgrimage, let my thought be remembrance of You, let my words be glorification of You. O Vishnu, let my activities, with my whole mind and body and soul, be engaged in You."

> *aparadha-sahasrani*
> *kriyante 'har-nisham maya*
> *daso 'ham iti mam matva*
> *kshamasva madhusudana*

"Thousands of offenses are performed by me day and night. But thinking of me as Your servant, kindly forgive those, O Madhusudana."

> *pratijna tava govinda*
> *na me bhaktah pranashyati*
> *iti samsmritya samsmritya*
> *pranan samdharayamy aham*

"O Govinda, Your promise is that Your devotee will never perish. By remembering this over and over again, I am able to retain my life-airs."

It is recommended that if anyone has committed any of the above offenses (the offenses in deity worship), one should read at least one chapter of the *Bhagavad-gita*. This is confirmed in the *Skanda Purana, Avanti-khanda*.

* * *

There are more details and explanations than what we are providing here, which you can learn later. We are only offering the basics. This is merely to help you get started. There are additional books that provide many more details about the proper standards and principles for doing deity worship and this aspect of bhakti-yoga, like the *Pancharatra Pradipa* or the *Hari-bhakti-vilasa*. But since this book is primarily for new *bhaktas*, or devotees who are just starting out, we will not go into so much detail here. Besides, when someone becomes initiated and more advanced, they are usually trained up in a personal way by those who are more experienced. This helps keep the proper standards intact over the years.

As you progress and learn more about deity worship, later you can also learn how to bathe and dress the deities, which has specific procedures that need to be learned when you are ready. Nonetheless, the basic procedures are provided in a later chapter of this book.

If, however, you have deities at home and are not initiated into deity worship yet, you can still learn from someone who is experienced and who can show you how to dress the deities so you can do it as best you can and not neglect caring for your deities, but knowing you will learn all of the proper procedures when you are more qualified.

CHAPTER TWENTY-THREE

Making our Cooking Part of Our Yoga

Some devotees who are not in the temple ashrama live at home and work at a career or occupation to support their family, and may not be able to visit the temple so often. So they will also need to cook their food at home. To make this a part of the bhakti-yoga process, we need to follow a vegetarian diet, and make our food so that it is offerable to the Supreme, especially if we have our own deities to which we offer our food on our home altar. This means that we are cooking for God.

So, no matter whether we cook at home or at the temple, there are certain standards that we need to keep to make sure that our cooking is also a form of yoga. This is "cooking-yoga" for the "yoga diet." Even if we live in the temple ashrama and are not yet initiated or qualified to cook in the temple kitchen, a new *bhakta* may still be able to assist those who are qualified. That is also a great way of learning. Otherwise, only initiated devotees should cook in the temple kitchen

Lord Krishna explains that the body is like a boat that has to be maintained in order to use it to cross over the ocean of material existence and reach the spiritual strata. The proper and regulated diet, or the yoga diet, can fulfill this need and prevents agitation to the mind and senses. Otherwise, eating impure and the wrong kinds of food can negatively affect the mind and drag us off the path of spiritual progress and back toward materialism.

SHOPPING

The first step is shopping for the type of food we will need. When we understand the purpose of the food we cook, then we also have to take care when shopping for the food and ingredients we will use. The first thing is it has to be purely vegetarian, no meat, fish, eggs, or insects, nor any derivatives of such things. The best way to avoid that is not to buy any processed foods, and no or few canned foods. Always buy fresh fruit and vegetables.

Naturally, shopping at local farmer's markets can help us acquire fresh and wholesome foods, or the organic section of large supermarkets, if they have them. Growing our own food, or knowing the person who is growing it is even better. We want to be free from unnecessary pesticides and foods that are genetically modified, or which may be contaminated with chemicals that are ingested if we eat them, all of which are known to have harmful effects on our bodies and health and consciousness. Certainly, this is also not what we want to offer to God.

Furthermore, precooked foods, which are sold at stores and often precooked by non-devotees, or those who may be devoid of spiritual consciousness, are also not to be offered to Krishna or His deity.

CLEANLINESS

Before cooking we should be clean, showered, and wear clean clothes, preferably devotional clothing. The kitchen is considered an extension of the altar, and we should treat it like that. It is also considered the domain of Srimati Radharani who also cooks for Krishna, but She never cooks the same thing twice. We may not be able to follow that standard, but we should be aware of the special environment of the kitchen.

You should also wash your hands when you enter the kitchen, and wash all food as you prepare it, and use nothing that touches or falls on the floor or other contaminated areas like the garbage pail, or even the sink unless it can be thoroughly cleansed. If you are at home, try not to wash the deity plates or the food you are preparing in the same sink that you wash the plates from which you have eaten. This helps keep things used for the deities from getting contaminated.

Also, do not mix any leftovers into new preparations, which actually should not be in the deity kitchen, though it may be necessary to store them in our home kitchen. Anything that has been offered before should not be offered a second time when it is already *prasadam*.

We also refrain from using things like garlic, onions, or mushrooms in food to be offered. These are considered foods in the mode of passion and also affect our consciousness in a similar way. We want to offer foods that are in the mode of goodness.

We also never taste the food while cooking. The first taste is always for Lord Krishna when it is offered. Plus, tasting the food while cooking, especially with utensils that are placed back in the food after we have tasted it, spreads germs and contaminates the preparations in such a way.

When cooking, the cook should also be barefoot or wear shoes that are designated only for kitchen use. No outdoor shoes should be worn in the kitchen, or in the temple or altar areas.

Also, no matter where the kitchen is, whether it is at the temple or at home, it is best if the kitchen can be divided into two areas: one for the cooking, and another area for storing the food and supplies, and the pots and utensils, and the clean up area.

Some consideration for the cooking utensils should be given. Aluminum pots are used in many areas, but the aluminum salts that accumulate in food that is cooked in them has a poisonous effect. So we do not use them, neither for ourselves or for making food to be offered to the deities. Other things like china, glass, or plastic, and even stainless steel are considered low class in Vedic culture, though we see them being used regularly. The best standard is to use eating utensils that are stone, brass, silver, or even gold. So, even if we do not use them for our own use, it is nice when we have such utensils for the deities that are made from any of these elements.

COOKING

When we cook we do so with the consciousness and intention that the food is meant to be first offered to God. Even while cooking one should not engage in unnecessary talking, which may divert our consciousness from the proper intention of what we are doing. But we can even mentally chant the Hare Krishna mantra or other devotional songs and meditate on how this will be offered to Lord Krishna, and how we are doing this for the Lord's pleasure, which is what turns it into bhakti-yoga.

We have to be thinking of Krishna while we cook. It is not that we can be thinking of some material subject matter and at the same time be cooking for Krishna. A very good way to keep our minds on Krishna is to listen to Srila Prabhupada giving a class while we are cooking for Krishna. While we are cooking our hands are busy but our ears are free. So while cooking for Krishna is the perfect opportunity to hear from recordings of advanced devotees giving lectures. This will help keep our mind on Krishna and stop it from wandering onto material subject matters. Or we may also have recordings of nice *bhajans* or *kirtanas* playing in the background, which helps provide a nice environment to uplift our consciousness while cooking.

It is important to cook in the right consciousness because the consciousness of the cook goes into the food, which affects the thoughts and consciousness of those who eat it. That is also why it is recommended that we not eat in restaurants because the cooks may be cooking in a poor attitude or consciousness, as if it is only a job to be done for money, or they may be intoxicated and treat the food poorly or even in unsanitary ways. Such food will affect our own consciousness in subtle and negative ways, which then hampers our spiritual progress.

Lord Krishna also states, "If one offers Me with love and devotion a leaf, flower, fruit, or water, I will accept it." (*Bhagavad-gita* 9.26) So He states what He prefers, and that is what we prepare, along with the combinations thereof. Plus, this indicates it is the love that motivates Lord Krishna to accept the offering, and which is what He accepts. Otherwise, we may prepare so many things, but if there is no love in the activities, why should He accept it? It is the *bhakti* which attracts the Supreme.

OFFERING

Offering the food to God is a type of sacrifice which spiritually energizes it and frees it from karma. It purifies us in this way. Whereas food that is not offered but merely eaten to satisfy our minds and senses still has karma, and we accumulate the results of that. Vegetarian food certainly has less karma than meat products which can only be acquired through cruel acts of violence and suffering for the living beings who are slaughtered and killed, but we should also go beyond mere vegetarianism.

In the *Bhagavad-gita* (3.13) Lord Krishna says: "The devotees of the Lord are released from all kinds of sins because they eat food which is offered first for sacrifice. Others, who prepare food for personal sense enjoyment, verily eat only sin."

This simply refers to the karma, however minor it may be, that goes with anything that is done for mere gratification of the mind or senses, or for one's own selfish interest. However, those devotees who engage in bhakti-yoga and offer their food or eat Krishna *prasada* become free from this, as mentioned in this verse.

When offering the food, use a separate metal plate or tray, and bowls or cups. These must be used only for this purpose and must not have been used or eaten from by anyone else. These are considered Krishna's plates only. They are special. Then after cooking all of the preparations, put a generous portion of each cooked preparation in each bowl or cup, along with a cup of fresh water or fruit juice, arranged nicely, and then take them to be presented to the deities, or to be placed in front of the pictures of Them on our home altar.

When the offering is ready, and you have done a simple *achamana*, then place the plate on the altar. Then prostrate yourself before the altar, or sit next to it, and while ringing the little altar bell, you make the offering to the deities or Their photos. The simplest prayer is to simply say, "My dear Lord Krishna, please accept this offering." But reciting the *pranam* mantras is proper for asking the deities to accept the offering. First you present it to your guru, and chant his *pranam* mantra three times, who then offers it to the lineage or *parampara* line of spiritual masters, who then offers it to the deity, such as Lord Krishna.

In the Hare Krishna tradition, you offer the food to your guru by chanting his *pranam* mantra three times. Then to Srila Prabhupada with his *pranam* mantra, chanted three times, as follows:

Chapter Twenty-Three

nama om vishnu-padaya krishna-preshthaya bhu-tale
shrimate bhaktivedanta-svamin iti namine

namas te sarasvate deve gaura-vani-pracharine
nirvishesha-shunyavadi-pashcatya-desha-tarine

"I offer my respectful obeisances unto His Divine Grace A. C. Bhaktivedanta Swami Prabhupada, who is very dear to Lord Krishna, having taken shelter at His lotus feet.

"Our respectful obeisances are unto you, O spiritual master, servant of Sarasvati Gosvami. You are kindly preaching the message of Lord Chaitanyadeva and delivering the Western countries, which are filled with impersonalism and voidism."

Then to Lord Chaitanya:

namo maha-vadanyaya krishna-prema-pradaya te
krishnaya krishna-caitanya-namne gaura-tvise namaha

"O most munificent incarnation! You are Krishna Himself appearing as Sri Krishna Chaitanya Mahaprabhu. You have assumed the golden color of Srimati Radharani, and You are widely distributing pure love of Krishna. We offer our respectful obeisances unto You."

Then to Lord Krishna:

namo brahmanya-devaya go-brahmana-hitaya cha
jagad-dhitaya krishnaya govindaya namo namaha

"I offer my respectful obeisances to the Supreme Absolute Truth, Krishna, who is the well-wisher of the cows and the brahmanas as well as the living entities in general. I offer my repeated obeisances to Govinda, who is the pleasure reservoir for all the senses."

Then to finish we chant: Hare Krishna, Hare Krishna, Krishna Krishna, Hare Hare / Hare Rama, Hare Rama, Rama Rama, Hare Hare.

Then leave the plate with portions of all the preparations on the altar for the deities to eat. About 10 to 15 minutes is good, and at the temple sometimes up to a half-hour. After the food is offered, the Lord glances over it and accepts the bhakti or love with which it is offered, and then the food becomes *prasada*, meaning the Lord's mercy, and the remnants of the offering are for us. Then, after the deities have eaten or accepted the offering, we come back, take the plate and transfer all of the items into a serving container to serve ourselves or the guests and devotees later. Then we wash and dry the deity plates and bowls and put them away to be stored for the next offering, and only then should you serve the *prasada* to others. Then you can take the *prasada* to the dining area to be served so others can honor the *prasada* by thankfully eating it.

The Lord is not hungry, but eager to accept our love with which we offer the food. It is not that God needs to eat, but He is so merciful that He accepts our love and blesses the food, which also spiritually energizes it, which then does the same to our bodies, minds and senses when we eat it. Thus, it uplifts our consciousness and purifies our existence, which also frees us from karma. However, we do not say we "eat" it, but we "honor" the *prasada* in this way.

Of course, many recipes and instructions on how to cook are available in other books or websites, including mine, but the best way to learn to cook is by assisting and watching other trained and experienced cooks in the kitchen and asking for their advice. Soon you will be knowing how to cook nice preparations, but, more importantly, doing so in the right consciousness.

CHAPTER TWENTY-FOUR

Caring for Tulasi Devi in Your Home

We have previously explained the special nature of the Tulasi plant in a previous chapter. So many people take care of Tulasi plants in their home, or would like to. Yet, Tulasi is a sensitive plant and requires particular growing conditions and care in order to do well. Furthermore, it is considered that how well Tulasi grows is a sign of one's devotional attitude to Lord Vishnu or Krishna. It is said that regardless of how much care Tulasi devi may receive, without the proper devotion, she will not grow well. On the other hand, I have seen many devotees who had plenty of devotion but did not do well in knowing how to take care of Tulasi.

So here a few instructions that may assist one in the care of Tulasi, both at home or in the temple. The following is a portion of a letter sent by Srila Prabhupada, dated October 25, 1976, which answers some important questions regarding the identity of Tulasi.

1) Is each Tulasi a separate *jiva* soul or a expansion of one pure devotee?

Answer by Srila Prabhupada: Tulasi is one devotee who appears wherever there is devotion to Krishna,

2) Where does her spirit soul go when she leaves this body?

Answer: Tulasi's body is spiritual.

3) May we place jewelry in her soil or just moon stones?

Answer: Yes, jewelry is alright.

4) When Tulasi is being cared for by householders in their home, must two *aratis* still be offered?

Answer: If possible.

5) When Tulasi is being cared for by householders in their home may they use her leaves and manjaris [blooms] on their home offerings or should they take them to the temple?

Answer: Tulasi leaves should be offered to the deity.

6) When Tulasi is being offered *arati* by the householders, must she have a ghee lamp?

Answer: If possible.

7) Is it offensive to turn the baby Tulasis back into the soil when they appear?

Answer! Yes.

8) There are even questions concerning Tulasi's *aratis*. We have always offered her incense, ghee lamp and flower. Is this correct?

Answer: Yes.

9) In the manual, it states that Tulasi should not be pruned. Does this also mean trimming the branches which no longer have leaves or life fluids flowing through them?

Answer: You may cut dead branches, but what is the necessity?

10) We were told you once spoke the "4 regulative principles of Tulasi care" which will keep her from getting sick: (a) keep her moist; (b) keep her clean; c) give her morning sunlight (at least); (d) give her two *aratis* a day. Is this bona fide?

Answer: I never said that.

11) May Tulasi be made into a tea after she has been offered?

Answer: No.

12) May devotees carve Tulasi wood for deity paraphernalia?

Answer: Yes.

13) When Tulasi leaves her body and the body is too soft for carving beads, how should she be used? Should a small fire sacrifice be performed?

Answer: Use the wood for beads as far as possible; the balance may be placed within the earth. [It is also accepted that one can take dead Tulasi and put it in the local river.]

14) We have a letter from you requesting that no sprays be used on Tulasi devi. May we use a spray of buttermilk, whole wheat flour dissolved in water which coats her leaves to keep spider-mites from causing Tulasi to leave her body?

Answer: I said no chemical sprays.

15) Does Tulasi sleep? Should she be left undisturbed after nightfall?

Answer: Undisturbed means what?

16) Is it permissible to use scissors to cut her manjaris; and when transplanting to use knives to loosen her from her pot?

Answer: Use common sense, and if you have none then consult with others.

17) Is it an offense to step on or across her shadow (or the shadow of any pure devotee)?

Answer: (As per letter of Jan. 1977, the answer is yes--it is offensive to step on the shadow of a pure devotee.)

18) For two years we have been waiting permission to use the following two prayers plus translations, and translation of the already existing prayer. [Prayers not reproduced here.] Are these bona fide?

Answer: Don't try to introduce something new. The most important thing is love and devotion.

Techniques of Caring for Tulasi Devi

IMPORTANT POINTS

If you have just received a Tulasi plant by mail, or from your local temple:

1. Repot the plant in a clay pot with soil recommended in the "potting" section.

2. If dry, water thoroughly.
3. If soggy, pot in moist soil and allow to dry out to normal moistness.

POTTING

Tulasis should be repotted immediately when they arrive as well as from time to time when roots occupy the whole inside of the pot. A Tulasi should never have a big pot if she is small as this tends to cause rotting and slow root system drainage should be provided by adding some pieces of broken pot over the hole at the bottom. A pot too small binds the plant, so repot in a slightly larger size pot.

In potting young seedlings, the pot may be partially filled with soil. The plant should then be held in place with the roots spread out in a natural way. The remaining soil should be added, and pressed firmly into place with the fingers. In small pots a space of ½ inch or so should be left on top between soil and rim of the pot. Don't bury the stem. You can use a good potting soil or make one from one part sand to three parts soil. Water thoroughly and do not place in full sun for a few days. Never pot in peat moss.

LIGHT

Light is essential to her growth. Full sunlight is preferable and a south window is excellent. In the summer you can put her in a protected place outside. Florescent plant lights are very good also; place seedlings six inches below and larger plants 6 to 14 inches below the light.

When plants are left in any one position for a long period of time, the leaves and stems will turn toward the light and growth will be unsymmetrical. So turn pots once a week.

TEMPERATURE

They will thrive well in temperature which ranges from 62 degrees to 70 degrees Fahrenheit during the day and which does not drop below 55 at night. Of course, she is used to a very hot climate and will do well at higher temperatures during the summer. During the winter protect her from frost near windows by a protective covering of newspaper between her and the window.

CONTROLLING THE ENEMIES OF TULASI DEVI

For control for aphids, use black leaf 40 (nicotine sulfate).
Spray Formula:
Black leaf 40—one teaspoon
Soap–1 cubic inch
Water–1 gallon
Spray every four to five days for one month.

For control of white fly—green house bugs. These are white bugs that fly and lay white eggs, and suck the juice of the plant. Do the same as for aphids.

For control of mealy bugs. These appear to be tiny dots of cotton, but if you look close they are bugs with many legs. These are found on the under sides of the leaves on new shoots. Control by wiping them off with cotton swab filled with alcohol.

Die back is one common, heartbreaking disease that begins on new shoots, gradually drying up and turning them brown until the entire plant dies this way. You should immediately control watering. Sometimes this is caused by bad soil, so check this and repot if necessary. The disease is carried by the soil.

Spider mites. These are tiny white spiders which make webs on the plant and suck her shoots. Control by using a syringe and spray frequently with light soapy water.

These are just a few of the many demons that plague Srimate Tulasi Devi, but you can help by checking her every day, especially the under sides of the leaves. Cut off dead branches and always make sure she is not too dry or too wet. Big beetles are often a problem as well as caterpillars because everyone loves her tender leaves. So destroy these creatures (while chanting Hare Krishna) when they decide to make their home on Tulasi Devi.

PLANTING

1. Buy a Jiffy Grower Seed Starter Kit (or similar brand) at a

garden store. This kit consists of small peat moss seed cups arranged like an egg carton with seed bed soil pre-mixed and sifted. So all you have to do is fill the cups with soil mix and moisten (according to package directions) and press the Tulasi seeds into the soil about 1/16" deep, about 6 seeds per cup. Keep in warm sunny room, avoiding temp changes, out of strong drafts, and away from gas fumes (the alternative is to mix 2 parts clean river sand (unsalted), sift into seed flat or peat moss pots and water from beneath, don't sprinkle them. This is more expensive, time consuming and not so successful.

    2. The first Tulasi sprouts appear in 6 or 7 days, and will continue appearing for several weeks. Keep the plastic seed germination bag from pressing on the seedlings—prop it up inside with sticks if necessary. This will keep the remaining unsprouted cups moist.

    3. Buy a dozen 4"-6" deep peat moss pots and some good planting soil-mix. If you mix your own planting soil, use 2 parts sifted loam, 1 part clean river sand (unsalted) and 1 part sifted peat moss or leaf mold. Generally it should be slightly fertile, light with good drainage. There is no objection to mixing your own--its cheaper; but these peat moss pots are very nice as they give good ventilation, and simplify the eventual transplanting job.

    4. In late afternoon, in a wind protected spot (preferably just in the vicinity of the seed kit so there will be no temperature changes) take a few handfuls of rocks, a water bottle as described herein) lots of tepid water, peat moss, and lots sand soil mix. The idea is to simply put the sprouted cups into deeper cups for more root-growing room. Plant the whole cup, just remove its bottom. Begin by lining the bottom of the 4" peat moss cups with rocks for drainage. Wet the soil mix and fill the peat pots leaving a depression for the seed cups to enter. With knife carefully remove the bottom of the peatmoss seed cup. Set the whole seed cup down into the moist depression, pressing down firmly on all sides. This eliminates air gaps. Water thoroughly making a moat or depression around the peat moss cup (planted) but avoid direct watering into the seed cup. Direct watering may disturb seeds that are still germinating in the seed cups. Use a squirt bottle and tepid (not hot or cold) water. Never hit the tiny seedlings directly with the water stream. (If by accident you do, pick Her up and try to prop Her with soil very gently.) When

finished, leave the pots in the same vicinity as the seed kit. Place the pots 2-3inches apart on 'oven racks' or the like so that they get good air circulation and drainage from beneath and sides. Allow light but no direct sun exposure.

5. In a few days, gradually introduce them to filtered sunlight, under a tree out doors or under a lath screen (if weather is nice and nights not very cold). Arrange the pots as above on an oven rack or better yet on old bare bed-springs is the ideal thing, one pot in each wire spiral, this also gives good insect protection. Shield them from sun and wind. Protection from wind may be afforded by attaching parrarin cloth, burlap muslin, or plywood to stakes, building a 4-sided box. Then fiberglass or aluminum window screen can be tacked to the box edge giving protection from sparrows, mynah birds and flying insects. (Flies are especially bad, they lay eggs in the leaves, so protect with screen.)

6. Water the Tulasi seedlings thoroughly each morning, using tepid water bottle. Keep a large pot of tepid water nearby for refilling the water bottles, as they should be kept nicely moist. If the seed-lings start turning purplish or grayish, then they're getting too much sun and not enough water. If this happens, keep them in shade for a few days till they recover, or else they may wither and disappear.

7. Care for the seedlings regularly in the above manner, offering obeisances and circumambulating twice daily, and in 2-3 weeks they will develop 2 or 3 more sets of leaves. Then if you have pots bearing more than one seedling (and you probably will) you will have to plan on separating them by transplanting each in a separate peatmoss pot (4-6 inches deep). This separation transplanting is difficult but it is necessary. So prepare the required number of peat moss pots as described in #3 and #4 and in late afternoon equip yourself with peat pots, a knife, spade, soil mix, water bottle, and lots of tepid water. Important: the seedlings must be put one to a pot as soon as possible when they have two sets of leaves. Beforehand be sure to water the plants to be transplanted thoroughly. This makes the soil stick to the roots protecting them. In transplanting, avoid breaking and loosening seedling roots. Transplant as quickly as possible because even momentary exposure to the air is damaging and keep as much moist soil as possible around the roots. After watering, begin by cutting an inch or so deep into the peatpot dividing it into two

or more sections, depending on the number of seedlings. Start sections by cutting them carefully, pull the sections apart, trying to avoid root breakage and root exposure as far as possible. Immediately plant the sections in the newly prepared peat pots, pressing down firmly and filling more with moist soil as needed and water thoroughly several times, (two devotees working together can do this more quickly). Press soil around the plants firmly to eliminate drying air pockets, and water thoroughly several times. Full shade and increased watering should continue for 3 days, and longer if they wilt. If you do it quickly and carefully, there will be little or no wilting or drying up.

8. After three days of shade (simply cover the screened bed with cloth to provide shade) and double watering, gradually introduce them to filtered sunlight and continue caring for them as in #5 & 6. Continue this program for 2-3 weeks, until they have 3 or 4 sets of leaves. When more leaves have appeared, you may check periodically to see if any tiny white roots are coming through the bottom of the pot. One of the advantages of peat moss pots, aside from easy transplant, is that the roots never become cramped, thus dwarfing Her. When the pot becomes too small the roots just start coming through it. When you begin to see the roots coming through the bottom, it is time to transplant Her.

9. Transplanting into Pots: It is advisable to put a few plants in pots for the winter, especially if your center or home is in a cold climate. Large 10-12" deep cement are sturdy (or redwood) and porous; clay pots are porous but break easily; plastic pots are non-porous and are not very good. Indoors in cold season with use of a plant lamp you should be able to continue growing Tulasi plants year round, so use durable and large pots. Cement and redwood pots usually have little logs beneath for drainage and air circulation, which is very important.

Soil mix: give Srimate Tulasi Devi a very nice planter and soil mix and she'll grow and flourish nicely. You can either buy a ready-mixed packaged soil, or mix your own, which is just as good, done properly and cheaper. A good planter mix is 2 parts garden loam (more or less; depending on whether soil is light or heavy in texture); 1 part compost; 1 part sand (coarse, clean & unsalted); 1 part peat moss/leaf mold; 1 part well-rotted dehydrated cow manure (cow manure must be dehydrated, fresh manure will burn the roots, buy it in a garden store).

Drainage: Be sure the pot drains freely. Place curved piece of crockery (broken clay pat) over the drainage hole, then line pot bottom with 1-2" of coarse gravel so that dirt will neither sift through holes nor clog them.

Procedure: In late afternoon prepare pot as directed and fill it with moist soil mix leaving a depression in the center of the pot. Water the Tulasi to be potted. Then with knife carefully remove the bottom of Tulasi's peatmoss pot and set peat pot and Tulasi (together) down into the depression, pressing firmly so there won't be any air pockets. Leave about 1 inch of room above the soil so there will be ease in watering. Water thoroughly by soaking pot in basin from below.

Care of Tulasi Devi in the Pots: The first thing is to water thoroughly when necessary and allow plant to absorb moisture or water a little each morning (about once every three days seems best). Be careful not to over or under water Her. She likes sun so give Her a sunny window or use a two bulb grow light.

ADDITIONAL NOTES

Sec. 1. When planting new seeds from Tulasi Devi, the seed pods must be dissected and the seeds removed from them. Each pod contains 4 seeds. Some might have already fallen from the pod. With fingernails, carefully pick apart pods, allowing seeds to fall onto a soft cloth. Don't smash the pods. Avoid bruising the seeds or exposing them to damp atmosphere. Do not plant more seeds than you can properly maintain

If Jiffy grower seed starter kits are not available in your area, then you can get pre-sifted planter soil mix, and put it into small peat moss pots, then cover with a piece of perforated plastic bag by means of a rubber band. And water from below.

Sec. 10. When plants are a little taller, for wind protection and to give them stability, drive a thin stake into the ground 1" or so beside the stalk base, and loosely tie stalk to it with a torn strip of soft cotton cloth (a strip at least 1" wide). Tie it loosely and in a place where it won't obstruct growth of new leaves. This gives the slender delicate stalk good support, even in wind, and makes for more rapid growth. In a few months, the stalk is no more soft and purple, but becomes hard and woody, like a little tree. Still, if the area is windy, best to leave the support stake in permanently.

When collecting the leaves, collect the ones that droop before they fall naturally. Don't cut terminal leaves and wait till plants are big before cutting many leaves from them.

Srila Prabhupad said there are two kinds of Tulasi: Rama Tulasi which is greener, and Krishna Tulasi which is purple. Srila Prabhupada said there will also be little fruits shaped like temples in a year or so. The flower stalks He called Manjaris. In temple court-yards, there are always Tulasis growing, sometimes in a 3 foot tall pillar that is like a big pot, and Srimate Tulasi devi is worshipped regularly by the devotees. Especially in villages, the women take very nice care of the Tulasi plant. They water and offer obeisances and circumambulate in the morning and in the evening they offer lamp and incense, like *arati*. She is a great devotee and She is very important and a necessary paraphernalia in our worship. The plants will continue to grow for about 5 years.

Srila Prabhupada once explained: "The Tulasi leaf is very, very dear to Lord Vishnu and Krishna. All Vishnu tattva deities profusely require Tulasi leaves. Lord Vishnu likes garlands of Tulasi leaves. Tulasi leaves mixed with sandalwood pulp and placed on the Lotus Feet of the Lord is the topmost worship. But we must be very careful that Tulasi leaves cannot be placed on the feet of anyone else except Lord Vishnu and His different forms. Tulasi leaves cannot be placed even on the lotus feet of Radharani or on the lotus feet of the Spiritual Master. It is entirely reserved for being placed on the lotus feet of Krishna. We can place, however, Tulasi leaves in the hands of Radharani for being placed on the lotus feet of Krishna as you have seen on the Govinda album."

PRAYERS

When bowing down to Tulasi devi (*panchanga pranam*)

Vrindaai Tulasi devyai priyasai kesavasya cha
Vishnu bhaktiprade devi satyavatyai namo namaha

"I offer my repeated obeiances to Vrinda, Srimati Tulasi Devi, who is very dear to Lord Keshava (Krishna). O goddess, you bestow devotional service to Lord Krishna and possess the highest truth."

When collecting leaves

tulasya mrita janmasi sada tvam keshavapriya
keshavarthi chinomi tvam barada bhava sobine

"O Tulasi, you were born from nectar. You are always very dear to Lord Keshava. Now in order to worship Lord Keshava, I am collecting your leaves and manjaris. Please bestow your benediction on me."

The songs for offering *arati* and for circumambulating Tulasi are found in Chapter Four.

CHAPTER TWENTY-FIVE

Additional Steps for Home Deity Worship

For those who have or want to have deities at home, and want additional information on what to do, or how to raise their treatment of the deities to a higher standard, here are some simple explanations and instructions for procedures that you can add to your home deity worship if or when you are ready.

The Sanskrit name for the deity form is *archa-vigraha*, which means the worshipful expansion form of God. *Archana* is the process of offering articles of worship to the deity for the pleasure of the deity. This is done after purificatory or cleansing rites are performed, such as bathing and doing *achamana*, as previously described. It is also a process that spiritualizes our consciousness by engaging all of our senses in bhakti-yoga.

Our imperfect senses do not allow us to directly see Lord Krishna in His spiritual form. So, in His unlimited mercy, Krishna expands to accept the form of the deity so we can see Him, and so He can accept our devotion, and so we can more easily approach the Lord to offer our service. That is bhakti. When our bhakti is more progressed and we develop a higher level of devotion, then we may indeed be able to reciprocate or even perceive God in so many ways.

BRINGING THE DEITIES TO YOUR HOME

Your home deities should be installed nicely, sometimes called a "Greeting Ceremony," at which time the deities are "Greeted" by the family and possibly a gathering of devotees, wherein a minimum standard of worship is begun. This worship is for the regulation of the family, such as doing chanting and service for the pleasure of the deities. If you cannot do that, then it may be best to simply keep pictures of the deities on your home altar, which do not require much regulated attention. Remember, we do this mostly for our own practice and purification and spiritual advancement.

In the greeting ceremony, we may have a feast especially prepared for the deities, possibly a fire *yajna* or ritual, an abhishek or bathing of the deities, then dressing Them in beautiful clothes, then Their first *arati* ceremony, lots of kirtana while this goes on, and then everyone can participate in the *prasada* feast.

Temple deities are installed by a full installation ceremony, wherein the personality of God is called or invited to dwell within the deity form. This is far more elaborate than the greeting ceremony at our house. However, even with home deities, our service to Them continues to call the Lord to accept the deity form and accept our service, which also makes the deities increasingly alive and willing to reciprocate with the devotees in various ways. I have seen this so many times. I have also written a whole book about such reciprocation and the interaction that Lord Krishna's deities have displayed with His devotees called *"Krishna Deities and Their Miracles,"* which anyone can read and be inspired by the descriptions and stories therein.

QUALIFICATIONS FOR DOING DEITY WORSHIP

In the temple one must be brahmana initiated to do regular deity worship. But at home, it is not necessary to be brahminically initiated, and they can keep the worship simple, provide a small food offering and *arati*, and then chant the *maha-mantra* to the home deities. It is not expected that one is always initiated to start taking care of their deities at home, and may start and practice the process until he or she is reaches the stage of initiation. But they should be sincere, serious, clean, and punctual, and get the right training to understand how best to worship their deities.

Children can also get involved, but they should be at least 10 years old or more. If they are younger, they can assist, such as in helping make flower garlands, cleaning around the temple room or in the kitchen and other places. At the age of ten, they can start getting trained in the process of worshiping the deities on a very basic level and gradually learn more.

YOUR DEITY PROGRAM

If you have the time, and if you wish to become more involved in taking care of your home deities, there can be a whole program that you can do. However, while at home, this is our choice. The best thing to do is to pick a standard you can maintain. You can always increase it later, but you should not decrease it once you have established a certain standard.

The program can begin with waking the deities in the morning, like waking a special guest who is staying at your house. So after we have bathed, put on clean clothes, then we can go to the temple room, knock on the door or ring the bell, then pay our obeisances to the spiritual master, all of which we do anytime we enter our temple room, and then we proceed to our altar.

What we have described as follows is a simple procedure you can do at home, but once you become familiar with this, it is not so different than what we find done in many Krishna temples. This means that when you become initiated, you will be fairly trained, but not completely, to do the *pujari* or priestly service in the temples.

WAKING THE DEITIES

Waking the deities can be done in a simple way, such as by merely clapping our hands softly and then preparing the altar for our *arati*. Or, a higher standard, we can simply touch the lotus feet of the deities and chant the mantras for waking Them. Or it can be done more elaborately, such as the following:

Chapter Twenty-Five

If the small deities are put to sleep at night in beds, as described later, then, if you are worshiping the deities of Gaura-Nitai (Lord Chaitanya and Lord Nityananda), we first wake our spiritual master, then we wake Gaura-Nitai, then Jagannatha, Balarama and Lady Subhadra (if you have these deities), and then Sri Sri Radha-Krishna (if you have these deities).

What you will need is a small bell on a plate (a special deity plate which is usually brass or even silver, and used only for our deity service), an *achamana* cup containing fresh water and a spoon, and a mat for you to sit on.

1. First we do *achamana*, at least a simple *achamana* as described earlier, then offer obeisances to your spiritual master while reciting his *pranama* mantra, and pray for his blessings to assist him in the worship of the Lord.

2. Then before entering the temple room, or the area where the altar is, you make a sound by softly clapping your hands, or ring the bell, or knock on the door. Then open the door or curtains, turn on the lights, and chant the names of the deities in a festive mood, such as:

> *jaya shri shri guru-gauranga*
> *jaya jagannatha-baladeva-subhadra*
> *radha-krishna ki jaya!*

If you are worshiping other or additional deities, then chant Their names instead or as well.

3. If you are using ghee or oil lamps on the altar, you may light them now. Now wash your hands with a few drops of water from the *achamana* cup.

4. Then wake your spiritual master first by ringing a bell with your left hand, touch the feet in his picture gently with your fingertips of your right hand, and request him to rise from bed by chanting:

> *uttishthottishtha shri-guro tyaja nidram kripa-maya*

"O all-merciful spiritual master, please rise from bed."

Then meditate that he is rising from bed.

5. Now approach the bed of Lord Nityananda, touch His lotus feet with your fingertips, and request Him to rise with the following

mantra:

> *uttishtha jahnaveshvara yoga-nidram tyaja prabho*
> *namno hatte divya-namam su-shraddartham vitarasi*

"O Lord Nityananda, Lord of Jahnava, please arise and give up Your divine sleep. At the marketplace of the holy name You distribute the divine name, asking only for one's faith as payment."

6. Then approach Lord Chaitanya and touch His lotus feet, and request Him to rise:

> *uttishthottishtha gauranga jahi nidram mahaprabho*
> *shubha-drishti-pradanena trailokya-mangalam kuru*

"O Lord Gauranga, please rise from sleep and bless the three worlds with Your auspicious glance."

7. Now approach the bed of Lord Jagannatha, Lord Balarama and Srimati Subhadra, touch Their lotus feet, first Jagannatha, then Balarama, and then Srimati Subhadra, and chant:

> *tyaja nidram jagan-natha shri baladevottishtha cha*
> *jagan-matar cha subhadre uttishthottishtha shubha-de*

"O Lord Jagannatha and Lord Baladeva, please give up your sleep and arise. O Srimati Subhadra, dear mother of the universe, please arise and bestow good fortune upon us."

8. Now approach Radha and Krishna's bed, touch Their lotus feet (first Krishna and then Radharani) and chant:

> *go-gopa-gokulananda yashoda-nanda-vardhana*
> *uttishtha radhaya sardham pratar asij jagat-pate*

"O master of the universes, O bliss of Gokula, the cowherds, and the cows, O You who gladden the hearts of Yashoda and Nanda, please rise from bed with Shri Radhika, for morning has come."

9. Now place any small deities that are in bed back on the altar.

If there are only large deities, meditate on waking Them and leading Them from Their beds to the altar.

10. Now put on any crowns, turbans or chadars, or veils that are part of the deities' nightdresses. They are offered the early morning *mangala-arati* in Their night dresses.

11. After removing any remaining flowers and garlands from the previous day, clean the deity room floor and then wash your hands with the three drops of water from the *achamana* cup.

12. Now that the deities have been awakened, offer obeisances to Them outside the altar area. Now you are ready to begin preparing to do a small food offering, followed by an *arati* ceremony, or if not offering any food at this time, you can simply prepare for doing an *arati*. This would be the first or early morning *mangala arati*. After that, we can prepare for dressing the deities.

BATHING AND DRESSING THE DEITIES

Temples dress the deities everyday as part of the regular morning program, but at home we may dress the deities once a week, or every Ekadasi, depending on time, place, facilities, and our finances, or how many dresses we have for our deities. The main ingredient is the heartfelt mood of devotion, with awe and reverence.

For metal deities, as with most Gaura-Nitai deities that are brass or made of five metals, bathing and dressing Them daily is the highest standard. Polishing Them is optional, but when you do polish Them, you can make a paste of *tilaka* and lemon juice and use a Q-tip or small cotton swab to polish Them.

To dress the deities, it is best to gather all the items you need first, and then go on the altar ready and prepared. Remember that while at home, you can decide how much of this procedure you can easily adopt from what is described. Such items you may need will include:

1. Small water pot or bowl with cover,
2. Small bowl with *tilaka* powder mixed with lemon juice if you are polishing the deities,
3. Scented oil,

4. Cotton swab,
5. Bathing receptacle or bowl,
6. Towels: one for each deity, and one for your hands (keep the deity towels separate for Them only),
7. The clothes and underclothing for the deities,
8. Whatever pins or Blu Tack that you may need to keep ornaments in place,
9. The jewelry you intend to use,
10. Sandalwood paste (on a small plate),
11. Tulasi (on a small plate)
12. Picture of your spiritual master,
13. Picture of Srila Prabhupada,
      Additional optional items:
1. Flowers (on a small plate),
2. Incense and ghee lamp,
3. Lighter or matches,
4. Bhoga (non-offered food) offering (such as small home-made sweets or fruit),
5. And bring this description if you need it.

The Procedure
    1. Gather the required paraphernalia from what is described above, arrange it nicely for performing the worship without having to look for things when needed.
    2. Sit on a mat, now perform *achamana* (if you have not already), and then lightly sprinkle yourself and the immediate area around you with a few drops of water from the *achamana* cup while chanting Hare Krishna.
    3. Then offer to your spiritual master and Srila Prabhupada flowers that have been dipped in sandalwood paste with your left hand, ringing the bell with your right, and place them at their feet or the base of the picture. Beg for blessings for performing the worship of the deities.
    4. Now remove the clothing from the deities. Keep Their night outfits nice and neat so they can be taken away later to be stored for later use. Keeping outfits on hangers or in nice plastic containers works well.

5. Invite the first deity to the bathing receptacle with a gesture of the hands,

6. Massage metal or marble deities with scented oils, do not massage wooden deities like Lord Jagannatha with oils. Oils are not good for the paint or the wood.

7. Now polish the metal deities, if you are going to do so, but be careful not to get the *tilaka* and lemon juice in Their eyes.

8. Clean off the paste with cotton.

9. Now place the metal deities in the bathing receptacle and, while ringing the bell with your left hand, pour water over the deity by holding the water bowl with your right hand, and let the water slowly flow over the deity. Do this three times. If you are bathing wooden deities, you simply bring the deity near the bathing receptacle and bathe the reflection in the water. You do not pour water directly over the wooden deity, except for the Snana-yatra festival which takes place a week or two before the Rathayatra festival.

While pouring water over the deities, chant the following mantras from the *Brahma-samhita*. Sometimes it is nice to simply play a tape of the chanting.

chintamani-prakara-sadmasu kalpa-vriksha-
lakshavriteshu surabhir abhipalayantam
lakshmi-sahasra-shata-sambhrama-sevyamanam
govindam adi-purusham tam aham bhajami

"I worship Govinda, the Primeval Lord, the First Progenitor Who is tending the cows, yielding all desires, in abodes built with spiritual gems, surrounded by millions of purpose-trees, always served with great reverence and affection by hundreds of thousands of Lakshmis or Gopis."

venum kvanantam aravinda-dalayataksam
barhavatam samasitambuda-sundarangam
kandarpa-koti-kamaniya vishesha-shobham
govindam adi-purusham tam aham bhajami

"I worship Govinda, the Primeval Lord, Who is adept in playing on His flute, with blooming eyes like lotus petals, with head bedecked with peacock's feather, with the figure of beauty tinged with the hue of blue clouds, and His unique loveliness charming millions of cupids."

Alternatively you can also simply chant the Hare Krishna maha-mantra.

10. Now remove the deity from the bowl or bathing receptacle which collects the water, and dry the deity with the soft towels. Now, similarly, bathe each of the other deities.

11. Now dress the deities with the undergarments and then the outfit for the day. Then add the ornaments and jewelry, and then the flower garlands. This part itself may require some explaining and demonstrations from someone who is experienced.

12. Now you can offer flowers and Tulasi leaves with sandalwood paste to the lotus feet of the deities.

13. Optionally you may also offer, A. incense with right hand while ringing the bell in your left hand, B. a ghee or camphor lamp, also while ringing the bell, C. and fruit or sweets and drinking water while ringing the bell.

Now that the deities are bathed and dressed, They are ready for being greeted, which is done in the temples by the opening of the curtains which reveal the deities in Their newly dressed outfits, flower garlands, etc., to all who have assembled to see Them. When this is performed, this is when the deities get a short *arati* called the *dhup-arati* ceremony, when They are offered incense, a flower, the *chamara* fan, and then a mirror to allow the deities to view Themselves and see how They look.

Shortly after this, the deities are also offered Their breakfast offering, which includes several items at the temples, but may include only whatever will be served later to the family at home. The process of offering food has been described earlier.

After this, we can use some time to spend chanting Hare Krishna on our *japa* beads as part of our morning program. However, if someone else was dressing the deities, it is during that time in which we do our *japa* meditation. If we do not complete chanting all of our *japa*, then we can finish later.

PUTTING THE DEITIES TO REST

In the Krishna temples and Bhakti Centers where they have deities, they will dress the deities in Their nightclothes before putting them to rest. This means to take Their day clothes off and dress Them for the evening. You may consider doing something similar if you have the means to get this involved with your home deities.

If you want to start doing this, then after being cleaned and doing *achamana*, you may bring the night dresses to the altar, then you can approach the deities and remove Their garlands and jewelry, take off Their day clothes, dress Them in Their night clothes, and prepare Them for bed. In the temples the deities get one last small *arati* before They take rest, and may even be offered some warm milk. After the deities have accepted this and we have transferred the milk from the deity's cups to a serving container, then we can accept it as *prasada* before we go to bed.

Whether we dress our home deities in the evening or not, if we also wish to put the deities to sleep in the evening, there are a few ways we can do that. We can place Their shoes next to the beds, and then chant the mantras inviting Them to take rest, maybe leave some cups of fresh water on the altar, and then leave the altar area, and turn out the lights. If you have no beds for Them, you can place little pillows in front of Them, or at Their feet, especially if They are large and cannot be moved so easily, and then chant the mantras for asking Them to take rest, and meditate that They are going to bed. If there is no room on the altar for the beds or pillows, then such items can also be placed on a small table in front of the altar. However, if you have small deities, you can have small beds made and then place the deities in the bed. There are different ways you can do this.

When putting the deities to rest, for Sri Sri Radha-Krishna you can chant this mantra from the *Hari-bhakti-vilasa* (11.40) while touching Their lotus feet: *agaccha shayana-sthanam priyabhih saha keshava*, "O Keshava, kindly come to Your bed along with Shrimati Radharani."

Then Krishna's flute should be placed under the pillow, and Krishna should be placed in bed alongside Shrimati Radharani, and this should be indicated by bringing the wooden slippers from the altar to the bedside. Before laying the deity down, a pot of milk and sugar can be offered to Him. After taking this thick milk, the deity should lie down and can be offered betel nuts and spices to chew. It is also nice to fluff up the pillow or bedding, or even place flower petals in the bed. This can also be done by meditation.

Once the deities are in bed, you can also massage Their lotus feet to relax Them, or meditate on doing so. Then cover Them with the bedding that is suitable to the room temperature. (Some of this may be a little difficult for some householders, but this is a nice standard if you can do it, which is followed by many temples, or something similar. And if you can not do all this, then do what you can do.) If you have other deities, then put Radha-Krishna to bed first, then Jagannatha, Baladeva and Subhadra, followed by Gaura-Nitai.

Now you can also ask your spiritual master to take rest, and meditate on his photo that he is taking rest. Offer obeisances, turn out the altar lights, or the lights to your temple room, and then leave the room. Now take any clothing and jewelry that have been taken off the deities from their day dress and put them into proper storage places.

When inviting the deities to take rest, you can chant the following Sanskrit verses, or the English translations, or simply ask the deities to please take rest. For Radha Krishna, you can chant:

agaccha shayana-sthanam priyabhih saha keshava
divya-pushpatya-shayyayam sukham vihara madhava

"Now come, O Keshava, along with Your beloved Shrimati Radharani and Her friends, to the bed covered with transcendental, aromatic flowers. Now happily enjoy Your pastimes, O Madhava."

For Jagannatha, Balarama and Subhadra:

agaccha shayana-sthanam agrajena hy adhokshaja
agaccha nija-shayyam cha subhadre me dayamkuru

"O Lord Jagannatha, if You please, You and Your elder brother Balarama may now come to Your beds. O Mother Subhadra, please come to your resting place and kindly bestow your mercy upon me."

For Lord Chaitanya:

*agaccha vishrama-sthanam sva-ganaih saha gauranga
kshanam vishramya sukhena lilaya vihara prabho*

"O Lord Gauranga, please come to Your resting place along with Your associates. O Lord, rest comfortably for a moment, enjoying Your pastimes."

For Lord Nityananda:

*agaccha shayana-sthanam nityananda jagad-guro
tava rupe maha-vishnor anante shayanam kuru*

"O spiritual master of the universe, Lord Nityananda, please come to Your place of rest. In your form of Maha-Vishnu, please rest upon the thousand-headed serpent known as Shesha."

If you have a deity of Srila Prabhupada, you may put him into a bed, or if you have a photo, touch the base of his picture as in touching his feet while chanting the following mantra and meditate that he is going to bed:

agaccha shayana-sthanam sva-ganaih saha parama-guro

"O grand spiritual master, please come to your resting place, along with all your associates."

For your own spiritual master:

agaccha shayana-sthanam sva-ganaih saha shri-guro

"O spiritual master, please come to your resting place, along with all your associates."

IF YOU MUST LEAVE THE DEITIES AT HOME

When you travel away from home, you may not be there to take care of your altar or deities, so what do we do? If you are going to be away for a short time, you may simply put the deities to rest and let Them remain until you return. Pray for forgiveness for any neglect, but that you will continue your worship when you return. Or you can also bring along photos of the deities when you travel so that the deities may be at rest at home, but you continue Their worship in a simple way through Their photos. Or you may also bring your deities to the house of another devotee friend, someone who will continue the worship for you while you are gone. This way They still get the worship and attention that you have maintained.

CONCLUSION

What to Expect From Your Practice

As I previously explained, this book is only about how to begin the basics of bhakti-yoga. Nonetheless, it will take you far in your spiritual progress by incorporating as much of the practices described herein as you can, and then also learning more about the philosophy as you continue your practice. No matter how much you accomplish materially, intellectually, physically, and so on, only by adding spirituality to your life can you actually reach your highest potential. And this practice, as outlined in this book, will help you do that.

Many years ago it was expected that the practicing yogi learn how to meditate for long periods of time, even years without interruption. This book teaches you how you can begin to apply the basics of bhakti-yoga into all aspects of your life, even up to 24 hours a day. Even sleeping can be done for Krishna's service, but not that we oversleep. This means that every minute of the day can have some connection with our practice of bhakti-yoga, and, thus, we can also be engaged in meditation for long periods of time.

The main thing is that if you chant the Hare Krishna mantra in your *japa* meditation, up to the standard of 16 rounds a day, follow the four regulative principles, learn how to do or attend the *arati* of the deity, associate with other devotees who are practicing bhakti-yoga, and honor Krishna *prasada* when eating, and continue to study such books as *Bhagavad-gita* or *Srimad-Bhagavatam* or other authorized texts, then you will make great strides in your spiritual development, up to attaining the direct reciprocation from Lord Krishna Himself. Then you will realize the importance and validity of this process as others have.

A person should also be serious and eager to take up this path. And he or she must continue if there are to be any significant results. It is like tending a garden: it must be done carefully and continuously if you want to have anything to harvest. You cannot change your mind later or change what crops you are growing halfway through the season if you want to see the results. You have to stick with it. So I have one other mantra that I use, which is: "Never give up. Never give up. Never give up." That mantra has served me better than anyone can know. No matter how I feel, or how things seem to be developing, never give up. Often I have seen that just when a person is about to make a major breakthrough, they give up or change their mind and lower their determination. Then they have to pick themselves up later and start again. Do not think that the illusory energy or our memories of past material attachments will not try to hold us back. But that is only the mind, which must be overcome. There are many instructions for that in the bhakti-yoga philosophy.

However, remember, this is a joyous process. And compared to other yoga systems, it is also very simple. You can easily get a taste for the things you do very quickly, which will help you continue in this process. Every step can offer greater and deeper insights, new perspectives about life and yourself, and how to be truly happy. As you go deeper, you will see your real identity as more than just this material body, and also your relationship with God will become increasingly apparent. God loves everyone, and He is only waiting for us to turn toward Him. And bhakti-yoga is the direct process of turning toward God and asking for His help. The more we ask and pray for it, the more that help will be there for us. We only need to become increasingly qualified to recognize the assistance and reciprocation from God that has always been available, like the shining of the sun. It is always there, though it may appear to be dark at times. But if we do not hide in our closet or somewhere, the sunshine is bound to reach us at some point. It is there for everyone, if we are willing to receive it. And bhakti-yoga is the process by which we become qualified to receive and recognize the loving mercy that God has been sending us in so many ways.

GLOSSARY

Acharya--the spiritual master who sets the proper standard by his own example.

Acintya-bhedabheda-tattva--simultaneously one and different. The doctrine Lord Sri Caitanya taught referring to the Absolute as being both personal and impersonal.

Advaita--nondual, meaning that the Absolute is one with the infinitesimal souls with no individuality between them. The philosophy of Sankaracharya.

Agni--fire, or Agni the demigod of fire.

Agnihotra--the Vedic sacrifice in which offerings were made to the fire, such as ghee, milk, sesame seeds, grains, etc. The demigod Agni would deliver the offerings to the demigods that were referred to in the ritual.

Ahankara--false ego, identification with matter.

Ahimsa--nonviolence.

Akarma--actions which cause no *karmic* reactions.

Akasha--the ether, or etheric plane; a subtle material element in which sound travels.

Ananda--spiritual bliss.

Ananta--unlimited.

Aranyaka--sacred writings that are supposed to frame the essence of the *Upanishads*.

Arati--the ceremony of worship when incense and ghee lamps are offered to the Deities.

Arca-vigraha--the worshipable Deity form of the Lord made of stone, wood, etc. Aryan--a noble person, one who is on the path of spiritual advancement.

Asana--postures for meditation, or exercises for developing the body into a fit instrument for spiritual advancement.

Asat--that which is temporary.

Ashrama--one of the four orders of spiritual life, such as *brahmachari* (celibate student), *grihastha* (married householder), *vanaprastha* (retired stage), and *sannyasa* (renunciate); or the abode of a spiritual teacher or *sadhu*.

Atma--the self or soul. Sometimes means the body, mind, and senses.

Avatara--an incarnation of the Lord who descends from the spiritual world.

Avidya--ignorance or nescience.

Aum--om or *pranava*

Ayurveda--the original holistic form of medicine as described in the Vedic literature.

Bhagavan--one who possesses all opulences, God.

Bhajan--song of worship.

Bhakta--a devotee of the Lord who is engaged in *bhakti-yoga*.

Bhakti--love and devotion for God.

Bhakti-yoga--the path of offering pure devotional service to the Supreme.

Brahma--the demigod of creation who was born from Lord Vishnu, the first created living being and the engineer of the secondary stage of creation of the universe when all the living entities were manifested.

Brahmachari--a celebate student who is trained by the spiritual master. One of the four divisions or ashramas of spiritual life.

Brahmajyoti--the great white light or effulgence which emanates from the body of the Lord.

Brahmaloka--the highest planet or plane of existence in the universe; the planet where Lord Brahma lives.

Brahman--the spiritual energy; the all-pervading impersonal aspect of the Lord; or the Supreme Lord Himself.

Brahmana or brahmin--one of the four orders of society; the intellectual class of men who have been trained in the knowledge of the *Vedas* and initiated by a spiritual master.

Brahmana--the supplemental books of the four primary *Vedas*. They usually contained instructions for performing Vedic *agnihotras*, chanting the *mantras*, the purpose of the rituals, etc. The *Aitareya* and *Kaushitaki Brahmanas* belong to the *Rig-veda*, the *Satapatha Brahmana* belongs to the *White Yajur-veda*, and the *Taittiriya Brahmana* belongs to the *Black Yajur-veda*. The *Praudha* and *Shadvinsa Brahmanas* are two of the eight *Brahmanas* belonging to the *Atharva-veda*.

Glossary

Brahminical--to be clean and upstanding, both outwardly and inwardly, like a brahmana should be.

Caitanya-caritamrita--the scripture by Krishnadasa Kaviraja which explains the teachings and pastimes of Lord Caitanya Mahaprabhu.

Caitanya Mahaprabhu--the most recent incarnation of the Lord who appeared in the 15th century in Bengal and who originally started the *sankirtana* movement, based on congregational chanting of the holy names.

Candala--a person in the lowest class, or dog-eater.

Darshan--the devotional act of seeing and being seen by the Deity in the temple.

Deity--the *arca-vigraha*, or worshipful form of the Supreme in the temple, or deity as the worshipful image of the demigod.

Devas--demigods or heavenly beings from higher levels of material existence, or a godly person.

Dharma--the essential nature or duty of the living being.

Diksha--spiritual initiation.

Dualism--as related in this book refers to the Supreme as both an impersonal force as well as a person.

Dvapara-yuga--the third age which lasts 864,000 years.

Dwaita--dualism, the principle that the Absolute Truth consists of the infinite Supreme Being and the infinitesimal individual souls.

Ekadasi--a fast day on the eleventh day of the waxing and waning moon.

Gandharvas--the celestial angel-like beings who have beautiful forms and voices, and are expert in dance and music, capable of becoming invisible and can help souls on the earthly plane.

Ganesh--a son of Shiva, said to destroy obstacles (as Vinayaka) and offer good luck to those who petition him.

Gaudiya *sampradaya*--the school of Vaishnavism founded by Sri Caitanya.

Gayatri--the spiritual vibration or *mantra* from which the other *Vedas* were expanded and which is chanted by those who are initiated as *brahmanas* and given the spiritual understanding of Vedic philosophy.

Goloka Vrindavana--the name of Lord Krishna's spiritual planet.

Gosvami--one who is master of the senses.

Govinda--a name of Krishna which means one who gives pleasure to the cows and senses.

Grihastha--the householder order of life. One of the four *ashramas* in spiritual life.

Gunas--the modes of material nature of which there is *sattva* (goodness), *rajas*(passion), and *tamas* (ignorance).

Guru--a spiritual master.

Hare--the Lord's pleasure potency, Radharani, who is approached for accessibility to the Lord.

Hari--a name of Krishna as the one who takes away one's obstacles on the spiritual path.

Haribol--a word that means to chant the name of the Lord, Hari.

Harinam--refers to the name of the Lord, Hari.

Hatha-yoga--a part of the yoga system which stresses various sitting postures and exercises.

Impersonalism--the view that God has no personality or form, but is only an impersonal force.

Impersonalist--those who believe God has no personality or form.

Incarnation--the taking on of a body or form.

Japa--the chanting one performs, usually softly, for one's own meditation.

Japa-mala--the string of beads one uses for chanting.

Jiva--the individual soul or living being.

Jivanmukta--a liberated soul, though still in the material body and universe.

Jnana--knowledge which may be material or spiritual.

Jnana-yoga--the process of linking with the Supreme through empirical knowledge and mental speculation.

Jnani--one engaged in jnana-yoga, or the process of cultivating knowledge to understand the Absolute.

Kali-yuga--the fourth and present age, the age of quarrel and confusion, which lasts 432,000 years and began 5,000 years ago.

Kalpa--a day in the life of Lord Brahma which lasts a thousand cycles of the four *yugas*.

Kama--lust or inordinate desire.

Kama sutra--a treatise on sex enjoyment.

Karanodakasayi Vishnu (Maha-Vishnu)--the expansion of Lord Krishna who created all the material universes.

Karma--material actions performed in regard to developing one's position or for future results which produce *karmic* reactions. It is also the reactions one endures from such fruitive activities.

Karma-yoga--the system of yoga for dovetailing one's activities for spiritual advancement.

Kirtana--chanting or singing the glories of the Lord.

Krishna--the name of the original Supreme Personality of Godhead which means the most attractive and greatest pleasure. He is the source of all other incarnations, such as Vishnu, Rama, Narasimha, Narayana, Buddha, Parashurama, Vamanadeva, Kalki at the end of Kali-yuga, etc.

Krishnaloka--the spiritual planet where Lord Krishna resides.

Kshatriya--the second class of *varna* of society, or occupation of administrative or protective service, such as warrior or military personel.

Ksirodakasayi Vishnu--the Supersoul expansion of the Lord who enters into each atom and the heart of each individual.

Lila--pastimes.

Mahabharata--the great epic of the Pandavas, which includes the *Bhagavad-gita*, by Vyasadeva.

Maha-mantra--the best mantra for self-realization in this age, called the Hare Krishna mantra.

Maha-Vishnu or Karanodakasayi Vishnu--the Vishnu expansion of Lord Krishna from whom all the material universes emanate.

Mandir--a temple.

Mantra--a sound vibration which prepares the mind for spiritual realization and delivers the mind from material inclinations. In some cases a mantra is chanted for specific material benefits.

Maya--illusion, or anything that appears to not be connected with the eternal Absolute Truth.

Mayavadi--the impersonalist or voidist who believes that the Supreme has no form.

Moksha--liberation from material existence.

Murti--a Deity of the Lord or spiritual master that is worshiped.

Om or *Omkara--pranava*, the transcendental *om mantra*, generally referring to the attributeless or impersonal aspects of the Absolute.

Paramahamsa--the highest level of self-realized devotees of the Lord.

Paramatma--the Supersoul, or localized expansion of the Lord.

Parampara--the system of disciplic succession through which transcendental knowledge descends.

Pranayama--control of the breathing process as in astanga or raja-yoga.

Prasada--food or other articles that have been offered to the Deity in the temple and then distributed amongst people as the blessings or mercy of the Deity.

Prema--matured love for Krishna.

Puja--the worship offered to the Deity.

Pujari--the priest who performs worship, *puja*, to the Deity.

Raja-yoga--the eightfold yoga system.

Ramayana--the great epic of the incarnation of Lord Ramachandra.

Sacrifice--in this book it in no way pertains to human sacrifice, as many people tend to think when this word is used. But it means to engage in an austerity of some kind for a higher, spiritual purpose.

Shabda-brahma--the original spiritual vibration or energy of which the *Vedas* are composed.

Sac-cid-ananda-vigraha--the transcendental form of the Lord or of the living entity which is eternal, full of knowledge and bliss.

Sadhana--a specific practice or discipline for attaining God realization.

Samsara--rounds of life; cycles of birth and death; reincarnation.

Sanatana-dharma--the eternal nature of the living being, to love and render service to the supreme lovable object, the Lord.

Sankirtana-yajna--the prescribed sacrifice for this age: congregational chanting of the holy names of God.

Sannyasa--the renounced order of life, the highest of the four *ashramas* on the spiritual path.

Sattva-guna--the material mode of goodness.

Satya-yuga--the first of the four ages which lasts 1,728,000 years.

Shaivites--worshipers of Lord Shiva.

Glossary

Shastra--the authentic revealed scripture.

Shiva--the benevolent one, the demigod who is in charge of the material mode of ignorance and the destruction of the universe. Part of the triad of Brahma, Vishnu, and Shiva who continually create, maintain, and destroy the universe. He is known as Rudra when displaying his destructive aspect.

Sikha or *shikha*--a tuft of hair on the back of the head signifying that one is a Vaishnava.

Smaranam--remembering the Lord.

Smriti--the traditional Vedic knowledge "that is remembered" from what was directly heard by or revealed to the *rishis*.

Sravanam--hearing about the Lord.

Srimad-Bhagavatam--the most ripened fruit of the tree of Vedic knowledge compiled by Vyasadeva.

Sruti--scriptures that were received directly from God and transmitted orally by brahmanas or *rishis* down through succeeding generations. Traditionally, it is considered the four primary *Vedas*.

Sudra--the working class of society, the fourth of the *varnas*.

Svami--one who can control his mind and senses.

Tamo-guna--the material mode of ignorance.

Tilaka--the clay markings that signify a person's body as a temple, and the sect or school of thought of the person.

Treta-yuga--the second of the four ages which lasts 1,296,000 years.

Tulasi--the small tree that grows where worship to Krishna is found. It is called the embodiment of devotion, and the incarnation of Vrinda-devi.

Upanishads--the portions of the *Vedas* which primarily explain philosophically the Absolute Truth. It is knowledge of Brahman which releases one from the world and allows one to attain self-realization when received from a qualified teacher. Except for the *Isa Upanishad*, which is the 40th chapter of the *Vajasaneyi Samhita* of the *Sukla* (*White*) *Yajur-veda*, the *Upanishads* are connected to the four primary *Vedas*, generally found in the *Brahmanas*.

Vaikunthas--the planets located in the spiritual sky.

Vaishnava--a worshiper of the Supreme Lord Vishnu or Krishna and His expansions or incarnations.

Vaishnava-*aparadha*--an offense against a Vaisnava or devotee, which can negate all of one's spiritual progress.

Vaisya--the third class of society engaged in business or farming.

Vanaprastha--the third of the four *ashramas* of spiritual life in which one retires from family life in preparation for the renounced order.

Varna--sometimes referred to as caste, a division of society, such as brahmana (a priestly intellectual), a kshatriya (ruler or manager), vaishya (a merchant, banker, or farmer), and sudra (common laborer).

Varnashrama--the system of four divisions of society and four orders of spiritual life.

Vedanta-sutras--the philosophical conclusion of the four *Vedas*.

Vedas--generally means the four primary *samhitas;* the *Rig, Yajur, Sama,* and *Atharva*.

Vrindavana--the place where Lord Krishna displayed His village pastimes 5,000 years ago, and is considered to be part of the spiritual abode.

Vyasadeva--the incarnation of God who appeared as the greatest philosopher who compiled all the *Vedas* into written form.

Yajna--a ritual or austerity that is done as a sacrifice for spiritual merit, or ritual worship of a demigod for good *karmic* reactions.

Yoga--linking up with the Absolute.

Yuga-avataras--the incarnations of God who appear in each of the four *yugas* to explain the authorized system of self-realization in that age.

REFERENCES

Art of Chanting Hare Krishna, Mahanidhia Swami, 2002.
Atharva-veda, translated by Devi Chand, Munshiram Manoharlal, Delhi, 1980
Bhagavad-gita As It Is, translated by A. C. Bhaktivedanta Swami, Bhaktivedanta Book Trust, New York/Los Angeles, 1972
Bhakti-rasamrita-sindhu, (Nectar of Devotion), translated by A. C. Bhaktivedanta Swami, Bhaktivedanta Book Trust, New York/Los Angeles, 1970
Bhakti Rasamarita Sindhu, by Srila Rupa Gosvami, trans. By Bhanu Swami, Sri Vaikuntha Enterprises, Chennai, 2003
Brahma-samhita, translated by Bhaktisiddhanta Sarasvati Gosvami Thakur, Bhaktivedanta Book Trust, New York/Los Angeles,
Brahma-Sutras, translated by Swami Vireswarananda and Adidevananda, Advaita Ashram, Calcutta, 1978
Brahma-Vaivarta Purana, translated by Shanti Lal Nagar, edited by Acharya Ramesh Chaturvedi, Parimal Publications, Delhi, 2005.
Brihan-naradiya Purana
Brihadaranyaka Upanishad
Caitanya-caritamrta, translated by A. C. Bhaktivedanta Swami, Bhaktivedanta Book Trust, Los Angeles, 1974
Caitanya Upanisad, translated by Kusakratha dasa, Bala Books, New York, 1970
Chandogya Upanishad,
Gitagovinda of Jayadeva, Barbara Stoller Miller, Motilal Banarsidass, Delhi, 1977
Gopal-tapani Upanishad, by Krsna Dvaipayana Vedavyasa, commentary by Visvanatha Cakravarti Thakura, translated by Bhumipati dasa, Ras Bihari Lal & Sons, Loi Bazaar, Vrindaban, UP, 281121, India, 2004
Hari-bhakti-vilasa,
Jaiva Dharma, Srila Thakur Bhakti Vinod, trans. By Bhakti Sadhaka Nishkinchana, Sree Gaudiya Math
Kali-santarana Upanishad,

The Law of Manu, [*Manu-samhita*], translated by Georg Buhlerg, Motilal Banarsidass, Delhi, 1970

Mahabharata, Kesari Mohan Ganguli, Munshiram Manoharlal Publisher Pvt., Ltd., New Delhi, 1970

Mahabharata, Sanskrit Text With English Translations, by M. N. Dutt, Parimal Publications, Delhi, 2001

Minor Upanishads, translated by Swami Madhavananda, Advaita Ashram, Calcutta, 1980; contains Paramahamsopanishad, Atmopanishad, Amritabindupanishad, Tejabindupanishad, Sarvopanishad, Brahmopanisad, Aruneyi Upanishad, Kaivalyopanishad.

Narada-Bhakti-Sutra, A. C. Bhaktivedanta Swami, Bhaktivedanta Book Trust, Los Angeles, 1991

Padma Purana, tr. by S. Venkitasubramonia Iyer, Banarsidass, Delhi, 1988

Siksashtaka, of Sri Caitanya Mahaprabhu.

Skanda Purana, by Srila Vyasadeva, Purnaprajna Dasa, Rasbihari Lal & Sons, Vrindavana, India, 2005.

Sri Brihat Bhagavatamritam, by Sri Srila Sanatana Gosvami, Sree Gaudiya Math, Madras, India, 1987

Sri Caitanya Bhagavat, by Sri Vrindavan dasa Thakura, 1538 AD.

Sri Caitanya Mangala, Locana Dasa Thakura, trans., by Subhag Swami, published by Mahanidhi Swami, Vrindavana, 1994

Sri Caitanya Upanishad, from the Atharva-veda

Sri Gopala-Tapani Upanishad, from the Atharva-Veda,

Sri Hari-bhakti-vilasa, Vilasas I & II, Srila Sanatana Gosvami, and *Panca-samskara*, by Saccidananda Thakura Bhaktivinoda, Brihat Mrdanga Press, Vrindavana, India, 2005

Svetasvatara Upanishad,

Twelve Essential Upanishads, by Tridandi Bhakti Prajnan Yati, Sree Gaudiya Math, Madras, 1983

Upadesamrta (Nectar of Instruction), translated by A. C. Bhaktivedanta Swami, Bhaktivedanta Book Trust, New York/Los Angeles, 1975

The Upanishads, translated by Swami Prabhavananda and Frederick Manchester, New American Library, New York, 1957; contains Katha, Isha, Kena, Prasna, Mundaka, Mandukya, Taittiriya,

Aitareya, Chandogya, Brihadaranyaka, Kaivalya, and Svetasvatara Upanishads.

Vedanta-Sutras of Badarayana with Commentary of Baladeva Vidyabhusana, translated by Rai Bahadur Srisa Chandra Vasu, Munshiram Manoharlal, New Delhi, 1979

White Yajurveda, translated by Griffith, The Chowkhamba Sanskrit Series Office, Varanasi, 1976

Yajurveda, translated by Devi Chand, Munshiram Manoharlal, Delhi, 1980

INDEX

Achamana 132
Achintya-bhedabheda-tattva. 68
Agamas. 105
Altar
    making one at home. . . 127
    taking care of it. 128
Arabic numerals
    from India. 123
Arati
    how to do this ceremony131
    learning to do this ceremony
    133
Arati ceremony 96
Archa-vigraha
    worshipable deity form of
    God. 71
Aryanakas.. 102
Asanas
    promotes better health. . 23
Association
    getting the best. 16
Astanga-yoga. 10
Atharva Veda 102
Ayurveda. 124
    meaning of the word. . . 124
    origin is lost in antiquity124
Bathing. 21
Being spiritual 23
Bells
    why ring them in the temple
    95
Bhagavad-gita. 104
Bhagavatam. 105
Bhakti-yoga. 10
    beginning the day. 20
    how this can affect you. 160
    the nine processes. 91
Bhakti-yogi
    at home or temple ashrama
    15
Brahma-muhurta hour. 20
Brahma-samhita. 39, 70
Brahmanas. 102
Chaitanya Mahaprabhu
    predictions of His
    appearance. 66
    who He is. 64
Chanting the holy names
    how to chant. 60
    the different stages. 60
Chaturmasya.. 90
Circumambulate
    its purpose.. 97
Cleanliness. 140
    in cooking and in kitchen
    140
Coconut
    its symbolism. 97
Conch shell
    significance of.. 96
Cooking
    making it bhakti-yoga. . 139
Cooking for God. 140
Damodarashtaka.. 48
Dance in India. 125
Dancing in the kirtana. 82

Index

Dandavat. 101
Darshan. 72, 125
Death. 111
Deities
    bathing and dressing Them
    154
    putting Them to rest. . . 157
    significance of Their worship. 70
    taking care of Them. . . 151
    waking Them in the morning. 152
Deity worship
    qualifications for. 152
Devotional Texts
    importance of reading them
    73
Dhoti. 99
Ekadasi
    the mother of devotion. . 88
    the special day. 85
Fasting
    its purpose. 98
Festivals. 89
Food
    offering it to God. 141
Gambling. 17
Gaura-Arati. 47
Gemology. 124
God
    has a form. 70
Greek
    mathematics. 123
Greeting the deities. 70
Guru
    purpose of having one. . . 94

Guru-Vandana. 39
Gurudeva. 53
Gurvashtaka. 25
Hare Krishna
    on chanting the mantra. . 58
Hare Krishna mantra
    contains everything for well-being. 61
    the process for chanting. 60
Hatha-yoga. 24
Instruments
    learning how to play. . . . 83
Intoxication. 18
Itihasas. 103
Jagannathashtaka. 51
Japa beads. 62
Japa mediation. 15
Jaya Radha-Madhava. 34
Jnana-yoga. 10, 16
Jyotish. 124
Karma. 114
    explanation of. 114
Karma-yoga. 10
Katha Upanishad. 109
Kirtana. 83
Krishna
    everything about Him is spiritually sweet. . . . 61
    explanation of the name.117
    instructs in Bhagavad-gita
    10
    the Supreme Being. . . . 116
    who is He?. 117
Lamps in the temple. 96
law of cause and effect. . . . 114
Lotus flower

its significance. 97
Mahabharata 103
Mangala-arati. 23
Mantra-yoga
    especially for this age. . . 25
Mantras
    for foregiveness of any offenses. 136
    used in bhakti-yoga. 25
Meat-eating
    giving it up. 17
Nama-Kirtana. 40
Nama-Sankirtana. 46
Namaste. 94
Nirjala Ekadasi. 89
Nrisimha Pranam 29
Obeisances. 101
Offering
    food to God. 141
Pancha-tattva mantra. 64
Pranam mantras. 28
Pranama Mantras. 36
Pranayama. 24
Prasada-sevaya. 42
Prasadam
    how to turn food into it. 121
    sacred food. 80
Puja
    doing a simple worship. 131
    doing simple worship. . 128
Punctuality   190
Puranas. 105
Pythagorean theorem
    already existing in Vedic mathematics. 124
Raja-yoga. 10

Ramayana. 103
Red forehead dots 94
Regulative principles. 16
Reincarnation
    explanation of. 111
Rig Veda 102
Sacred thread. 100
Sadhana
    regular spiritual practice. . 7
Saffron
    the meaning of this color.99
Sama Veda. 102
Sanatana-dharma
    the Vedic process. 98
Sari. 99
Sat-chit-ananda vigraha
    form of God. 71
Shikha
    the tuft of hair. 100
Shikshashtaka. 32
Shiva
    known as Nataraja. . . . 125
Shopping
    for our food. 139
Shri Shri Shad-Goswamy-Ashtaka. 43
Shruti. 101
Shulba Sutras. 123
Shulba Sutras 123
Smriti. 101
Songs
    used in bhakti-yoga. 25
Soul
    explanation of. 108
Spiritually, we do not die. . 108
Srimad Bhagavata Purana . 105

Srimad-Bhagavatam
    its importance. 73
Srimad-Bhagavatam 108
Svetasvatara Upanishad. . . 109
Tantras. 106
Temple Etiquette. 82
Ten offenses to chanting. . . 31
Tilaka. 21, 95
Tulasi
    taking care of her. 144
Tulasi arati kirtan. 29
Tulasi puja 75
Tulasi tree
    her importance. 76
    how to worship her. 75
    who she is. 75
Unnecessary sex 18
Upanishads. 101, 102
Vaikuntha. 61
Vastu. 124

Vedanta Sutras 103
Vedic art 124
Vedic culture
    how it is still relevant today
    123
Vedic dance 125
Vedic mathematics 123
    continues to be important in
        modern society. . . . 123
Vedic process
    who may practice it. 98
Vegetarian
    why be one. 119
Vegetarianism
    going beyond that. 121
Yajur Veda. 102
Yoga
    benefits. 23

ABOUT THE AUTHOR

Stephen Knapp grew up in a Christian family, during which time he seriously studied the Bible to understand its teachings. In his late teenage years, however, he sought answers to questions not easily explained in Christian theology. So he began to search through other religions and philosophies from around the world and started to find the answers for which he was looking. He also studied a variety of occult sciences, ancient mythology, mysticism, yoga, and the spiritual teachings of the East. After his first reading of the *Bhagavad-gita*, he felt he had found the last piece of the puzzle he had been putting together through all of his research. Therefore, he continued to study all of the major Vedic texts of India to gain a better understanding of the Vedic science.

It is known amongst all Eastern mystics that anyone, regardless of qualifications, academic or otherwise, who does not engage in the spiritual practices described in the Vedic texts cannot actually enter into understanding the depths of the Vedic spiritual science, nor acquire the realizations that should accompany it. So, rather than pursuing his research in an academic atmosphere at a university, Stephen directly engaged in the spiritual disciplines that have been recommended for hundreds of years. He continued his study of Vedic knowledge and spiritual practice under the guidance of a spiritual master. Through this process, and with the sanction of His Divine Grace A. C. Bhaktivedanta Swami Prabhupada, he became initiated into the genuine and authorized spiritual line of the Brahma-Madhava-Gaudiya *sampradaya*, which is a disciplic succession that descends back through Sri Chaitanya Mahaprabhu and Sri Vyasadeva, the compiler of Vedic literature, and further back to Sri Krishna. At that time he was given the spiritual name of Sri Nandanandana dasa. In this way, he has been practicing yoga, especially bhakti-yoga, for forty plus years, and has attained many insights and realizations through this means. Besides being *brahminically* initiated, Stephen has also been to India several times and traveled extensively throughout the country, visiting most of the major holy places and gaining a wide variety of spiritual experiences that only such places can give. He has also spent nearly 40 years in the management of various temples.

About the Author

Stephen has put the culmination of over forty years of continuous research and travel experience into his books in an effort to share it with those who are also looking for spiritual understanding. More books are forthcoming, so stay in touch through his website to find out further developments.

More information about Stephen, his projects, books, free ebooks, and numerous articles and videos can be found on his website at: www.stephen-knapp.com or http://stephenknapp.info or his blog at http://stephenknapp.wordpress.com.

Stephen has continued to write books that include in *The Eastern Answers ot the Mysteries of Life* series:
1. *The Secret Teachings of the Vedas: The Eastern Answers to the Mysteries of Life*
2. *The Universal Path to Enlightenment*
3. *The Vedic Prophecies: A New Look into the Future*
4. *How the Universe was Created and Our Purpose In It*
     He has also written:
5. *Toward World Peace: Seeing the Unity Between Us All*
6. *Facing Death: Welcoming the Afterlife*
7. *The Key to Real Happiness*
8. *Proof of Vedic Culture's Global Existence*
9. *The Heart of Hinduism: The Eastern Path to Freedom, Enlightenment and Illumination*
10. *The Power of the Dharma: An Introduction to Hinduism and Vedic Culture*
11. *Vedic Culture: The Difference it can Make in Your Life*
12. *Reincarnation & Karma: How They Really Affect Us*
13. *The Eleventh Commandment: The Next Step for Social Spiritual Development*
14. *Seeing Spiritual India: A Guide to Temples, Holy Sites, Festivals and Traditions*
15. *Crimes Against India: And the Need to Protect its Ancient Vedic Tradition*
16. *Yoga and Meditation: Their Real Purpose and How to Get Started*

17. *Avatars, Gods and Goddesses of Vedic Culture: Understanding the Characteristics, Powers and Positions of the Hindu Divinities*
18. *The Soul: Understanding Our Real Identity*
19. *Prayers, Mantras and Gayatris: A Collection for Insights, Protection, Spiritual Growth, and Many Other Blessings*
20. *Krishna Deities and Their Miracles: How the Images of Lord Krishna Interact with Their Devotees*
21. *Defending Vedic Dharma: Tackling the Issues to Make a Difference*
22. *Advancements of the Ancient Vedic Culture*
23. *Spreading Vedic Traditions Through Temples*
24. *Destined for Infinity*, an exciting novel for those who prefer lighter reading, or learning spiritual knowledge in the context of an action oriented, spiritual adventure.

If you have enjoyed this book, or if you are serious about finding higher levels of real spiritual Truth, and learning more about the mysteries of India's Vedic culture, then you will also want to get other books written by Stephen Knapp, which include:

The Secret Teachings of the Vedas
The Eastern Answers to the Mysteries of Life

This book presents the essence of the ancient Eastern philosophy and summarizes some of the most elevated and important of all spiritual knowledge. This enlightening information is explained in a clear and concise way and is essential for all who want to increase their spiritual understanding, regardless of what their religious background may be. If you are looking for a book to give you an in-depth introduction to the Vedic spiritual knowledge, and to get you started in real spiritual understanding, this is the book!

The topics include: What is your real spiritual identity; the Vedic explanation of the soul; scientific evidence that consciousness is separate from but interacts with the body; the real unity between us all; how to attain the highest happiness and freedom from the cause of suffering; the law of karma and reincarnation; the karma of a nation; where you are really going in life; the real process of progressive evolution; life after death—heaven, hell, or beyond; a description of the spiritual realm; the nature of the Absolute Truth—personal God or impersonal force; recognizing the existence of the Supreme; the reason why we exist at all; and much more. This book provides the answers to questions not found in other religions or philosophies, and condenses information from a wide variety of sources that would take a person years to assemble. It also contains many quotations from the Vedic texts to let the texts speak for themselves, and to show the knowledge the Vedas have held for thousands of years. It also explains the history and origins of the Vedic literature. This book has been called one of the best reviews of Eastern philosophy available.

Trim size 6"x9", 320 pages, ISBN: 0-9617410-1-5, $14.95.

The Universal Path to Enlightenment
The Way to Spiritual Success for Everyone

This book brings together the easy and joyful principles and practices that are common to all major religions of the world. These are what can be used by all people from any culture or tradition for the highest spiritual progress, and to bring about a united, one world religion. This is a happy process of spiritual success for everyone. This is much easier to recognize than most people think, and is a way to bring down the differences, barriers and separations that seem to exist between religions. This book also presents:

- A most interesting and revealing survey of the major spiritual paths of the world, describing their histories, goals, and how they developed, which are not always what we would expect of a religion;
- The philosophical basis of Christianity, Judaism, Islam, Hinduism, Buddhism, Zoroastrianism, Jainism, Sikhism, etc., and the types of spiritual knowledge they contain;
- How Christianity and Judaism were greatly influenced by the early pre-Christian or "pagan" religions and adopted many of their legends, holidays, and rituals that are still accepted and practiced today;
- The essential teachings of Jesus;
- Benefits of spiritual advancement that affect all aspects of a person's life, and the world in which we live;
- How spiritual enlightenment is the real cure for social ills;
- And, most importantly, how to attain the real purpose of a spiritual process to be truly successful, and how to practice the path that is especially recommended as the easiest and most effective for the people of this age.

This book is 6"x9" trim size, 340 pages, ISBN: 1453644660, $19.95.

The Vedic Prophecies:
A New Look into the Future

The Vedic prophecies take you to the end of time! This is the first book ever to present the unique predictions found in the ancient Vedic texts of India. These prophecies are like no others and will provide you with a very different view of the future and how things fit together in the plan for the universe.

Now you can discover the amazing secrets that are hidden in the oldest spiritual writings on the planet. Find out what they say about the distant future, and what the seers of long ago saw in their visions of the destiny of the world.

This book will reveal predictions of deteriorating social changes and how to avoid them; future droughts and famines; low-class rulers and evil governments; whether there will be another appearance (second coming) of God; and predictions of a new spiritual awareness and how it will spread around the world. You will also learn the answers to such questions as:

- Does the future get worse or better?
- Will there be future world wars or global disasters?
- What lies beyond the predictions of Nostradamus, the Mayan prophecies, or the Biblical apocalypse?
- Are we in the end times? How to recognize them if we are.
- Does the world come to an end? If so, when and how?

Now you can find out what the future holds. The Vedic Prophecies carry an important message and warning for all humanity, which needs to be understood now!

Trim size 6"x9", 325 pages, ISBN:0-9617410-4-X, $20.95.

How the Universe was Created And Our Purpose In It

This book provides answers and details about the process of creation that are not available in any other traditions, religions, or areas of science. It offers the oldest rendition of the creation and presents insights into the spiritual purpose of it and what we are really meant to do here.

Every culture in the world and most religions have their own descriptions of the creation, and ideas about from where we came and what we should do. Unfortunately, these are often short and generalized versions that lack details. Thus, they are often given no better regard than myths. However, there are descriptions that give more elaborate explanations of how the cosmic creation fully manifested which are found in the ancient Vedic *Puranas* of India, some of the oldest spiritual writings on the planet. These descriptions provide the details and answers that other versions leave out. Furthermore, these Vedic descriptions often agree, and sometimes disagree, with the modern scientific theories of creation, and offer some factors that science has yet to consider.

Now, with this book, we can get a clearer understanding of how this universe appears, what is its real purpose, from where we really came, how we fit into the plan for the universe, and if there is a way out of here. Some of the many topics included are:
- Comparisons between other creation legends.
- Detailed descriptions of the dawn of creation and how the material energy developed and caused the formation of the cosmos.
- What is the primary source of the material and spiritual elements.
- Insights into the primal questions of, "Who am I? Why am I here? Where have I come from? What is the purpose of this universe and my life?"
- An alternative description of the evolutionary development of the various forms of life.
- Seeing beyond the temporary nature of the material worlds, and more.

This book will provide some of the most profound insights into these questions and topics. It will also give any theist more information and understanding about how the universe is indeed a creation of God.

This book is 6" x 9" trim size, $19.95, 308 pages, ISBN: 1456460455.

Proof of Vedic Culture's Global Existence

This book provides evidence which makes it clear that the ancient Vedic culture was once a global society. Even today we can see its influence in any part of the world. Thus, it becomes obvious that before the world became full of distinct and separate cultures, religions and countries, it was once united in a common brotherhood of Vedic culture, with common standards, principles, and representations of God.

No matter what we may consider our present religion, society or country, we are all descendants of this ancient global civilization. Thus, the Vedic culture is the parent of all humanity and the original ancestor of all religions. In this way, we all share a common heritage.

This book is an attempt to allow humanity to see more clearly its universal roots. This book provides a look into:

- How Vedic knowledge was given to humanity by the Supreme.
- The history and traditional source of the Vedas and Vedic Aryan society.
- Who were the original Vedic Aryans. How Vedic society was a global influence and what shattered this world-wide society. How Sanskrit faded from being a global language.
- Many scientific discoveries over the past several centuries are only rediscoveries of what the Vedic literature already knew.
- How the origins of world literature are found in India and Sanskrit.
- The links between the Vedic and other ancient cultures, such as the Sumerians, Persians, Egyptians, Romans, Greeks, and others.
- Links between the Vedic tradition and Judaism, Christianity, Islam, and Buddhism.
- How many of the western holy sites, churches, and mosques were once the sites of Vedic holy places and sacred shrines.
- The Vedic influence presently found in such countries as Britain, France, Russia, Greece, Israel, Arabia, China, Japan, and in areas of Scandinavia, the Middle East, Africa, the South Pacific, and the Americas.
- Uncovering the truth of India's history: Powerful evidence that shows how many mosques and Muslim buildings were once opulent Vedic temples, including the Taj Mahal, Delhi's Jama Masjid, Kutab Minar, as well as buildings in many other cities, such as Agra, Ahmedabad, Bijapur, etc.
- How there is presently a need to plan for the survival of Vedic culture.

This book is sure to provide some amazing facts and evidence about the truth of world history and the ancient, global Vedic Culture. This book has enough startling information and historical evidence to cause a major shift in the way we view religious history and the basis of world traditions.

This book is 6"x9" trim size, 431 pages, ISBN: 978-1-4392-4648-1, $20.99.

Toward World Peace: Seeing the Unity Between Us All

This book points out the essential reasons why peace in the world and cooperation amongst people, communities, and nations have been so difficult to establish. It also advises the only way real peace and harmony amongst humanity can be achieved.

In order for peace and unity to exist we must first realize what barriers and divisions keep us apart. Only then can we break through those barriers to see the unity that naturally exists between us all. Then, rather than focus on our differences, it is easier to recognize our similarities and common goals. With a common goal established, all of humanity can work together to help each other reach that destiny.

This book is short and to the point. It is a thought provoking book and will provide inspiration for anyone. It is especially useful for those working in politics, religion, interfaith, race relations, the media, the United Nations, teaching, or who have a position of leadership in any capacity. It is also for those of us who simply want to spread the insights needed for bringing greater levels of peace, acceptance, unity, and equality between friends, neighbours, and communities. Such insights include:

- The factors that keep us apart.
- Breaking down cultural distinctions.
- Breaking down the religious differences.
- Seeing through bodily distinctions.
- We are all working to attain the same things.
- Our real identity: The basis for common ground.
- Seeing the Divinity within each of us.
- What we can do to bring unity between everyone we meet.

This book carries an important message and plan of action that we must incorporate into our lives and plans for the future if we intend to ever bring peace and unity between us.

This book is $6.95, 90 pages, 6" x 9" trim size, ISBN: 1452813744.

Facing Death
Welcoming the Afterlife

Many people are afraid of death, or do not know how to prepare for it nor what to expect. So this book is provided to relieve anyone of the fear that often accompanies the thought of death, and to supply a means to more clearly understand the purpose of it and how we can use it to our advantage. It will also help the survivors of the departed souls to better understand what has happened and how to cope with it. Furthermore, it shows that death is not a tragedy, but a natural course of events meant to help us reach our destiny.

This book is easy to read, with soothing and comforting wisdom, along with stories of people who have been with departing souls and what they have experienced. It is written especially for those who have given death little thought beforehand, but now would like to have some preparedness for what may need to be done regarding the many levels of the experience and what might take place during this transition.

To assist you in preparing for your own death, or that of a loved one, you will find guidelines for making one's final days as peaceful and as smooth as possible, both physically and spiritually. Preparing for deathcan transform your whole outlook in a positive way, if understood properly. Some of the topics in the book include:
- The fear of death and learning to let go.
- The opportunity of death: The portal into the next life.
- This earth and this body are no one's real home, so death is natural.
- Being practical and dealing with the final responsibilities.
- Forgiving yourself and others before you go.
- Being the assistant of one leaving this life.
- Connecting with the person inside the disease.
- Surviving the death of a loved one.
- Stories of being with dying, and an amazing near-death-experience.
- Connecting to the spiritual side of death.
- What happens while leaving the body.
- What difference the consciousness makes during death, and how to attain the best level of awareness to carry you through it, or what death will be like and how to prepare for it, this book will help you.

Published by iUniverse.com, $13.95, 135 pages, ISBN: 978-1-4401-1344-4

Destined for Infinity

Deep within the mystical and spiritual practices of India are doors that lead to various levels of both higher and lower planes of existence. Few people from the outside are ever able to enter into the depths of these practices to experience such levels of reality.

This is the story of the mystical adventure of a man, Roman West, who entered deep into the secrets of India where few other Westerners have been able to penetrate. While living with a master in the Himalayan foothills and traveling the mystical path that leads to the Infinite, he witnesses the amazing powers the mystics can achieve and undergoes some of the most unusual experiences of his life. Under the guidance of a master that he meets in the mountains, he gradually develops mystic abilities of his own and attains the sacred vision of the enlightened sages and enters the unfathomable realm of Infinity. However, his peaceful life in the hills comes to an abrupt end when he is unexpectedly forced to confront the powerful forces of darkness that have been unleashed by an evil Tantric priest to kill both Roman and his master. His only chance to defeat the intense forces of darkness depends on whatever spiritual strength he has been able to develop.

This story includes traditions and legends that have existed for hundreds and thousands of years. All of the philosophy, rituals, mystic powers, forms of meditation, and descriptions of the Absolute are authentic and taken from narrations found in many of the sacred books of the East, or gathered by the author from his own experiences in India and information from various sages themselves.

This book will will prepare you to perceive the multi-dimensional realities that exist all around us, outside our sense perception. This is a book that will give you many insights into the broad possibilities of our life and purpose in this world.

Published by iUniverse.com, 255 pages, 6" x 9" trim size, $16.95, ISBN: 0-595-33959-X.

Reincarnation and Karma: How They Really Affect Us

Everyone may know a little about reincarnation, but few understand the complexities and how it actually works. Now you can find out how reincarnation and karma really affect us. Herein all of the details are provided on how a person is implicated for better or worse by their own actions. You will understand why particular situations in life happen, and how to make improvements for one's future. You will see why it appears that bad things happen to good people, or even why good things happen to bad people, and what can be done about it.

Other topics include:

- Reincarnation recognized throughout the world
- The most ancient teachings on reincarnation
- Reincarnation in Christianity
- How we transmigrate from one body to another
- Life between lives
- Going to heaven or hell
- The reason for reincarnation
- Free will and choice
- Karma of the nation
- How we determine our own destiny
- What our next life may be like
- Becoming free from all karma and how to prepare to make our next life the best possible.

Combine this with modern research into past life memories and experiences and you will have a complete view of how reincarnation and karma really operate.

Published by iUniverse.com, 135 pages, 6" x 9" trim size, $13.95, ISBN: 0-595-34199-3.

Vedic Culture
The Difference It Can Make In Your Life

The Vedic culture of India is rooted in Sanatana-dharma, the eternal and universal truths that are beneficial to everyone. It includes many avenues of self-development that an increasing number of people from the West are starting to investigate and use, including:

- Yoga
- Meditation and spiritual practice
- Vedic astrology
- Ayurveda
- Vedic gemology
- Vastu or home arrangement
- Environmental awareness
- Vegetarianism
- Social cooperation and arrangement
- The means for global peace
- And much more

Vedic Culture: The Difference It Can Make In Your Life shows the advantages of the Vedic paths of improvement and self-discovery that you can use in your life to attain higher personal awareness, happiness, and fulfillment. It also provides a new view of what these avenues have to offer from some of the most prominent writers on Vedic culture in the West, who discovered how it has affected and benefited their own lives. They write about what it has done for them and then explain how their particular area of interest can assist others. The noted authors include, David Frawley, Subhash Kak, Chakrapani Ullal, Michael Cremo, Jeffrey Armstrong, Robert Talyor, Howard Beckman, Andy Fraenkel, George Vutetakis, Pratichi Mathur, Dhan Rousse, Arun Naik, Parama Karuna Devi, and Stephen Knapp, all of whom have numerous authored books or articles of their own.

For the benefit of individuals and social progress, the Vedic system is as relevant today as it was in ancient times. Discover why there is a growing renaissance in what the Vedic tradition has to offer in *Vedic Culture*.

Published by iUniverse.com, 300 pages, 6"x 9" trim size, $22.95, ISBN: 0-595-37120-5.

The Heart of Hinduism:
The Eastern Path to Freedom, Empowerment and Illumination

This is a definitive and easy to understand guide to the essential as well as devotional heart of the Vedic/Hindu philosophy. You will see the depths of wisdom and insights that are contained within this profound spiritual knowledge. It is especially good for anyone who lacks the time to research the many topics that are contained within the numerous Vedic manuscripts and to see the advantages of knowing them. This also provides you with a complete process for progressing on the spiritual path, making way for individual empowerment, freedom, and spiritual illumination. All the information is now at your fingertips.

Some of the topics you will find include:

- A complete review of all the Vedic texts and the wide range of topics they contain. This also presents the traditional origins of the Vedic philosophy and how it was developed, and their philosophical conclusion.
- The uniqueness and freedom of the Vedic system.
- A description of the main yoga processes and their effectiveness.
- A review of the Vedic Gods, such as Krishna, Shiva, Durga, Ganesh, and others. You will learn the identity and purpose of each.
- You will have the essential teachings of Lord Krishna who has given some of the most direct and insightful of all spiritual messages known to humanity, and the key to direct spiritual perception.
- The real purpose of yoga and the religious systems.
- What is the most effective spiritual path for this modern age and what it can do for you, with practical instructions for deep realizations.
- The universal path of devotion, the one world religion.
- How Vedic culture is the last bastion of deep spiritual truth.
- Plus many more topics and information for your enlightenment.

So to dive deep into what is Hinduism and the Vedic path to freedom and spiritual perception, this book will give you a jump start. Knowledge is the process of personal empowerment, and no knowledge will give you more power than deep spiritual understanding. And those realizations described in the Vedic culture are the oldest and some of the most profound that humanity has ever known.

Published by iUniverse.com, 650 pages, $35.95, 6" x 9" trim size, ISBN: 0-595-35075-5.

The Power of the Dharma
An Introduction to Hinduism and Vedic Culture

The Power of the Dharma offers you a concise and easy-to-understand overview of the essential principles and customs of Hinduism and the reasons for them. It provides many insights into the depth and value of the timeless wisdom of Vedic spirituality and why the Dharmic path has survived for so many hundreds of years. It reveals why the Dharma is presently enjoying a renaissance of an increasing number of interested people who are exploring its teachings and seeing what its many techniques of Self-discovery have to offer.

Herein you will find:
- Quotes by noteworthy people on the unique qualities of Hinduism
- Essential principles of the Vedic spiritual path
- Particular traits and customs of Hindu worship and explanations of them
- Descriptions of the main Yoga systems
- The significance and legends of the colorful Hindu festivals
- Benefits of Ayurveda, Vastu, Vedic astrology and gemology,
- Important insights of Dharmic life and how to begin.

The Dharmic path can provide you the means for attaining your own spiritual realizations and experiences. In this way it is as relevant today as it was thousands of years ago. This is the power of the Dharma since its universal teachings have something to offer anyone.

Published by iUniverse.com, 170 pages, 6" x 9" trim size, $16.95, ISBN: 0-595-39352-7.

Seeing Spiritual India
A Guide to Temples, Holy Sites, Festivals and Traditions

This book is for anyone who wants to know of the many holy sites that you can visit while traveling within India, how to reach them, and what is the history and significance of these most spiritual of sacred sites, temples, and festivals. It also provides a deeper understanding of the mysteries and spiritual traditions of India.

This book includes:

- Descriptions of the temples and their architecture, and what you will see at each place.
- Explanations of holy places of Hindus, Buddhists, Sikhs, Jains, Parsis, and Muslims.
- The spiritual benefits a person acquires by visiting them.
- Convenient itineraries to take to see the most of each area of India, which is divided into East, Central, South, North, West, the Far Northeast, and Nepal.
- Packing list suggestions and how to prepare for your trip, and problems to avoid.
- How to get the best experience you can from your visit to India.
- How the spiritual side of India can positively change you forever.

This book goes beyond the usual descriptions of the typical tourist attractions and opens up the spiritual venue waiting to be revealed for a far deeper experience on every level.

Published by iUniverse.com, 592 pages, $33.95, ISBN: 978-0-595-50291-2.

Crimes Against India:
And the Need to Protect its Ancient Vedic Traditions

1000 Years of Attacks Against Hinduism and What to Do about It

India has one of the oldest and most dynamic cultures of the world. Yet, many people do not know of the many attacks, wars, atrocities and sacrifices that Indian people have had to undergo to protect and preserve their country and spiritual tradition over the centuries. Many people also do not know of the many ways in which this profound heritage is being attacked and threatened today, and what we can do about it.
Therefore, some of the topics included are:
- How there is a war against Hinduism and its yoga culture.
- The weaknesses of India that allowed invaders to conquer her.
- Lessons from India's real history that should not be forgotten.
- The atrocities committed by the Muslim invaders, and how they tried to destroy Vedic culture and its many temples, and slaughtered thousands of Indian Hindus.
- How the British viciously exploited India and its people for its resources.
- How the cruelest of all Christian Inquisitions in Goa tortured and killed thousands of Hindus.
- Action plans for preserving and strengthening Vedic India.
- How all Hindus must stand up and be strong for Sanatana-dharma, and promote the cooperation and unity for a Global Vedic Community.

India is a most resilient country, and is presently becoming a great economic power in the world. It also has one of the oldest and dynamic cultures the world has ever known, but few people seem to understand the many trials and difficulties that the country has faced, or the present problems India is still forced to deal with in preserving the culture of the majority Hindus who live in the country. This is described in the real history of the country, which a decreasing number of people seem to recall.

Therefore, this book is to honor the efforts that have been shown by those in the past who fought and worked to protect India and its culture, and to help preserve India as the homeland of a living and dynamic Vedic tradition of Sanatana-dharma (the eternal path of duty and wisdom).

Available from iUniverse.com. 370 pages, $24.95, ISBN: 978-1-4401-1158-7.

The Eleventh Commandment
The Next Step in Social Spiritual Development

A New Code to Bring Humanity to a Higher Level of Spiritual Consciousness

This is some of Stephen's boldest and most direct writing. Based on the Universal Spiritual Truths, or the deeper levels of spiritual understanding, it presents a new code in a completely nonsectarian way that anyone should be able and willing to follow. Herein is the next step for consideration, which can be used as a tool for guidance, and for setting a higher standard in our society today. This new commandment expects and directs us toward a change in our social awareness and spiritual consciousness. It is conceived, formulated, and now provided to assist humanity in reaching its true destiny, and to bring a new spiritual dimension into the basic fabric of our ordinary every day life. It is a key that unlocks the doors of perception, and opens up a whole new aspect of spiritual understanding for all of us to view. It is the commandment which precepts us to gain the knowledge of the hidden mysteries, which have for so long remained an enigma to the confused and misdirected men of this world. It holds the key which unlocks the answers to man's quest for peace and happiness, and the next step for spiritual growth on a dynamic and all-inclusive social level.

This 11th Commandment and the explanations provided show the means for curing social ills, reducing racial prejudices, and create more harmony between the races and cultures. It shows how to recognize the Divine within yourself and all beings around you. It shows how we can bring some of the spiritual atmosphere into this earthly existence, especially if we expect to reach the higher domain after death. It also explains how to:

- Identify our real Self and distinguish it from our false self.
- Open our hearts to one another and view others with greater appreciation.
- Utilize higher consciousness in everyday life.
- Find inner contentment and joy.
- Attain a higher spiritual awareness and perception.
- Manifest God's plan for the world.
- Be a reflection of God's love toward everyone.
- Attain the Great Realization of perceiving the Divine in all beings.

The world is in need of a new direction in its spiritual development, and this 11th Commandment is given as the next phase to manifest humanity's most elevated potentials.

This book is $13.95, Size: 6" x 9", Pages: 128, ISBN: 0-595-46741-5.

Yoga and Meditation Their Real Purpose and How to Get Started

Yoga is a nonsectarian spiritual science that has been practiced and developed over thousands of years. The benefits of yoga are numerous. On the mental level it strengthens concentration, determination, and builds a stronger character that can more easily sustain various tensions in our lives for peace of mind. The assortment of *asanas* or postures also provide stronger health and keeps various diseases in check. They improve physical strength, endurance and flexibility. These are some of the goals of yoga.

Its ultimate purpose is to raise our consciousness to directly perceive the spiritual dimension. Then we can have our own spiritual experiences. The point is that the more spiritual we become, the more we can perceive that which is spiritual. As we develop and grow in this way through yoga, the questions about spiritual life are no longer a mystery to solve, but become a reality to experience. It becomes a practical part of our lives. This book will show you how to do that. Some of the topics include:

- Benefits of yoga
- The real purpose of yoga
- The types of yoga, such as Hatha yoga, Karma yoga, Raja and Astanga yogas, Kundalini yoga, Bhakti yoga, Mudra yoga, Mantra yoga, and others.
- The Chakras and Koshas
- Asanas and postures, and the Surya Namaskar
- Pranayama and breathing techniques for inner changes
- Deep meditation and how to proceed
- The methods for using mantras
- Attaining spiritual enlightenment, and much more

This book is 6"x9" trim size, $17.95, 240 pages, 32 illustration, ISBN: 1451553269.

Avatars, Gods and Goddesses of Vedic Culture

The Characteristics, Powers and Positions of the Hindu Divinities

Understanding the assorted Divinities or gods and goddesses of the Vedic or Hindu pantheon is not so difficult as some people may think when it is presented simply and effectively. And that is what you will find in this book. This will open you to many of the possibilities and potentials of the Vedic tradition, and show how it has been able to cater to and fulfill the spiritual needs and development of so many people since time immemorial. Here you will find there is something for everyone.

This takes you into the heart of the deep, Vedic spiritual knowledge of how to perceive the Absolute Truth, the Supreme and the various powers and agents of the universal creation. This explains the characteristics and nature of the Vedic Divinities and their purposes, powers, and the ways they influence and affect the natural energies of the universe. It also shows how they can assist us and that blessings from them can help our own spiritual and material development and potentialities, depending on what we need.

Some of the Vedic Divinities that will be explained include Lord Krishna, Vishnu, Their main avatars and expansions, along with Brahma, Shiva, Ganesh, Murugan, Surya, Hanuman, as well as the goddesses of Sri Radha, Durga, Sarasvati, Lakshmi, and others. This also presents explanations of their names, attributes, dress, weapons, instruments, the meaning of the Shiva lingam, and some of the legends and stories that are connected with them. This will certainly give you a new insight into the expansive nature of the Vedic tradition.

This book is: $17.95 retail, 230 pages, 11 black & white photos, ISBN: 1453613765, EAN: 9781453613764.

The Soul
Understanding Our Real Identity
The Key to Spiritual Awakening

This book provides a summarization of the most essential spiritual knowledge that will give you the key to spiritual awakening. The descriptions will give you greater insights and a new look at who and what you really are as a spiritual being.

The idea that we are more than merely these material bodies is pervasive. It is established in every religion and spiritual path in this world. However, many religions only hint at the details of this knowledge, but if we look around we will find that practically the deepest and clearest descriptions of the soul and its characteristics are found in the ancient Vedic texts of India.

Herein you will find some of the most insightful spiritual knowledge and wisdom known to mankind. Some of the topics include:

- How you are more than your body
- The purpose of life
- Spiritual ignorance of the soul is the basis of illusion and suffering
- The path of spiritual realization
- How the soul is eternal
- The unbounded nature of the soul
- What is the Supersoul
- Attaining direct spiritual perception and experience of our real identity

This book will give you a deeper look into the ancient wisdom of India's Vedic, spiritual culture, and the means to recognize your real identity.

This book is 5 1/2"x8 1/2" trim size, 130 pages, $7.95, ISBN: 1453733833.

Prayers, Mantras and Gayatris
A Collection for Insights, Spiritual Growth, Protection, and Many Other Blessings

Using mantras or prayers can help us do many things, depending on our intention. First of all, it is an ancient method that has been used successfully to raise our consciousness, our attitude, aim of life, and outlook, and prepare ourselves for perceiving higher states of being.

The Sanskrit mantras within this volume offer such things as the knowledge and insights for spiritual progress, including higher perceptions and understandings of the Absolute or God, as well as the sound vibrations for awakening our higher awareness, invoking the positive energies to help us overcome obstacles and oppositions, or to assist in healing our minds and bodies from disease or negativity. They can provide the means for requesting protection on our spiritual path, or from enemies, ghosts, demons, or for receiving many other benefits. In this way, they offer a process for acquiring blessings of all kinds, both material and spiritual. There is something for every need. Some of what you will find includes:

- The most highly recommended mantras for spiritual realization in this age.
- A variety of prayers and gayatris to Krishna, Vishnu and other avatars, Goddess Lakshmi for financial well-being, Shiva, Durga, Ganesh, Devi, Indra, Sarasvati, etc., and Surya the Sun-god, the planets, and for all the days of the week.
- Powerful prayers of spiritual insight in Shiva's Song, along with the Bhaja Govindam by Sri Adi Shankaracharya, the Purusha Sukta, Brahma-samhita, Isha Upanishad, Narayana Suktam, and Hanuman Chalisa.
- Prayers and mantras to Sri Chaitanya and Nityananda.
- Strong prayers for protection from Lord Narasimha. The protective shield from Lord Narayana.
- Lists of the 108 names of Lord Krishna, Radhika, Goddess Devi, Shiva, and Sri Rama.
- The Vishnu-Sahasranama or thousand names of Vishnu, Balarama, Gopala, Radharani, and additional lists of the sacred names of the Vedic Divinities;
- And many other prayers, mantras and stotras for an assortment of blessings and benefits.

This book is 6"x9" trim size, 760 pages, ISBN:1456545906, $31.95.

Krishna Deities and Their Miracles
How the Images of Lord Krishna Interact with Their Devotees

This book helps reveal how the Deities of Krishna in the temple are but another channel through which the Divine can be better understood and perceived. In fact, the Deities Themselves can exhibit what some would call miracles in the way They reveal how the Divine accepts the Deity form. These miracles between the Deities of Krishna and His devotees happen in many different ways, and all the time. This is one process through which Krishna, or the Supreme Being, reveals Himself and the reality of His existence. Stories of such miracles or occurrences extend through the ages up to modern times, and all around the world. This book relates an assortment of these events to show how the images in the temples have manifested Their personality and character in various ways in Their pastimes with Their devotees, whether it be for developing their devotion, instructing them, or simply giving them His kindness, mercy or inspiration.

This book helps show that the Supreme Reality is a person who plays and exhibits His pastimes in any manner He likes. This is also why worship of the Deity in the temple has been and remains a primary means of increasing one's devotion and connection with the Supreme Being.

Besides presenting stories of the reciprocation that can exist between Krishna in His Deity form and the ordinary living beings, other topics include:
- The antiquity of devotion to the Deity in the Vedic tradition.
- Historical sites of ancient Deity worship.
- Scriptural instructions and references to Deity veneration.
- The difference between idols and Deities.
- What is darshan and the significance of Deities.
- Why God would even take the initiative to reveal Himself to His devotees and accept the position of being a Deity.

This book will give deeper insight into the unlimited personality and causeless benevolence of the Supreme, especially to those who become devoted to Him.

This book is 6"x9" trim size, 210 pages, $14.95, ISBN: 1463734298.

Defending Vedic Dharma
Tackling the Issues to Make a Difference

The Vedic culture and its philosophy is one of the most deeply spiritual and all encompassing traditions in the world, and has been a major contributor to philosophical thought and the development of civilization. It does not take that long to understand, but it can take some serious consideration. Until then, there can be some aspects of it that are misunderstood or misinterpreted.

Therefore, this book takes some of the issues of the day and describes what they are and the remedies for dealing with them in order to make a difference in how we participate in Vedic culture, how we can make it more effective in our lives, and how it can be perceived in a more positive way. All of this makes a difference in the objectives of preserving, protecting, promoting, and perpetuating the Vedic spiritual path.

So this book shows some of the many uplifting and insightful qualities we can find in the Vedic tradition, of which everyone should be aware and can appreciate. Some of the important issues discussed within include:

- Why it is important to use the proper vocabulary to express Vedic concepts.
- Why all religions really are not the same, though many Hindus and gurus like to think they are. Time to wake up to reality.
- The power of a united Vedic community, and how it could rapidly change things if Hindus actually became more united and worked together.
- The importance of becoming a Dharmic leader and to do your part, and the danger of Hindu teachers who really do not lead in a way they should.
- The long-term but realistic cure for the corruption in India.
- The importance of Vedic temples as centers of sacred knowledge, and why temples should be open to everyone.
- How and why the Vedic texts say that the knowledge within them must be shared with everyone.
- The real purpose of the natural Vedic way of social arrangement, but why the present caste system in India should be changed or thrown out completely.
- An eight point action plan for how Hindus in America can best use the freedoms they have, which often exceed the decreasing freedoms in India, to cultivate their tradition to its fullest extent while they have the means to do so.

The clarity with which these and other issues are addressed make this an important book for consideration.

This book is 6" x 9" trim size, $12.95, 214 pages, ISBN: 1466342277.

Advancements of Ancient India's Vedic Culture
The Planet's Earliest Civilization and How it Influenced the World

This book shows how the planet's earliest civilization lead the world in both material and spiritual progress. From the Vedic culture of ancient India thousands of years ago, we find for example the origins of mathematics, especially algebra and geometry, as well as early astronomy and planetary observations, many instances of which can be read in the historical Vedic texts. Medicine in Ayurveda was the first to prescribe herbs for the remedy of disease, surgical instruments for operations, and more.

Other developments that were far superior and ahead of the rest of the world included:

- Writing and language, especially the development of sophisticated Sanskrit;
- Metallurgy and making the best known steel at the time;
- Ship building and global maritime trade;
- Textiles and the dying of fabric for which India was known all over the world;
- Agricultural and botanical achievements;
- Precise Vedic arts in painting, dance and music;
- The educational systems and the most famous of the early universities, like Nalanda and Takshashila;
- The source of individual freedom and fair government, and the character and actions of rulers;
- Military and the earliest of martial arts;
- Along with some of the most intricate, deep and profound of all philosophies and spiritual paths, which became the basis of many religions that followed later around the world.

These and more are the developments that came from India, much of which has been forgotten, but should again be recognized as the heritage of the ancient Indian Vedic tradition that continues to inspire humanity.

This book is 6"x9" trim size, 350 pages, $20.95, ISBN: 1477607897.

Spreading Vedic Traditions Through Temples
Proven Strategies that Make them More Effective

After forty years of managing Vedic temples or Mandirs in many different ways, as well as traveling all over India and seeing how others utilize successful plans, Stephen Knapp has put together a book that explains the most important programs that any temple can use for more effectively protecting and perpetuating the Vedic traditions. In a non-sectarian way, he lists and describes how the Dharmic temples of all kinds can increase their congregations as well as engage their members in service to help in maintaining the temples and traditions, and expanding their influence. Some of what is included are:

- The primary mission of the temple.
- Services the guests can easily offer in seva to the temple or deity.
- Giving Vedic culture to the next generation.
- Temple classes, the Sunday program and children's schools and youth camps.
- Vedic temples as centers of sacred knowledge.
- The power of adult study groups, cultural and outreach programs, and festivals.
- Utilizing temple restaurants, gift shops, exhibits, and support groups.
- Ways of reaching more people, both in India and the USA.
- The need and ways for promotion, and radio, television, and newspapers.
- An action plan on how to cultivate Vedic culture in America.
- Attracting and welcoming non-Indians and Western seekers for more support.
- Starting a spiritual revolution in India and elsewhere.
- Working with priests, rituals, and teaching the culture and traditions.
- Unifying and organizing the Vedic community.

This book covers many more methods that are not merely ideas, but are already being used in practical and successful ways to help preserve, promote and spread what is the last bastion of deep spiritual truth. As more temples are built in Western countries, these strategies will become increasingly important. Using these techniques as the basis of your ideas, your temple cannot help but be successful.

This book is 6"x9" trim size, 186 pages, $11.95, ISBN: 1478222999.

www.Stephen-Knapp.com
http://stephenknapp.info
http://stephenknapp.wordpress.com

Be sure to visit Stephen's web site. It provides lots of information on many spiritual aspects of Vedic and spiritual philosophy, and Indian culture for both beginners and the scholarly. You will find:

- All the descriptions and contents of Stephen's books, how to order them, and keep up with any new books or articles that he has written.
- Reviews and unsolicited letters from readers who have expressed their appreciation for his books, as well as his website.
- Free online booklets are also available for your use or distribution on meditation, why be a Hindu, how to start yoga, meditation, etc.
- Helpful prayers, mantras, gayatris, and devotional songs.
- Over a hundred enlightening articles that can help answer many questions about life, the process of spiritual development, the basics of the Vedic path, or how to broaden our spiritual awareness. Many of these are emailed among friends or posted on other web sites.
- Over 150 color photos taken by Stephen during his travels through India. There are also descriptions and 40 photos of the huge and amazing Kumbha Mela festival.
- Directories of many Krishna and Hindu temples around the world to help you locate one near you, where you can continue your experience along the Eastern path.
- Postings of the recent archeological discoveries that confirm the Vedic version of history.
- Photographic exhibit of the Vedic influence in the Taj Mahal, questioning whether it was built by Shah Jahan or a pre-existing Vedic building.
- A large list of links to additional websites to help you continue your exploration of Eastern philosophy, or provide more information and news about India, Hinduism, ancient Vedic culture, Vaishnavism, Hare Krishna sites, travel, visas, catalogs for books and paraphernalia, holy places, etc.
- A large resource for vegetarian recipes, information on its benefits, how to get started, ethnic stores, or non-meat ingredients and supplies.
- A large "Krishna Darshan Art Gallery" of photos and prints of Krishna and Vedic divinities. You can also find a large collection of previously unpublished photos of His Divine Grace A. C. Bhaktivedanta Swami.

This site is made as a practical resource for your use and is continually being updated and expanded with more articles, resources, and information. Be sure to check it out.

Printed in France by Amazon
Brétigny-sur-Orge, FR

20750238R00157